How to Become a U.S. Citizen

5th Edition

PETERSON'S

Publishing

About Peterson's Publishing

To succeed on your lifelong educational journey, you will need accurate, dependable, and practical tools and resources. That is why Peterson's is everywhere education happens. Because whenever and however you need education content delivered, you can rely on Peterson's to provide the information, know-how, and guidance to help you reach your goals. Tools to match the right students with the right school. It's here. Personalized resources and expert guidance. It's here. Comprehensive and dependable education content— delivered whenever and however you need it. It's all here.

For more information, contact Peterson's Publishing, 2000 Lenox Drive, Lawrenceville, NJ 08648; 800-338-3282 Ext. 54229; or find us online at petersonspublishing.com.

Petersonspublishing.com/publishingupdates

Check out our Web site at www.petersonspublishing.com/publishingupdates to see if there is any new information regarding the test and any revisions or corrections to the content of this book. We've made sure the information in this book is accurate and up-to-date; however, the test format or content may have changed since the time of publication.

Stephen Clemente, Managing Director, Publishing and Institutional Research; Bernadette Webster, Director of Publishing; Jill C. Schwartz, Editor; Ray Golaszewski, Manufacturing Manager; Linda M. Williams, Composition Manager

ISBN-13: 978-0-7689-2905-8
ISBN-10: 0-7689-2905-9

Printed in the United States of America

10 9 8 7 6 5 4 3 2 1   12 11 10

Fifth Edition

Contents

PART III: 5 PRACTICE TESTS

PART IV: APPENDIXES

INTRODUCTION

Becoming a U.S. Citizen

Many people consider the United States to be the greatest country in the world, and most of us who live here agree. It's not surprising that so many people from other parts of the world come to the United States or that many of them want to stay here. With such a demand to become part of this great country, it is important that there is a well-defined process for legally entering this country and staying here for a short time or permanently.

It is a complicated and lengthy process, but if you decide you want to stay here permanently, the information presented in this book will provide you with resources and guidance you need to become a U.S. citizen so that you can enjoy all of the many benefits this great country has to offer.

RIGHTS AND BENEFITS

The United States has been called "The Land of Opportunity" and a place where you can "live the American Dream." Although the Constitution and laws of the United States extend many rights to both citizens and noncitizens, some rights are extended to U.S. citizens only, for example:

Voting: Only U.S. citizens can vote in federal elections, and most states also restrict the right to vote to U.S. citizens.

Bringing family members to the United States: Citizens generally get priority when petitioning to bring family members permanently to this country.

Obtaining citizenship for children born abroad: In most cases, a child born abroad to a U.S. citizen is automatically a U.S. citizen.

Traveling with a U.S. passport: A U.S. passport enables you to get assistance from the U.S. government when you are overseas.

Becoming eligible for federal jobs: Most jobs with government agencies require U.S. citizenship.

Becoming an elected official: Many elected offices in this country require U.S. citizenship.

In addition to these and many other benefits, U.S. citizenship also comes with certain responsibilities. When you take the Oath of Allegiance, you make several promises as a U.S. citizen, including that you will:

- Give up all prior allegiance to any other nation or sovereignty
- Swear allegiance to the United States
- Support and defend the Constitution and U.S. laws
- Serve the country when required

U.S. citizens also have a responsibility to participate in the political process by registering and voting in elections. Serving on a jury is another responsibility of citizenship. In addition, the United States becomes stronger when all of its citizens respect the different opinions, cultures, ethnic groups, and religions found in this country. Thus, tolerance for differences is another responsibility of citizenship.

As you can see, becoming a citizen of this great country is not something that should be taken lightly. However, it is a decision that certainly comes with many benefits. Before you are granted citizenship, you will be interviewed by an officer of the U.S. Citizenship and Immigration Services (USCIS). It is likely that you will be asked about why you want to become a citizen and whether you accept these responsibilities willingly. Be sure to consider these questions carefully before beginning this process.

YOU'RE WELL ON YOUR WAY TO SUCCESS

You've made the decision to become a citizen of the United States. *Peterson's How to Become a U.S. Citizen* will help you prepare for the steps you will need to take to achieve your goal—from becoming a permanent resident to passing the necessary tests and achieving U.S. citizenship. The editors at Peterson's Publishing wish you the best of luck as you begin this endeavor.

GIVE US YOUR FEEDBACK

Peterson's publications can be found at high school guidance offices, college and university libraries and career centers, and your local bookstore and library. Peterson's publications are also available as e-books. Check our Web site, www.petersonspublishing.com, for more information about our e-book program.

We welcome any comments or suggestions you may have about this publication. Your feedback will help us make educational and career goals possible for you—and others like you.

PART I

The Immigration System

CHAPTER 1

A Look at the Immigration System

OBJECTIVES AND GOALS OF THE U.S. IMMIGRATION SYSTEM

Immigration policies in the United States are set by the U.S. Citizenship and Immigration Services (USCIS). The USCIS is the bureau within the Department of Homeland Security that directs the immigration process in this country, including citizenship, permanent residency, family- and employment-related immigration, employment authorization, and inter-country adoptions. The USCIS also handles foreign student authorization, asylum and refugee status, and replacement immigration documents.

Policies and regulations established by the U.S. immigration system are designed to allow visitors, temporary workers, and immigrants lawful entry into the United Sates. The immigration system has two main objectives. First, it gives those seeking permanent residency a clear process for obtaining U.S. citizenship (naturalization). It also provides information for those who would like to visit the United States temporarily as students, tourists, or workers. Second, the immigration system protects the rights of current citizens by stopping illegal entry, benefit distribution, or employment.

The U.S. immigration system strives to meet the following goals:

- *Safety:* First and foremost, immigration laws are in place to keep U.S. citizens safe. Although many new immigrants are welcomed into the country each year, the immigration system also has safeguards to prevent unlawful entry into the United States.
- *Family reunification:* Policies established by the USCIS are intended to keep families intact. Immigration laws make it easier for those with immediate family members (parents, children, or spouses) already living in the United States to enter the country.
- *Asylum:* Immigration laws provide political, religious, and social asylum for those fleeing discrimination or maltreatment in their native countries.
- *Integration:* The immigration system supports those seeking permanent residency or citizenship by providing helpful resources and information.

VISAS: IMMIGRANT AND NONIMMIGRANT

Whether you would like to visit the United States temporarily or stay permanently, the first step is to obtain a visa. A visa allows a person to travel to the United States and apply for admission to stay for longer periods of time. However, having a visa does not guarantee entrance into the United States. At the port of entry, an immigration inspector will determine the visa holder's eligibility for admission into the country.

Operated by the U.S. Department of State, the National Visa Center (NVC) is a visa processing center that collects visa application forms and fees. Although visas are not issued in the United States, visa applications are processed through the NVC in New Hampshire. The NVC processes applications by first ensuring that an applicant's dates of visitation are acceptable. Then, the NVC contacts the applicant for the required processing fees and visa documentation. Once the visa application has been approved, the NVC sends these records to a U.S. embassy or consulate, so that the applicant may obtain the visa. The length of time needed to issue an immigrant visa varies and depends on the applicant's country of origin and the type of visa requested.

There are two types of visas available for travel to the United States:

- *Nonimmigrant Visa:* This type of visa is issued to those visiting the United States on a temporary basis, including students, tourists, businesspeople, workers, or patients receiving medical treatment. Unless you qualify for the Visa Waiver Program (generally for stays of ninety days or less) or are exempt from the visa requirement, a nonimmigrant visa is necessary for short-term admission into the country.

- *Immigrant Visa:* If you are seeking permanent resident status in the United States, you will need to apply for an immigrant visa. When immigrant visa holders enter the country, they obtain a permanent resident card, also known as a green card. People with green cards may live and work in the United States for as long as they would like. Immigrant visa holders keep their native citizenships and passports and do not have to become naturalized citizens of the United States. Anyone with a green card may file an application to become a naturalized U.S. citizen after five years (three years if the applicant is married to a U.S. citizen).

CHAPTER 2

Nonimmigrant Visas

TYPES OF NONIMMIGRANT VISAS

Visitors to the United States who are interested in staying temporarily are issued a type of visa called a nonimmigrant visa. Nonimmigrant visas fall into several categories. People may enter the United States temporarily for business (B-1) or for pleasure or medical treatment (B-2). There are also specific visa categories for students, crewmen, temporary workers, and journalists. In addition, many countries participate in the Visa Waiver Program that allows foreign nationals to visit the United States without first obtaining a visa.

In order to obtain a nonimmigrant visa, applicants must meet the provisions of the Immigration and Nationality Act. U.S. immigration law assumes that visitors to the United States intend to immigrate to this country. Thus, applicants for nonimmigrant visas must prove that they are not seeking immigration to the United States by demonstrating the following:

- They plan to enter the United States for medical treatment, business, or pleasure.
- They will stay in the United States for a limited and specific time period.
- They have sufficient funds to cover their expenses in the United States.
- They maintain a residence in their native country.
- They have familial, economic, and social ties abroad.

Visitors to the United States should realize that having a nonimmigrant visa does not guarantee entry into the country. They may be denied admission by immigration authorities, who may also determine the length of their stay. When visitors to the United States arrive at the port of entry, their admission to the country will be authorized by a U.S. Customs and Border Protection (CBP) official. He or she will stamp the visitor's Form I-94: Record of Arrival-Departure and approve the length of the visit. Travelers who would like to extend their visit should contact the USCIS and request Form I-539: Application to Extend/Change Nonimmigrant Status.

As with most visas, the sooner you apply the better. As a result of the terrorist attacks on the United States on September 11, 2001, visa applications are screened even more thoroughly than they were previously—a time-consuming process. It's a good idea to start the visa application process as soon as you begin making travel plans.

B-1 and B-2 Visitors

For those wishing to travel to the United States temporarily, a nonimmigrant visa called the "visitor" visa is available. There are two types of visitor visas.

- *B-1 Visa:* This visa is reserved for business travelers. If you plan to visit the United States to attend a professional, educational, or business conference or convention, a B-1 visa would be a good choice. The B-1 visa may also be used for business meetings, contract negotiations, or estate settlements.

- *B-2 Visa:* This visa is for those seeking recreational travel or medical treatment in the United States. If you are planning to visit the United States for reasons that include tourism, visits with family or friends, social or service activities, rest, or amusement, you should apply for a B-2 visa. The B-2 visa is also for patients who plan to visit the United States for medical treatment.

You may apply for a visitor visa at any U.S. consular office overseas. However, it is recommended that you visit the U.S. embassy or consulate that has jurisdiction over the area where you live. It is quicker and easier to qualify for a visa within your country of permanent residence.

There are currently thirty-five countries that participate in the Visa Waiver Program (VWP). Citizens of these countries may travel to the United States without a visa if they meet certain requirements. To be eligible for the VWP, travelers should be visiting the United States for the purpose of business or tourism and stay in the country for fewer than 90 days. They must also be authorized through the Electronic System for Travel Authorization (ESTA) before coming to the United States, have a current passport and sufficient funds for the duration of their stay, and travel on an approved carrier.

Detailed information about the Visa Waiver Program is available by accessing the U.S. Department of State's Web site at http://travel.state.gov. This site provides the most up-to-date information about the VWP program, explains passport and other travel requirements, and lists the participating countries.

F-1 and M-1 Students

There are two nonimmigrant visa categories for students: the "F" visa and the "M" visa. Nonimmigrants coming to the United States for academic or language training programs are issued an "F" visa. An "M" visa is given to those pursuing vocational or nonacademic studies in the United States.

To be eligible for the F-1 or M-1 visa, students must meet certain criteria. First, they must be enrolled full-time in a vocational, educational, or language-training program at a USCIS-approved school. Second, students must display English proficiency or be registered for English language courses. They are also required to have necessary funds to support themselves during their studies and maintain a residence abroad. Students may obtain these funds through a sponsor living in the United States. The sponsor will need to complete Form I-134: Affidavit of Support on the student's behalf. This form proves that the student has financial support from the sponsor and will not become a "public charge" (meaning dependent on public assistance programs, like food stamps or Medicaid) while living in the United States.

If you are interested in visiting the United States on a student F-1 or M-1 visa, the first step is to apply to a USCIS-approved school. Once you are accepted into a program, your educational institution will provide you with the needed approval documentation, including Form I-20: Certificate of Eligibility for Nonimmigrant (F-1) Student Status. You will submit Form I-20 to the Department of Homeland Security as part of your visa application. To begin the student visa application process, you'll need to contact your local U.S. embassy.

J-1 Exchange Visitors

Travelers are encouraged to visit the United States through the Exchange Visitor Program (J-1). This type of visa was created to promote cultural awareness between countries, allowing visitors to exchange ideas, knowledge, and skills in a variety of fields. J-1 nonimmigrant visas are issued to travelers who have been approved to participate in a sponsoring organization's U.S. exchange visitor program. Anyone requesting a

J-1 visa must have been accepted into an exchange program before applying for a visa. Sponsors of exchange programs provide participants with the documentation needed to apply for a J-1 visa.

H-1B Specialty Occupation Worker

Another type of visa included in the nonimmigrant visa category is the H-1B for specialty occupation workers. U.S. employers may use this visa program to hire foreign workers with specialized knowledge or expertise. Workers coming to the United States on an H-1B visa should have a bachelor's degree (or the equivalent). Some examples of H-1B occupations include college professors, architects, computer programmers, accountants, and engineers. The U.S. Congress sets an annual limit on the number of workers who may be issued a visa each year for certain nonimmigrant classifications. This limit is referred to as the annual cap. Currently, the H-1B visa has an annual cap of 65,000.

H-2B Temporary Workers

U.S. employers may also hire foreign workers on a temporary basis through the H-2B visa category. These employers may hire seasonal or intermittent workers during their peak production times to increase their labor force. Employers might also add to their workforce temporarily for a one-time occurrence, such as a large building project. Many H-2B workers are hired for manufacturing, construction, health care, landscaping, food service, lumber, and hospitality services jobs.

Current annual caps on H-2B visas are set at 66,000 per year. Half of these visas (33,000) are reserved for workers hired from October 1 through March 31, and the other half are for those working from April 1 through September 30. These limitations were set as a result of the Save Our Small and Seasonal Businesses Act of 2005. Starting in 2010, an H-2B petition cannot be filed more than 120 days before the actual start of the job that is identified on the labor certificate. In many cases, workers are able to extend their stays in H-2B status.

L-1 Intracompany Transferees

Yet another type of nonimmigrant visa issued to foreign workers is the L-1 classification. The L-1 visa is intended for those holding positions with companies overseas where they have worked for at least one year. If the company decides to transfer the employee to a U.S.-based branch, subsidiary, parent, or affiliate, a worker may apply for an L-1 visa to work for the company in the United States. Employees in this classification, called intracompany transferees, must stay with the same employer. They also must work in an executive, managerial, or specialized knowledge position with the company.

E-1 and E-2 Treaty Traders and Investors

Nonimmigrant visas are also available to foreign nationals coming to the United States for the purpose of trade or investment. These workers must live in a country that has a treaty of commerce and navigation with the United States. A complete list of treaty countries may be found at the Department of State's Web site at http://travel.state.gov.

E-1 visas are issued to treaty traders coming to the United States to conduct significant trade between the U.S. and the treaty country. Applicants must be executives or supervisors, must be citizens of a treaty country, and must handle "substantial" (large and continuing) trade agreements. E-2 visas are reserved for treaty investors or those who direct and develop the resulting enterprise. Investors are also required to be nationals of a treaty country and have the expertise to manage large investments.

TN Visas for Canadian and Mexican Professionals

As a result of the North American Free Trade Agreement (passed in 1993), qualified Canadian and Mexican workers may enter the United States for professional business activities on a TN visa. Those entering the United States on a TN nonimmigrant visa should have a bachelor's degree or other required credentials. Many TN visa holders work as engineers, lawyers, teachers, accountants, pharmacists, and scientists. Currently, there is no annual cap on the number of TN visas issued each year. A TN visa is valid for up to three years.

Canadian workers do not need to apply for a visa. When they arrive in the United States, they must provide proof of Canadian citizenship and their educational credentials and a letter from their future employer explaining the worker's position, length of stay, and education credentials. They will be inspected by a U.S. CBP officer, admitted as a TN nonimmigrant, and given Form I-94 as proof of admission. Mexican workers are required to obtain visas and should apply for a TN visa at a U.S. consular office in Mexico. They will also need a letter from their prospective employer and proof of Mexican citizenship and their educational qualifications. Mexican workers will also be issued a Form I-94 showing their TN nonimmigrant status by a U.S. CBP inspector.

K-1 Fiancé(e)s

If you are engaged to a foreign national and would like to marry in the United States, you will need to file a petition for a K-1 nonimmigrant visa for your fiancé(e). If the petition is approved, your fiancé(e) must apply for a visa at a U.S. embassy or consulate office abroad. To be eligible for the K-1 visa, you and your fiancé(e) must be free to marry and have met in person within the past two years. You must also agree to marry within ninety (90) days of your fiancé(e)'s arrival in the United States. If your fiancé(e) has children, you may apply to bring them to the United States if they are under 21 years of age. To begin the application process, you will need to file a petition with your local USCIS Service Center.

After you are married, your fiancé(e) should apply for permanent resident status if he or she wants to live and work in the United States. Your spouse's permanent resident status will be conditional for the first two years of your marriage.

K-3 and K-4 Spouses and Children of U.S. Citizens Who Are Abroad

Following passage of the Legal Immigration Family Equity Act (LIFE Act), the spouse and children of a U.S. citizen living abroad may now enter the United States on a nonimmigrant visa. The K-3 and K-4 visas permit the spouse and child (or children) of a U.S. citizen to apply for permanent resident status while living in the United States. While they adjust their status, those on a K-3 or K-4 visa are allowed to find employment in the United States. To be eligible for a K-3 visa, an applicant must be married to a U.S. citizen and seek permanent resident status. The applicant's spouse must file a relative petition (Form I-130) and send Form I-129F: Petition for Alien Fiancé(e) to the spouse's U.S. consulate abroad. To be eligible for a K-4 visa, a person must be the unmarried child of the K-3 applicant and under 21 years of age.

V Visas for Spouses and Children of Permanent Residents

The spouse and child (or children) of lawful permanent residents in the United States may also apply to live and work in the U.S. as nonimmigrants. This nonimmigrant category (V) allows the spouse and child to stay in the United States while they wait for either an immigrant visa or lawful permanent resident status. To apply for this type of visa, an applicant must either be married to a lawful permanent resident of the United States (V-1) or have a parent who is a lawful permanent resident (V-2). The spouse or parent with lawful permanent resident status must file a relative petition (Form I-130) on behalf of the spouse or child. To begin the application process abroad, applicants should contact their U.S. embassy or consulate. Spouses and children of lawful permanent residents who are already living in the United States will need to file Form I-539: Application to Change Nonimmigrant Status, undergo a medical examination, and pay an application fee.

Other Nonimmigrant Visas

In addition to the more popular nonimmigrant visa categories previously outlined, visa categories also exist for foreign government, organization, and media employees; aliens in transit and crewmembers; and witnesses and victims. Within all the nonimmigrant visa categories, there are numerous classifications, including those for religious workers, artists and performers, and people with exceptional talents and abilities. For a comprehensive list of all nonimmigrant visa categories and classifications, details about who is eligible to apply, and application instructions, see the link to "Nonimmigrant Visa Classifications" on the USCIS Web site at www.uscis.gov.

WHAT U.S. VISITORS WITH NONIMMIGRANT VISAS NEED TO KNOW

If you are visiting the United States on a nonimmigrant visa, you need to be careful to follow your visa's terms and restrictions. This is especially important if you are hoping to stay in the United States through an extension of your current nonimmigrant visa, another nonimmigrant visa, an adjustment to lawful permanent resident status, or an application for citizenship. The following are a few points to consider regarding your visa.

Observe All Laws

Be very careful not to let your current nonimmigrant visa expire. If your visa has certain restrictions or conditions, be sure not to violate these policies. Any future visa applications or status adjustment requests will be looked at more favorably if you have followed the immigration laws governing your current visa.

Be Mindful of Important Dates

When a foreign national enters the United States on a visa, he or she is admitted for a specific time period. The visa holder's I-94 Arrival-Departure record shows how long he or she may remain in the United States. If you are visiting on a nonimmigrant visa, take note of this departure date and make plans to either leave the United States or apply to extend your stay before your visa expires. If you stay in the Unites States past the departure date on your I-94 Arrival-Departure record, you will lose your legal status and jeopardize any plans you might have to remain in the country.

It is also a good idea to watch the dates of your passport to make sure this document remains current. Although you are visiting the United States on a visa, you must maintain citizenship in your native country and keep your passport valid. Updating your passport in the United States might prove to be a slow process, so be sure to start the renewal process early.

Do Not Disobey the Terms of Your Visa

Each nonimmigrant visa has specific terms and conditions. It is important to note these restrictions and follow them carefully. For example, many visitor and student visas do not allow recipients to work. If you are visiting the United States on one of these visas and accept employment, you risk losing your legal status. Similarly, if you are visiting the United States on a temporary employment visa, you may not continue to work past your visa's expiration date. Be sure that you completely understand the conditions of your visa. If you violate these terms, you may limit your chances to adjust your status or gain citizenship in the future.

Avoid Changes during the First Three Months

After entering the United States on a nonimmigrant visa, try to avoid making any changes to your visa or your status during the first three months. If you attempt to extend your stay or adjust your status in the United States before three months have passed, immigration officials may doubt your original intentions and question other information you've submitted as part of your visa application. Therefore, it is better to let a few months go by before you decide to extend your visa or change your status. After several months, it is more plausible that your plans, situation, or reasoning has legitimately changed.

EMILIA'S STORY: PART 1

To make the process more understandable, we've created a "real-life" example to show what might actually be involved in taking the steps toward citizenship.

When she was 16 years old, Emilia Alvarez was a citizen of Chile with a Chilean passport. Her mother had come to the United States as an exchange student as part of a program that would help her to be a more effective English teacher in Chile. As an exchange visitor, Emilia's mother, Rene, was issued a J-1 visa that would be valid for the two years she would be in the United States for her studies. (J visas are issued for a specific period of time. This is referred to as the *duration of status* and is noted as "D/S" on a person's Form I-94.) The terms of Rene's grant included tuition and living expenses. Emilia came with her mother as a dependent child and was issued a J-2 visa. While her mother was attending her classes, Emilia attended the local high school and earned her high school diploma.

At the end of the two years, Rene had completed her studies and prepared to return to Chile. However, Emilia wanted to stay in the United States. Emilia applied to a local university that offered courses in pre-school education, the field she was interested in studying. Her mother agreed to pay for Emilia's tuition, but she couldn't afford to also pay for her room and board. Fortunately, Emilia was invited to stay with a family that she and her mother had come to know during the previous two years. Michael Williams, his wife, Virginia, and their two children, Susan and Richard, were delighted to invite Emilia to stay with them in their home.

To prepare for this transition, Emilia went to the USCIS Web site at www.uscis.gov and downloaded the following forms:

- I-539: Application to Extend/Change Nonimmigrant Status
- I-134: Affidavit of Support

(The following are examples of what these two forms might look like when properly filled out. Blank practice forms, as well as instructions for filling them out, can be found in Appendix A.)

OMB No. 1615-0003; Expires 02/29/12

Department of Homeland Security
U.S. Citizenship and Immigration Services

I-539, Application to Extend/ Change Nonimmigrant Status

START HERE - Please type or print in black ink

Part 1.   Information About You

Family Name	Given Name	Middle Name
Alvarez	Emilia	Rosalia

Address -
In care of -

Street Number and Name		Apt. Number
1224 S. Gaylord Street		462

City	State	Zip Code	Daytime Phone Number
Denver	CO	80231	303-123-4567

Country of Birth	Country of Citizenship
Chile	Chile

Date of Birth (mm/dd/yyyy)	U.S. Social Security # (if any)	A-Number (if any)
03/19/1986	000-00-0000	A00000000

Date of Last Arrival Into the U.S.	I-94 Number
05/07/2003	00000000

Current Nonimmigrant Status	Expires on (mm/dd/yyyy)
J-2	04/21/2013

Part 2. Application Type (See instructions for fee)

1. I am applying for: (Check one)
- **a.** ☐ An extension of stay in my current status.
- **b.** ☒ A change of status. The new status I am requesting is: F-1
- **c.** ☐ Reinstatement to student status.

2. Number of people included in this application: (Check one)
- **a.** ☒ I am the only applicant.
- **b.** ☐ Members of my family are filing this application with me.
  The total number of people (including me) in the application is: _____
  (Complete the supplement for each co-applicant.)

Part 3. Processing Information

1. I/We request that my/our current or requested status be extended until (mm/dd/yyyy): D/S

2. Is this application based on an extension or change of status already granted to your spouse, child, or parent?
☒ No ☐ Yes. USCIS Receipt # _____

3. Is this application based on a separate petition or application to give your spouse, child, or parent an extension or change of status? ☒ No ☐ Yes, filed with this I-539.

☐ Yes, filed previously and pending with USCIS. Receipt #: _____

4. If you answered "Yes" to Question 3, give the name of the petitioner or applicant:

If the petition or application is pending with USCIS, also give the following data:

Office filed at	Filed on (mm/dd/yyyy)

Part 4. Additional Information

1. For applicant #1, provide passport information: Valid to: (mm/dd/yyyy)
Country of Issuance: Chile   12/02/2010

2. Foreign Address: Street Number and Name | Apt. Number
Avenida Diego Bravo 12345 | 320

City or Town	State or Province
Las Condes	Santiago

Country	Zip/Postal Code
Chile	N/A

For USCIS Use Only

Returned	Receipt
Date	
Resubmitted	
Date	
Reloc Sent	
Date	
Reloc Rec'd	
Date	

☐ Applicant Interviewed on _____ Date

☐ Extension Granted to (Date): _____

Change of Status/Extension Granted
New Class: From (Date): _____
_____ To (Date): _____

If Denied:
☐ Still within period of stay
☐ S/D to: _____
☐ Place under docket control

Remarks:

Action Block

To Be Completed by Attorney or Representative, if any

☐ Fill in box if G-28 is attached to represent the applicant.

ATTY State License #

Form I-539 (Rev. 06/12/09)Y

3. Answer the following questions. If you answer "Yes" to any question, describe the circumstances in detail and explain on a separate sheet of paper.

		Yes	No
a.	Are you, or any other person included on the application, an applicant for an immigrant visa?	☐	☒
b.	Has an immigrant petition ever been filed for you or for any other person included in this application?	☐	☒
c.	Has Form I-485, Application to Register Permanent Residence or Adjust Status, ever been filed by you or by any other person included in this application?	☐	☒
d.1.	Have you, or any other person included in this application, ever been arrested or convicted of any criminal offense since last entering the United States?	☐	☒

d.2. Have you EVER ordered, incited, called for, commited, assisted, helped with, or otherwise participated in any of the following:

(a) Acts involving torture or genocide?

(b) Killing any person?

(c) Intentionally and severely injuring any person?

(d) Engaging in any kind of sexual contact or relations with any person who was being forced or threatened?

(e) Limiting or denying any person's ability to exercise religious beliefs?   ☐   ☒

d.3. Have you EVER:

(a) Served in, been a member of, assisted in, or participated in any military unit, paramilitary unit, police unit, self-defense unit, vigilante unit, rebel group, guerrilla group, militia, or insurgent organization?

(b) Served in any prison, jail, prison camp, detention facility, labor camp, or any other situation that involved detaining persons?   ☐   ☒

d.4. Have you EVER been a member of, assisted in, or participated in any group, unit, or organization of any kind in which you or other persons used any type of weapon against any person or threatened to do so?   ☐   ☒

d.5. Have you EVER assisted or participated in selling or providing weapons to any person who to your knowledge used them against another person, or in transporting weapons to any person who to your knowledge used them against another person?   ☐   ☒

d.6. Have you EVER received any type of military, paramilitary, or weapons training?   ☐   ☒

e.	Have you, or any other person included in this application, done anything that violated the terms of the nonimmigrant status you now hold?	☐	☒
f.	Are you, or any other person included in this application, now in removal proceedings?	☐	☒
g.	Have you, or any other person included in this application, been employed in the United States since last admitted or granted an extension or change of status?	☐	☒

1. If you answered "Yes" to Question 3f, give the following information concerning the removal proceedings on the attached page entitled "**Part 4. Additional information. Page for answers to 3f and 3g.**" Include the name of the person in removal proceedings and information on jurisdiction, date proceedings began, and status of proceedings.

2. If you answered "No" to Question 3g, fully describe how you are supporting yourself on the attached page entitled "**Part 4. Additional information. Page for answers to 3f and 3g.**" Include the source, amount, and basis for any income.

3. If you answered "Yes" to Question 3g, fully describe the employment on the attached page entitled "**Part 4. Additional information. Page for answers to 3f and 3g.**" Include the name of the person employed, name and address of the employer, weekly income, and whether the employment was specifically authorized by USCIS.

		Yes	No

h.   Are you currently or have you ever been a J-1 exchange visitor or a J-2 dependent of a J-1 exchange visitor?   ☒   ☐

If "Yes," you must provide the dates you maintained status as a J-1 exchange visitor or J-2 dependent. Willful failure to disclose this information (or other relevant information) can result in your application being denied. Also, provide proof of your J-1 or J-2 status, such as a copy of Form DS-2019, Certificate of Eligibility for Exchange Visitor Status, or a copy of your passport that includes the J visa stamp.

Part 5. Applicant's Statement and Signature *(Read the information on penalties in the instructions before completing this section. You must file this application while in the United States.)*

Applicant's Statement (Check One):

☒   I can read and understand English, and have read and understand each and every question and instruction on this form, as well as my answer to each question.

☐   Each and every question and instruction on this form, as well as my answer to each question, has been read to me by the person named below in _____, a language in which I am fluent. I understand each and every question and instruction on this form, as well as my answer to each question.

Applicant's Signature

I certify, under penalty of perjury under the laws of the United States of America, that this application and the evidence submitted with it is all true and correct. I authorize the release of any information from my records that U.S. Citizenship and Immigration Services needs to determine eligibility for the benefit I am seeking.

Signature *Emilia R. Roberts*	Print your Name Emilia Rosalia Alvarez	Date 09/22/2004
Daytime Telephone Number 303-123-4567	E-Mail Address	

NOTE: *If you do not completely fill out this form or fail to submit required documents listed in the instructions, you may not be found eligible for the requested benefit and this application may be denied.*

Part 6. Interpreter's Statement

Language used: _____

I certify that I am fluent in English and the above-mentioned language. I further certify that I have read each and every question and instruction on this form, as well as the answer to each question, to this applicant in the above-mentioned language, and the applicant has understood each and every instruction and question on the form, as well as the answer to each question.

Signature	Print Your Name	Date
Firm Name (if applicable)	Daytime Telephone Number *(Area Code and Number)*	
Address	Fax Number *(Area Code and Number)*	E-Mail Address

Part 7. Signature of Person Preparing Form, if Other Than Above *(Sign Below)*

Signature	Print Your Name	Date
Firm Name (if applicable)	Daytime Telephone Number *(Area Code and Number)*	
Address	Fax Number *(Area Code and Number)*	E-Mail Address

I declare that I prepared this application at the request of the above person and it is based on all information of which I have knowledge.

Part 4. (Continued) Additional Information. (Page 2 for answers to 3f and 3g.)

If you answered "Yes" to Question 3f in Part 4 on Page 3 of this form, give the following information concerning the removal proceedings. Include the name of the person in removal proceedings and information on jurisdiction, date proceedings began, and status of proceedings.

If you answered "No" to Question 3g in Part 4 on Page 3 of this form, fully describe how you are supporting yourself. Include the source, amount and basis for any income.

```
I have been a dependant of my mother, who was visiting the United States on a J-1 visa.
```

If you answered "Yes" to Question 3g in Part 4 on Page 3 of this form, fully describe the employment. Include the name of the person employed, name and address of the employer, weekly income, and whether the employment was specifically authorized by USCIS.

Department of Homeland Security
U.S. Citizenship and Immigration Services

Form I-134, Affidavit of Support

(Answer all items. Type or print in black ink.)

I, ___Michael R. Williams___   residing at ___1145 Pearl Street___
         (Name)   (Street and Number)

___Denver___   ___CO___   ___80234___   ___USA___
    (City)   (State)   (Zip Code if in U.S.)   (Country)

certify under penalty of perjury under U.S. law, that:

1. I was born on ___06/22/1959___ in ___Iowa City, Iowa___   ___USA___
          (Date-mm/dd/yyyy)   (City)   (Country)

If you are not a U.S. citizen based on your birth in the United States, or a non-citizen U.S. national based on your birth in American Samoa (including Swains Island), answer the following as appropriate:

    a. If a U.S.citizen through naturalization, give certificate of naturalization number _____

    b. If a U.S. citizen through parent(s) or marriage, give citizenship certificate number _____

    c. If U.S. citizenship was derived by some other method, attach a statement of explanation.

    d. If a lawfully admitted permanent resident of the United States, give A-Number _____

    e. If a lawfully admitted nonimmigrant, give Form I-94, Arrival-Departure Document, number _____

2. I am ___50___ years of age and have resided in the United States since (date) ___06/22/1959___

3. This affidavit is executed on behalf of the following person:

Name (Family Name)	(First Name)	(Middle Name)	Gender	Age
Alvarez	Emilia	Rosalia	F	18

Citizen of (Country)		Marital Status	Relationship to Sponsor	
Chile		single	none	

Presently resides at (Street and Number)	(City)	(State)	(Country)
1234 Dahlia Street, Apt. 1-A	Denver	CO	80224

Name of spouse and children accompanying or following to join person:

Spouse	Gender	Age	Child		Gender	Age
N/A						
Child	Gender	Age	Child		Gender	Age
Child	Gender	Age	Child		Gender	Age

4. This affidavit is made by me for the purpose of assuring the U.S. Government that the person(s) named in **item (3)** will not become a public charge in the United States.

5. I am willing and able to receive, maintain, and support the person(s) named in **item 3**. I am ready and willing to deposit a bond, if necessary, to guarantee that such person(s) will not become a public charge during his or her stay in the United States, or to guarantee that the above named person(s) will maintain his or her nonimmigrant status, if admitted temporarily, and will depart prior to the expiration of his or her authorized stay in the United States.

6. I understand that:

    a. Form I-134 is an "undertaking" under section 213 of the Immigration and Nationality Act, and I may be sued if the person named in **item 3** becomes a public charge after admission to the United States; and

    b. Form I-134 may be made available to any Federal, State, or local agency that may receive an application from the person named in **item 3** for Food Stamps, Supplemental Security Income, or Temporary Assistance to Needy Families;

    c. If the person named in **item 3** does apply for Food Stamps, Supplemental Security Income, or Temporary Assistance for Needy Families, my own income and assets may be considered in deciding the person's application. How long my income and assets may be attributed to the person named in **item 3** is determined under the statutes and rules governing each specific program.

7. I am employed as or engaged in the business of ___Engineering___ with ___Colorado Professional [+]___

              (Type of Business)   (Name of Concern)

at   ___4500 S. Broadway___   ___Littleton___   ___CO___   ___80241___

      (Street and Number)   (City)   (State)   (Zip Code)

I derive an annual income of: *(If self-employed, I have attached a copy of my last income tax return or report of commercial rating concern which I certify to be true and correct to the best of my knowledge and belief. See instructions for nature of evidence of net worth to be submitted.)* $ 163,000

I have on deposit in savings banks in the United States: $ 75,000

I have other personal property, the reasonable value of which is: $ 85,000

I have stocks and bonds with the following market value, as indicated on the attached list, which I certify to be true and correct to the best of my knowledge and belief: $ 100,000

I have life insurance in the sum of: $ 500,000

With a cash surrender value of: $ none

I own real estate valued at: $ 350,000

    With mortgage(s) or other encumbrance(s) thereon amounting to: $ ___175,000___

    Which is located at: ___1145 Pearl Street___   ___Denver___   ___CO___   ___80234___

                       (Street and Number)   (City)   (State)   (Zip Code)

8. The following persons are dependent upon me for support: *(Check the box* in the appropriate column to indicate whether the person named is *wholly* or *partially* dependent upon you for support.)

Name of Person	Wholly Dependent	Partially Dependent	Age	Relationship to Me
Virginia Williams	☐	☒	47	spouse
Susan Williams	☒	☐	17	child
Richard Williams	☒	☐	15	child

9. I have previously submitted affidavit(s) of support for the following person(s). If none, state "None".

Name of Person	Date submitted
none	

10. I have submitted a visa petition(s) to U.S. Citizenship and Immigration Services on behalf of the following person(s). If none, state "None".

Name of Person	Relationship	Date submitted
none		

11. I ☒ intend   ☐ do not intend to make specific contributions to the support of the person(s) named in **item 3**.

(If you check "intend," indicate the exact nature and duration of the contributions. For example, if you intend to furnish room and board, state for how long and, if money, state the amount in U.S. dollars and whether it is to be given in a lump sum, weekly or monthly, and for how long.

___Room and board for Emilia's four years in college___

Oath or Affirmation of Sponsor

I acknowledge that I have read "Sponsor and Alien Liability" on Page 2 of the instructions for this form, and am aware of my responsibilities as a sponsor under the Social Security Act, as amended, and the Food Stamp Act, as amended.

I certify under penalty of perjury under United States law that I know the contents of this affidavit signed by me and that the statements are true and correct.

Signature of sponsor ___Michael R. Williams___   Date ___09/22/2004___

Because she decided to stay in the United States, Emilia needed to change her visa status from a J-2 to an F-1. To begin this process, Emilia made copies of her completed I-539 and I-134 forms, as well as of the I-94 form she received at the airport when she arrived in the United States. The Form I-94 would be proof that she had remained in the United States legally because it was stamped with her date of entry, date of intended departure, and nonimmigrant status. In addition, Emilia made copies of her passport, her birth certificate, her high school diploma, her university admissions letter, and her Form I-20. She sent all of these documents along with the required filing fee by certified mail, return receipt requested, to the appropriate USCIS office as directed on Form I-539.

It is important to note that the USCIS always wants originals of forms that must be signed; however, you will want to make copies to keep for yourself. Photocopies of other documents are acceptable. Also keep in mind that mail sometimes gets lost. Although it is an added expense, it can be worth it to pay a little extra so you have receipts that prove when documents were mailed in the event a deadline is involved and your documents don't arrive on time.

Emilia requested that the university file a copy of Form I-20 with the USCIS on her behalf. Her copy of Form I-20 looked like that shown on the next page.

U.S. Department of Justice
Immigration and Naturalization Service
Please Read Instructions on Page 2

Certificate of Eligibility for Nonimmigrant (F-1) Student Status - For Academic and Language Students

OMB No. 1115-0051

Page 1

This page must be completed and signed in the U.S. by a designated school official.

1. Family Name (surname) **Alvarez**
   First (given) name (do not enter middle name) **Emilia**
   Country of birth **Chile**   Date of birth (mo./day/year) **03/19/1986**
   Country of citizenship **Chile**   Admission number (Complete if known) **N/A**

2. School (school district) name **Knowledge University**
   School official to be notified of student's arrival in U.S. (Name and Title) **Edward Fisher, International Student Advisor**
   School address (include zip code) **123 Knowledge St., Denver, CO 80224**
   School code (including 3-digit suffix, if any) and approval date **CO 214F 000 000** approved on **06/30/2004**

For Immigration Official Use

Visa issuing post   Date Visa issued

Reinstated, extension granted to:

3. This certificate is issued to the student named above for:
   a. ☒ Initial attendance at this school
   b. ☐ Continued attendance at this school
   c. ☐ School transfer. Transferred from
   d. ☐ Use by dependents for entering the United States.
   e. ☐ Other

4. Level of education the student is pursuing or will pursue in the United States:
   a. ☐ Primary   e. ☐ Master's
   b. ☐ Secondary   f. ☐ Doctorate
   c. ☐ Associate   g. ☐ Language training
   d. ☒ Bachelor's   h. ☐ Other

5. The student named above has been accepted for a full course of study at this school, majoring in **pre-school education**
   The student is expected to report to the school no later than (date) **08/15/2004** and complete studies not later than (date) **08/15/2008**
   The normal length of study is **4 years**

6. ☒ English proficiency is required:
   ☒ The student has the required English proficiency
   ☐ The student is not yet proficient, English instructions will be given at the school.
   ☐ English proficiency is not required because

7. This school estimates the student's average costs for an academic term of **9** (up to 12) months to be:
   a. Tuition and fees $ **75,000**
   b. Living expenses $ **25,000**
   c. Expenses of dependents $ **none**
   d. Other(specify): $ **none**
   Total $ **100,000**

8. This school has information showing the following as the students means of support, estimated for an academic term of **9** months (Use the same number of months given in item 7).
   a. Student's personal funds $ **15,000**
   b. Funds from this school (specify type) $ **none**
   c. Funds from another source (specify type and source) $ **10,000; Mr.Williams Room and Board**
   d. On-campus employment (if any) $ **none**
   Total $ **25,000**

9. Remarks:

10. School Certification: I certify under penalty of perjury that all information provided above in items 1 through 8 was completed before I signed this form and is true and correct; I executed this form in the United States after review and evaluation in the United States by me or other officials of the school of the student's application, transcripts or other records of courses taken and proof of financial responsibility, which were received at the school prior to the execution of this form; the school has determined that the above named student's qualifications meet all standards for admission to the school; the student will be required to pursue a full course of study as defined by 8 CFR 214.2(f)(6); I am a designated official of the above named school and I am authorized to issue this form.
Edward Fisher **Edward Fisher International Student Advisor 7/15/04 Denver, CO**
Signature of designated school official   Name of school official (print or type)   Title   Date issued   Place issued (city and state)

11. Student Certification: I have read and agreed to comply with the terms and conditions of my admission and those of any extension of stay as specified on page 2. I certify that all information provided on this form refers specifically to me and is true and correct to the best of my knowledge. I certify that I seek to enter or remain in the United States temporarily, and solely for the purpose of pursuing a full course of study at the school named on page 1 of this form. I also authorize the named school to release any information from my records which is needed by the INS pursuant to 8 CFR 214.3(g) to determine my nonimmigrant status.
Emilia Alvarez **Emilia Alvarez** **7/15/2004**
Signature of student   Name of student   Date
Rene Alvarez **Rene Alvarez 1234 Dahlia St. Apt. 1-A, Denver, CO USA 7/15/04**
Signature of parent or guardian if student is under 18   Name of parent/guardian (Print or type)   Address(city)   (State or province)   (Country)   (Date)

Form I20 A-B/I20ID(Rev 04-27-88)N

For official use only
Microfilm Index Number

I-20 SCHOOL

CHAPTER 3

Immigrant Visas: Becoming a Legal Permanent Resident

ALL ABOUT IMMIGRANT VISAS

If you are interested in becoming a permanent resident of the United States, you will need to apply for an immigrant visa. Possession of an immigrant visa proves that a person is registered to live and work in the United States and is compliant with U.S. immigration laws. The U.S. Citizenship and Immigration Services (USCIS) issues immigrant visas.

After you have obtained an immigrant visa, you may stay in the United States for as long as you would like. Immigrant visa holders are considered permanent residents, but they are not U.S. citizens. To gain citizenship, you will need to begin the process of naturalization, which is the legal process of acquiring a new nationality.

Obtaining Your Immigrant Visa

To become a legal immigrant in the United States, you must follow a three-step process. This process normally begins when an employer or relative files an immigrant petition on your behalf. The USCIS will inform the petitioner if the visa petition has been approved. If the USCIS approves your immigrant petition, the agency will send it to the Department of State's National Visa Center (NVC). Your petition will remain with the NVC until an immigrant visa number is available. The NVC will contact you when your visa petition is received and when an immigrant visa number is available. When you receive an immigrant visa number, you have been assigned an immigrant visa (or green card). Once you are in the United States, you may apply for permanent resident status. If you are outside the United States when you obtain your immigrant visa number, you will be asked to visit your local U.S. consulate to complete your immigrant visa application.

GREEN CARDS

Also known as a permanent resident card, a green card is an identification card that proves that you are a lawful permanent resident of the United States. There are many privileges granted to those with green cards, including the right to live and work in the United States, the right to travel abroad (for limited periods of time), and the right to apply for citizenship following a certain number of years as a U.S. resident.

Although green cards issued years ago were green in color, today's green cards are actually white with black lettering. About the size and shape of a credit card, a green card contains the holder's name, photograph, and other information. A green card may be revoked for various reasons, such as leaving the country for an extended period of time, breaking certain laws, or failing to maintain permanent residency in the United States.

Following the terrorist attacks of September 11, 2001, permanent residents are now required to carry their green cards with them at all times as proof of their legal status as visitors. It is very important to keep your proof of permanent residence in the United States current and up-to-date. If your green card is lost, stolen, or damaged, you should apply for a replacement card immediately. Similarly, if any of your personal information has changed, for example, if your name has changed because of marriage, your green card will need to be updated. To replace or update your green card, you'll need to contact USCIS at 800-870-3676 (toll-free). If you are outside the United States, you should visit the nearest U.S. consulate.

Obtaining Your Green Card

There are several ways to qualify for a green card. If you are interested in obtaining an immigrant visa, or green card, you may qualify based on a relative, your employment, or your need for refugee status or asylum. You might also choose to apply for a green card through a program called the Diversity Visa Lottery. Each of these options will be explained in detail later in this chapter.

To begin the process of obtaining your green card, you will need to provide the USCIS with a number of forms. Most of these can easily be obtained by visiting the USCIS Web site at http://www.uscis.gov/portal/site/uscis. You will also find detailed information about how to fill out the forms and where to file the forms once they are completed. The following forms will get you started on the path to obtaining your green card:

- Form I-485: Application to Register Permanent Residence or Adjust Status. You may also obtain this form by going to the USCIS Web site, by calling 800-870-3676 (toll-free), or by sending a request through the USCIS's forms-by-mail system.

- Form G-325A: Biographic Data Sheet (for those applicants ages 14 to 79).

- Form I-693: Medical Examination Sheet (unless you have already had a medical exam when applying for a fiancé(e) visa or have been a continuous resident since before 1972).

- Two recent, color photographs (taken within the past thirty days of your application). For instructions on photographs, please consult Form I-485 and Form M-603 in the appendix of this book.

- Form I-864: Affidavit of Support. Your sponsor should fill out this form. If you are adjusting to permanent resident status based on an employment petition, this requirement may not apply.

- Form I-765: Authorization for Employment. This form is necessary if you would like to work in the United States while your application is being processed.

- Form I-94: Arrival-Departure Record (presents evidence of admission, inspection, or parole in the United States). This form will be provided to you by the U.S. Customs and Border Patrol when you enter the country. You need to fill it out, and after your entry has been processed, the CPB officer will return the form to you. You must keep this form because it will be the basis for all other immigration-related activity.

Family-based Immigration

If you have a relative who is either a U.S. citizen or a permanent resident, you may become a permanent resident through family-based immigration. To begin this process, your relative must file an immigrant visa petition form, the I-130: Petition for Alien Relative, on your behalf. This form must also include proof of your relationship to the petitioner. Next, the Department of State will check if an immigrant visa number is available. Once an immigrant visa number is available, you may apply to have it assigned to you (even if you are already living in the United States). You can check on the status of your visa number through the visa bulletin available at the Department of State's Web site at http://travel.state.gov or by calling the Department of State's Visa Office at 202-663-1541.

A relative may sponsor your immigration to the United States if he or she is either a citizen or a lawful permanent resident of this country. Sponsors who are U.S. citizens may petition for a husband or wife, an unmarried child under 21 years of age, an unmarried son or daughter over 21 years of age, or a married son or daughter. If the sponsor is at least 21 years old, he or she may petition to have a brother, sister, or parent immigrate to the U.S. A lawful permanent resident of the United States may petition for a husband, wife, or unmarried son or daughter to immigrate to the U.S. In all cases, proof of the relationship will be required.

People hoping to come to the United States through family-based immigration must wait for an immigrant visa number based on certain preference categories. Parents, spouses, and unmarried children under 21 years of age will receive an immigrant visa number immediately. Other relatives, however, will obtain a visa number according to the following preference categories:

- *First preference:* Sons and daughters of U.S. citizens who are unmarried and at least 21 years of age

- *Second preference:* Spouses, spouses' unmarried children, and unmarried sons and daughters of lawful permanent residents of the United States

- *Third preference:* Married children of U.S. citizens, their spouses, and their children who are under age 21

- *Fourth preference:* Adult U.S. citizens' brothers and sisters, their spouses, and their children who are under age 21

Following its review of your Form I-130, the USCIS will either approve or deny your petition. If your petition is approved, it will then follow the process described earlier in the "Obtaining Your Immigrant Visa" section. Very likely, you and your petitioning relative will be asked to interview at a local USCIS office. It is a good idea to contact the USCIS to report any changes in your address or personal situation, or those of your sponsor.

Employment-based Immigration

Another path you might take to immigrate to the United States is through employment. If you have been offered permanent employment in the United States, you may follow steps outlined by the USCIS to obtain an immigration visa. Employers may sponsor those wishing to become lawful permanent residents based on employment. To apply for employment-based immigration, you (or your employer) need to complete the following steps:

- First, the U.S. employer should fill out Form ETA 750: Application for Alien Employment Certification for the employee seeking immigration. This form and instructions for filling it out can be obtained from the U.S. Department of Labor Employment and Training Administration at http://www.foreignlaborcert.doleta.gov/. The completed form should be returned to the Labor Department, which will either approve or deny the application.

- If the application is approved, the employer will submit Form I-140: Immigrant Petition for Alien Worker to the USCIS. Form I-140 is an immigrant visa petition filed by the employer to allow an employee to work and live in the United States on a permanent basis.

- Next, the State Department must issue the employee an immigrant visa number, even if he or she is already living and working in the United States. Once the immigration visa number has been assigned, the employee has been assigned an immigrant visa. Applicants may check on the status of their visa numbers by checking the Department of State's visa bulletin.

- After the visa number is issued, if the employee is already in the United States, he or she must apply for permanent resident status (a green card). If the employee has not yet arrived in the United States, he or she will complete this process at a local U.S. consulate office. While the employee's application for permanent resident status is pending, he or she may apply for a work permit.

To be eligible for permanent resident status based on employment, potential immigrants to the United States should be in one of the following categories:

1. *EB-1 Priority workers:* Foreign nationals (those seeking immigration to the United States) who are skilled in education, business, science, art, or athletics

2. *EB-2 Professionals:* Professionals with graduate degrees, qualified physicians, and foreign nationals with extraordinary abilities in business, science, or the arts

3. *EB-3 Skilled or professional workers:* Those with either a bachelor's degree or at least two years of work experience or training, as well as some unskilled workers

4. *EB-4 Special immigrants:* Former and current U.S. government employees working abroad and religious workers

Investor Visas

It is also possible to immigrate to the United States through investment. More than 10,000 investor visas are available each year to those who want to invest in a U.S. commercial enterprise. Applicants for this type of visa must prove that their business would create ten or more new jobs in this country and improve the local economy where the business operates. Investors are required to spend a specific amount of capital and may create, purchase, or expand a business based on USCIS guidelines. If you would like to apply for permanent resident status based on investment, you may do so alone or with your spouse and unmarried children.

Individuals Seeking Asylum and Refugees

Some people are able to immigrate to the United States as a result of persecution or fear of persecution. These individuals, called asylees or refugees, are persecuted because of their nationality, religion, race, political views, or social group. The United States offers a form of protection for those fearing persecution called asylum. Asylum allows asylees who are either already in the country or just arriving the right to remain in the United States. If asylum is granted, asylees are eligible to apply for lawful permanent resident status.

The U.S. Asylum Program differs from the U.S. Refugee Program that brings groups of refugees to the United States for resettlement. In contrast, those seeking asylum must already be in the United States or at a port of entry. Ports of entry include airports, seaports, or border crossings. People may apply for asylum without regard to their immigration status or their country of origin. An unlimited number of people may apply for asylum each year. Refugees must apply for lawful permanent resident status (a green card) within one year of entering the United States. Although asylees are not required to apply for lawful permanent resident status, they are free to do so after one year in the United States.

Diversity or Green Card Lottery

In addition to family-based and employment-based immigration, many people are able to immigrate to the United States through the Diversity Lottery Program (also known as the Green Card Lottery). This program makes 55,000 immigrant visas available each year to people in countries with low rates of immigration to the United States. The Department of State administers the Diversity Lottery and selects applications at random. The program closes once 55,000 immigration visas are issued or the fiscal year ends. Applicants who receive a visa through this program are permitted to live and work in the United States. They are also authorized to bring their spouses and unmarried children (under age 21) to this country.

In order to be eligible for the Diversity Lottery, you, your spouse, or, in some cases, your parent must be a citizen of a country designated by the Department of State to participate in the lottery. Before each year's lottery, the Department of State publishes a list of eligible countries. You will also need a high school diploma (or the equivalent) or two years of recent work experience. This work experience must be in an occupation requiring two years of training or experience.

To apply for the Diversity Lottery Program, you will complete an online application for the program. The form is only available during the online registration period and may be found at the State Department's Diversity Visa Web site, http://www.dvlottery.state.gov.

Adjusting Your Status

At one time, foreign nationals were only allowed to obtain immigrant visas abroad at a U.S. consulate. Now, this process is much easier. Foreign nationals who are living and working in the United States may become lawful permanent residents without leaving the country. This process is known as adjustment of status and allows applicants to file for green cards without having to return to their native countries. Adjustment of status refers only to the process of becoming a lawful permanent resident—it does not include changing status from one nonimmigrant category to another. Filing an adjustment of status requires applicants to fill out forms and pay application fees.

When You May Change Your Status

A foreign national who is living in the United States may apply for permanent resident status if the USCIS has approved his or her immigrant petition and an immigrant number is immediately available from the Department of State. You may also apply for permanent resident status if you were first admitted to the United States as a conditional resident. Conditional residents are usually those who came to this country through marriages of less than two years or through investment-based immigration.

Although conditional residents may live and work in the United States, they must apply for a green card after two years in the country. If you obtained status as a conditional resident through marriage and would like to adjust to permanent resident status, you'll need to complete Form I-751: Petition to Remove Conditions on Residence. When you adjust your status to that of a permanent resident, you share most of the rights enjoyed by U.S. citizens. Permanent residents have the right to live and work permanently in the United States and to be protected by federal, state, and local laws.

How to Change Your Status

There are several ways to adjust your status to that of a lawful permanent resident of the United States. First, if you are already living in the United States, you may apply to change your status after you've been issued a visa number from the Department of State. You will then need to complete Form I-485: Application to Register Permanent Residence or Adjust Status. If a visa number becomes available and you are outside the United States, you must visit your local U.S. consulate to complete the application process. You should receive a green card within a few months after your adjustment of status is approved.

If you would like to change your legal status to become a lawful permanent resident, you must file the following materials with the USCIS:

- Form I-485: Application to Register Permanent Residence or Adjust Status
- Form G-325A: Biographic Data Sheet (for those aged 14 to 79)
- Form I-693: Medical Examination Sheet
- Two recent color photos (taken within thirty days)
- Form I-864: Affidavit of Support (completed by the sponsor and not applicable to those applying for permanent resident status based on employment)
- Form I-765: Authorization for Employment (for those who intend to work while their applications are pending)
- Form I-94: Arrival-Departure Record (provides evidence of admission, inspection, or parole into the United States)

To obtain the necessary forms, you may call the forms line provided by the USCIS at 800-870-3676 (toll-free) or submit a request using the USCIS's forms-by-mail system. Many forms and instructions for filling them out may also be available on the USCIS Web site at http://www.uscis.gov/portal/site/uscis. In some cases, these forms can be filed online. Depending on your particular circumstances, you may also need to provide the following items as part of your application for adjustment of status:

- Your approval notice sent by the USCIS if you have already been approved for an immigrant petition
- A copy of the completed petition filed on your behalf that will make an immigrant number immediately available to you if approved
- Copies of the fiancé(e) petition approval notice and marriage certificate if you were admitted into the United States as a U.S. citizen's fiancé(e)
- A copy of Form I-94: Arrival-Departure Record showing the date you were granted refuge or asylum in the United States
- Evidence of citizenship or nationality (along with Form I-485) for Cuban citizens or natives
- Evidence proving that you entered the United States prior to January 1, 1972, and have lived in the United States continually since that date (for those who have been continuous residents of the United States)
- A copy of your birth certificate and proof of relationship to your parent if your parent became a lawful permanent resident after you were born
- A copy of your marriage certificate, proof that any previous marriages were terminated, and evidence that your spouse became a permanent resident, if your spouse gained legal status following your marriage

Waiting for a Decision on Your Status

You may find it difficult to wait for a decision while your adjustment of status application is being reviewed. The USCIS processes applications of the same type (employment-based, for example) in the order they were filed. You will usually be notified by mail when a decision has been made. There are several ways for you to check on the status of your application while you wait.

First, you may check the USCIS's Web site at www.uscis.gov and follow the links to "Case Status Online." Here, you'll find the filing dates of cases that are currently pending for every USCIS office and service center. This information will give you a good idea of how much time it will take to complete your case. To check on your application status online, you will need to enter the receipt number assigned to your case. This number starts with the letters "VSC" and is followed by ten digits. Your receipt number allows you to obtain case status information and also to register for automatic case status updates.

You may also check on the status of your application by calling the USCIS's National Customer Service Center at 800-375-5283 (toll-free). Be sure to have your receipt number with you when you call. One other option is to write to the local office or service center where you filed your application. If you submit a written request, be sure to include the following:

- Your name and address
- An "A" number if one was assigned to your application
- Your date of birth
- The date and place where you filed your application
- Your receipt number
- Any recent notices from the USCIS
- The date and office where you were fingerprinted and interviewed (if completed)
- A copy of your Confirmation Receipt notice if you filed electronically

Be sure to sign your request and write ATTN: STATUS INQUIRY on your envelope. You may also bring these materials to your local USCIS office and inquire about your case status in person.

Travel Plans

If you need to travel outside the United States while your application is pending, you must secure advanced permission to leave the country. This advanced permission, called Advance Parole, is required before you leave the United States. If you do not obtain Advance Parole before leaving the country, your application with the USCIS will be abandoned, and you may not be permitted to return to the United States.

Change of Address

It is very important to notify the USCIS if you change your address while your adjustment of status application is pending. Be sure to update this information by calling the National Customer Service Center at 800-375-5283 (toll-free) or write to your local USCIS office. You'll need to include your full name, "A" number, old address, and current address.

Be sure to write ATTN: CHANGE OF ADDRESS on the envelope.

The USCIS Interview

The last stage of the adjustment of status process is an interview at your local USCIS office. During the interview, a USCIS staff member will review all of your forms and other documentation and correct any errors. He or she will place you under oath, ask you a number of questions, and review your medical examination results. If you are applying for marriage-based permanent resident status, the examiner may question both you and your spouse and ask for evidence of your life together, including proof of shared residence. Be sure to keep copies of your marriage certificate, wedding announcements, receipts for wedding-related expenses, pictures, and other materials documenting your wedding and marriage. If you are seeking permanent resident status based on your employment, you will be asked questions about your job in the United

States. At the end of the interview, you may be informed of the outcome of your case, or you might be asked to supply more evidence so a decision can be reached.

Fingerprints

The USCIS also requires most immigration applicants to be fingerprinted. Fingerprints are needed to conduct criminal background checks through the Federal Bureau of Investigation (FBI). Applicants must obtain fingerprint cards at an authorized fingerprint site, including USCIS offices, freestanding fingerprint sites called Application Support Centers (ASCs), and U.S. consulates and military installations overseas. Most fingerprints are submitted to the FBI using electronic fingerprint technology, making the processing time for criminal background checks much faster.

EMILIA'S STORY: PART 2

Although each person's experience is unique, following one person's story can help you sort out the steps. Let's check in again with Emilia.

After carefully filing the appropriate forms and documentation, Emilia was granted an F-1 visa and entered the university. She proceeded with her studies, getting good grades and making many new friends. Emilia kept track of the expiration date on her Chilean passport, and several months before it was due to expire, she renewed it. During her final year of school, Emilia met Christopher Roberts. They dated all through the year, fell in love, and decided to get married. Because Emilia and Christopher had friends who had become U.S. citizens, they were aware of many of the USCIS requirements for documentation. Wanting to make sure they did everything correctly, Emilia and Christopher announced their engagement in the local newspaper and took lots of photos at their engagement party. As their wedding approached, they rented a hall and made arrangements with a variety of contractors to provide all of the services for their wedding. They kept a folder with copies of all of the orders and receipts, a list of the invited wedding guests, and eventually a copy of their marriage license and certificate. The wedding and reception were videotaped by a friend.

After their wedding, Emilia moved from the Williamses' residence to Christopher's apartment. They quickly outgrew that space and so rented a larger apartment in both their names as husband and wife. Then, it was time to fill out more forms to complete the process of obtaining citizenship for Emilia.

Christopher filled out Form I-130: Petition for Alien Relative.

Department of Homeland Security
U.S. Citizenship and Immigration Services

OMB #1615-0012; Expires 01/31/11

I-130, Petition for Alien Relative

DO NOT WRITE IN THIS BLOCK - FOR USCIS OFFICE ONLY

A#	Action Stamp	Fee Stamp

Section of Law/Visa Category
- [ ] 201(b) Spouse - IR-1/CR-1
- [ ] 201(b) Child - IR-2/CR-2
- [ ] 201(b) Parent - IR-5
- [ ] 203(a)(1) Unm. S or D - F1-1
- [ ] 203(a)(2)(A)Spouse - F2-1
- [ ] 203(a)(2)(A) Child - F2-2
- [ ] 203(a)(2)(B) Unm. S or D - F2-4
- [ ] 203(a)(3) Married S or D - F3-1
- [ ] 203(a)(4) Brother/Sister - F4-1

Petition was filed on: _____ (priority date)
- [ ] Personal Interview
- [ ] Pet. [ ] Ben. " A" File Reviewed
- [ ] Field Investigation
- [ ] 203(a)(2)(A) Resolved
- [ ] Previously Forwarded
- [ ] I-485 Filed Simultaneously
- [ ] 204(g) Resolved
- [ ] 203(g) Resolved

Remarks:

A. Relationship   You are the petitioner. Your relative is the beneficiary.

1. I am filing this petition for my:	2. Are you related by adoption?	3. Did you gain permanent residence through adoption?
[X] Husband/Wife [ ] Parent [ ] Brother/Sister [ ] Child	[ ] Yes [X] No	[ ] Yes [X] No

B. Information about you

1. Name (Family name in CAPS) (First) (Middle)
ROBERTS   Christopher   J.

2. Address (Number and Street) (Apt. No.)
1224 S. Gaylord St.   462

(Town or City) (State/Country) (Zip/Postal Code)
Denver   CO   80231

3. Place of Birth (Town or City) (State/Country)
Royal Oak   MI

4. Date of Birth **5. Gender** **6. Marital Status**
02/12/1984   [X] Male [ ] Female   [X] Married [ ] Single [ ] Widowed [ ] Divorced

7. Other Names Used (including maiden name)

8. Date and Place of Present Marriage (if married)
05/15/2008   Denver, CO

9. U.S. Social Security Number (If any)   **10. Alien Registration Number**
111-11-1111

11. Name(s) of Prior Husband(s)/Wive(s)   **12. Date(s) Marriage(s) Ended**
none   N/A

13. If you are a U.S. citizen, complete the following:

My citizenship was acquired through (check one):
- [X] Birth in the U.S.
- [ ] Naturalization. Give certificate number and date and place of issuance.

- [ ] Parents. Have you obtained a certificate of citizenship in your own name?
  - [ ] Yes. Give certificate number, date and place of issuance. [ ] No

14. If you are a lawful permanent resident alien, complete the following:
Date and place of admission for or adjustment to lawful permanent residence and class of admission.

14b. Did you gain permanent resident status through marriage to a U.S. citizen or lawful permanent resident?
[ ] Yes [ ] No

C. Information about your relative

1. Name (Family name in CAPS) (First) (Middle)
ROBERTS   Emilia   Rosalia

2. Address (Number and Street) (Apt. No.)
1224 S. Gaylord St.   462

(Town or City) (State/Country) (Zip/Postal Code)
Denver   CO   80231

3. Place of Birth (Town or City) (State/Country)
Las Condes   Santiago/Chi

4. Date of Birth **5. Gender** **6. Marital Status**
03/19/1986   [ ] Male [X] Female   [X] Married [ ] Single [ ] Widowed [ ] Divorced

7. Other Names Used (including maiden name)
Emilia Rosalia Alvarez (maiden)

8. Date and Place of Present Marriage (if married)
05/15/2008   Denver, CO

9. U.S. Social Security Number (If any)   **10. Alien Registration Number**
000-00-0000   A00000000

11. Name(s) of Prior Husband(s)/Wive(s)   **12. Date(s) Marriage(s) Ended**
none   N/A

13. Has your relative ever been in the U.S.? [X] Yes [ ] No

14. If your relative is currently in the U.S., complete the following:
He or she arrived as a:
(visitor, student, stowaway, without inspection, etc.)   J-2

Arrival/Departure Record (I-94)   Date arrived
1 1 1 ▮ 1 1 1 1 1 1 1 1 1 1   05/07/2003

Date authorized stay expired, or will expire, as shown on Form I-94 or I-95   D/S

15. Name and address of present employer (if any)
none

Date this employment began   N/A

16. Has your relative ever been under immigration proceedings?
[X] No [ ] Yes Where _____ When _____
[ ] Removal [ ] Exclusion/Deportation [ ] Rescission [ ] Judicial Proceedings

INITIAL RECEIPT	RESUBMITTED	RELOCATED: Rec'd	Sent	COMPLETED: Appv'd	Denied	Ret'd

Form I-130 (Rev. 05/27/08)Y

C. Information about your alien relative (continued)

17. List husband/wife and all children of your relative.

(Name)	(Relationship)	(Date of Birth)	(Country of Birth)
N/A			

18. Address in the United States where your relative intends to live.

(Street Address)	(Town or City)	(State)
1224 S. Gaylord Street	Denver	CO

19. Your relative's address abroad. (Include street, city, province and country)

Avenida Diego Bravo 12345, Apt. 320, Las Condes, Santiago, Chile

Phone Number (if any)   303-123-4567

20. If your relative's native alphabet is other than Roman letters, write his or her name and foreign address in the native alphabet.

(Name)   Address (Include street, city, province and country):

21. If filing for your husband/wife, give last address at which you lived together. (Include street, city, province, if any, and country):

1224 S. Gaylord Street, Denver, CO, USA

From: 05/15/2008   To: present

22. Complete the information below if your relative is in the United States and will apply for adjustment of status.

Your relative is in the United States and will apply for adjustment of status to that of a lawful permanent resident at the USCIS office in:

If your relative is not eligible for adjustment of status, he or she will apply for a visa abroad at the American consular post in:

Denver	CO		
(City)	(State)	(City)	(Country)

NOTE: Designation of a U.S. embassy or consulate outside the country of your relative's last residence does not guarantee acceptance for processing by that post. Acceptance is at the discretion of the designated embassy or consulate.

D. Other information

1. If separate petitions are also being submitted for other relatives, give names of each and relationship.

N/A

2. Have you ever before filed a petition for this or any other alien? ☐ Yes ☒ No

If "Yes," give name, place and date of filing and result.

WARNING: USCIS investigates claimed relationships and verifies the validity of documents. USCIS seeks criminal prosecutions when family relationships are falsified to obtain visas.

PENALTIES: By law, you may be imprisoned for not more than five years or fined $250,000, or both, for entering into a marriage contract for the purpose of evading any provision of the immigration laws. In addition, you may be fined up to $10,000 and imprisoned for up to five years, or both, for knowingly and willfully falsifying or concealing a material fact or using any false document in submitting this petition.

YOUR CERTIFICATION: I certify, under penalty of perjury under the laws of the United States of America, that the foregoing is true and correct. Furthermore, I authorize the release of any information from my records that U.S. Citizenship and Immigration Services needs to determine eligiblity for the benefit that I am seeking.

E. Signature of petitioner.

Christopher J. Roberts   Date 09/21/2009   Phone Number (303) 987-6543

F. Signature of person preparing this form, if other than the petitioner.

I declare that I prepared this document at the request of the person above and that it is based on all information of which I have any knowledge.

Print Name _____   Signature _____   Date _____

Address _____   G-28 ID or VOLAG Number, if any. _____

Form I-130 (Rev. 05/27/08)Y Page 2

Emilia completed Form I-485: Application to Register Permanent Residence or Adjust Status.

OMB No. 1615-0023; Expires 11/30/2011

Department of Homeland Security
U.S. Citizenship and Immigration Services

**I-485, Application to Register
Permanent Residence or Adjust Status**

START HERE - Type or print in black ink.

For USCIS Use Only	
Returned	Receipt

Part 1.   Information About You

Family Name	Given Name	Middle Name
Roberts	Emilia	Rosalia

Address- C/O

Street Number and Name	Apt. #
1224 S. Gaylord Street	462

City

Denver

State	Zip Code
CO	80231

Date of Birth *(mm/dd/yyyy)*   Country of Birth: Chile
03/19/1986
Country of Citizenship/Nationality: Chile

U.S. Social Security #
000-00-0000

A # *(if any)*
A00000000

Date of Last Arrival *(mm/dd/yyyy)*
05/07/2003

I-94 #
111-111111

Current USCIS Status
F-1

Expires on *(mm/dd/yyyy)*
D/S

For USCIS Use Only
Resubmitted
Reloc Sent
Reloc Rec'd
Applicant Interviewed

Part 2.   Application Type *(Check one)*

I am applying for an adjustment to permanent resident status because:

a. ☒ An immigrant petition giving me an immediately available immigrant visa number that has been approved. (Attach a copy of the approval notice, or a relative, special immigrant juvenile, or special immigrant military visa petition filed with this application that will give you an immediately available visa number, if approved.)

b. ☐ My spouse or parent applied for adjustment of status or was granted lawful permanent residence in an immigrant visa category that allows derivative status for spouses and children.

c. ☐ I entered as a K-1 fiancé(e) of a U.S. citizen whom I married within 90 days of entry, or I am the K-2 child of such a fiancé(e). (Attach a copy of the fiancé(e) petition approval notice and the marriage certificate).

d. ☐ I was granted asylum or derivative asylum status as the spouse or child of a person granted asylum and am eligible for adjustment.

e. ☐ I am a native or citizen of Cuba admitted or paroled into the United States after January 1, 1959, and thereafter have been physically present in the United States for at least one year.

f. ☐ I am the husband, wife, or minor unmarried child of a Cuban described above in (e), and I am residing with that person, and was admitted or paroled into the United States after January 1, 1959, and thereafter have been physically present in the United States for at least one year.

g. ☐ I have continuously resided in the United States since before January 1, 1972.

h. ☐ Other basis of eligibility. Explain (for example, I was admitted as a refugee, my status has not been terminated, and I have been physically present in the United States for one year after admission). If additional space is needed, use a separate piece of paper.

I am already a permanent resident and am applying to have the date I was granted permanent residence adjusted to the date I originally arrived in the United States as a nonimmigrant or parolee, or as of May 2, 1964, whichever date is later, and: *(Check one)*

i. ☐ I am a native or citizen of Cuba and meet the description in (e) above.

j. ☐ I am the husband, wife, or minor unmarried child of a Cuban and meet the description in (f) above.

Section of Law
☐ Sec. 209(b), INA
☐ Sec. 13, Act of 9/11/57
☐ Sec. 245, INA
☐ Sec. 249, INA
☐ Sec. 1 Act of 11/2/66
☐ Sec. 2 Act of 11/2/66
☐ Other

Country Chargeable

Eligibility Under Sec. 245
☐ Approved Visa Petition
☐ Dependent of Principal Alien
☐ Special Immigrant
☐ Other

Preference

Action Block

To be Completed by
Attorney or Representative, if any
☐ Fill in box if G-28 is attached to represent the applicant.
VOLAG #
ATTY State License #

Form I-485 (Rev. 12/16/08)Y

Part 3. Processing Information

A. City/Town/Village of Birth	Current Occupation
Las Condes	none

Your Mother's First Name	Your Father's First Name
Rene	Carlos

Give your name exactly as it appears on your Arrival-Departure Record (Form I-94)
Emilia Rosalia Alvarez

Place of Last Entry Into the United States (City/State)	In what status did you last enter? (Visitor, student, exchange alien, crewman, temporary worker, without inspection, etc.)
Denver, CO	
Were you inspected by a U.S. Immigration Officer? ☒ Yes ☐ No	J-2

Nonimmigrant Visa Number	Consulate Where Visa Was Issued
11111	Santiago, Chile

Date Visa Was Issued (mm/dd/yyyy) 04/01/2003	Gender: ☐ Male ☒ Female	Marital Status: ☒ Married ☐ Single ☐ Divorced ☐ Widowed

Have you ever before applied for permanent resident status in the U.S.? ☒ No ☐ Yes. If you checked "Yes," give date and place of filing and final disposition.

B. List your present husband/wife, all of your sons and daughters (If you have none, write "None." If additional space is needed, use separate paper).

Family Name	Given Name	Middle Initial	Date of Birth (mm/dd/yyyy)
Roberts	Christopher	J.	02/12/1984
Country of Birth USA	**Relationship** husband	**A** # N/A	**Applying with you?** ☐ Yes ☒ No
Family Name	Given Name	Middle Initial	Date of Birth (mm/dd/yyyy)
Country of Birth	Relationship	A #	Applying with you? ☐ Yes ☐ No
Family Name	Given Name	Middle Initial	Date of Birth (mm/dd/yyyy)
Country of Birth	Relationship	A #	Applying with you? ☐ Yes ☐ No
Family Name	Given Name	Middle Initial	Date of Birth (mm/dd/yyyy)
Country of Birth	Relationship	A #	Applying with you? ☐ Yes ☐ No
Family Name	Given Name	Middle Initial	Date of Birth (mm/dd/yyyy)
Country of Birth	Relationship	A #	Applying with you? ☐ Yes ☐ No

C. List your present and past membership in or affiliation with every organization, association, fund, foundation, party, club, society, or similar group in the United States or in other places since your 16th birthday. Include any foreign military service in this part. If none, write "None." Include the name(s) of organization(s), location(s), dates of membership from and to, and the nature of the organization(s). If additional space is needed, use a separate piece of paper.

Form I-485 (Rev. 12/16/08)Y Page 2

Part 3.   Processing Information *(Continued)*

Answer the following questions. (If your answer is **"Yes"** on any one of these questions, explain on a separate piece of paper and refer to "What Are the General Filing Instructions? Initial Evidence" to determine what documentation to include with your application. Answering **"Yes"** does not necessarily mean that you are not entitled to adjust status or register for permanent residence.)

1. Have you ever, in or outside the United States:

    a. Knowingly committed any crime of moral turpitude or a drug-related offense for which you have not been arrested? ☐ Yes ☒ No

    b. Been arrested, cited, charged, indicted, fined, or imprisoned for breaking or violating any law or ordinance, excluding traffic violations? ☐ Yes ☒ No

    c. Been the beneficiary of a pardon, amnesty, rehabilitation decree, other act of clemency, or similar action? ☐ Yes ☒ No

    d. Exercised diplomatic immunity to avoid prosecution for a criminal offense in the United States? ☐ Yes ☒ No

2. Have you received public assistance in the United States from any source, including the U.S.Government or any State, county, city, or municipality (other than emergency medical treatment), or are you likely to receive public assistance in the future? ☐ Yes ☒ No

3. Have you ever:

    a. Within the past ten years been a prostitute or procured anyone for prostitution, or intend to engage in such activities in the future? ☐ Yes ☒ No

    b. Engaged in any unlawful commercialized vice, including, but not limited to, illegal gambling? ☐ Yes ☒ No

    c. Knowingly encouraged, induced, assisted, abetted, or aided any alien to try to enter the United States illegally? ☐ Yes ☒ No

    d. Illicitly trafficked in any controlled substance, or knowingly assisted, abetted, or colluded in the illicit trafficking of any controlled substance? ☐ Yes ☒ No

4. Have you ever engaged in, conspired to engage in, or do you intend to engage in, or have you ever solicited membership or funds for, or have you through any means ever assisted or provided any type of material support to any person or organization that has ever engaged or conspired to engage in sabotage, kidnapping, political assassination, hijacking, or any other form of terrorist activity? ☐ Yes ☒ No

5. Do you intend to engage in the United States in:

    a. Espionage? ☐ Yes ☒ No

    b. Any activity a purpose of which is opposition to, or the control or overthrow of, the Government of the United States, by force, violence, or other unlawful means? ☐ Yes ☒ No

    c. Any activity to violate or evade any law prohibiting the export from the United States of goods, technology, or sensitive information? ☐ Yes ☒ No

6. Have you ever been a member of, or in any way affiliated with, the Communist Party or any other totalitarian party? ☐ Yes ☒ No

7. Did you, during the period from March 23, 1933, to May 8, 1945, in association with either the Nazi Government of Germany or any organization or government associated or allied with the Nazi Government of Germany, ever order, incite, assist, or otherwise participate in the persecution of any person because of race, religion, national origin, or political opinion? ☐ Yes ☒ No

8. Have you ever engaged in genocide, or otherwise ordered, incited, assisted, or otherwise participated in the killing of any person because of race, religion, nationality, ethnic origin, or political opinion? ☐ Yes ☒ No

9. Have you ever been deported from the United States, or removed from the United States at government expense, excluded within the past year, or are you now in exclusion, deportation, removal, or rescission proceedings? ☐ Yes ☒ No

10. Are you under a final order of civil penalty for violating section 274C of the Immigration and Nationality Act for use of fraudulent documents or have you, by fraud or willful misrepresentation of a material fact, ever sought to procure, or procured, a visa, other documentation, entry into the United States, or any immigration benefit? ☐ Yes ☒ No

11. Have you ever left the United States to avoid being drafted into the U.S. Armed Forces? ☐ Yes ☒ No

12. Have you ever been a J nonimmigrant exchange visitor who was subject to the two-year foreign residence requirement and have not yet complied with that requirement or obtained a waiver? ☐ Yes ☒ No

13. Are you now withholding custody of a U.S. citizen child outside the United States from a person granted custody of the child? ☐ Yes ☒ No

14. Do you plan to practice polygamy in the United States? ☐ Yes ☒ No

Form I-485 (Rev. 12/16/08)Y Page 3

Part 4.   Signature (Read the information on penalties in the instructions before completing this section. You must file this application while in the United States.)

Your Registration With U.S. Citizenship and Immigration Services

"I understand and acknowledge that, under section 262 of the Immigration and Nationality Act (Act), as an alien who has been or will be in the United States for more than 30 days, I am required to register with U.S. Citizenship and Immigration Services. I understand and acknowledge that, under section 265 of the Act, I am required to provide USCIS with my current address and written notice of any change of address within **ten** days of the change. I understand and acknowledge that USCIS will use the most recent address that I provide to USCIS, on any form containing these acknowledgements, for all purposes, including the service of a Notice to Appear should it be necessary for USCIS to initiate removal proceedings against me. I understand and acknowledge that if I change my address without providing written notice to USCIS, I will be held responsible for any communications sent to me at the most recent address that I provided to USCIS. I further understand and acknowledge that, if removal proceedings are initiated against me and I fail to attend any hearing, including an initial hearing based on service of the Notice to Appear at the most recent address that I provided to USCIS or as otherwise provided by law, I may be ordered removed in my absence, arrested, and removed from the United States."

Selective Service Registration

The following applies to you if you are a male at least 18 years of age, but not yet 26 years of age, who is required to register with the Selective Service System: "I understand that my filing Form I-485 with U.S. Citizenship and Immigration Services authorizes USCIS to provide certain registration information to the Selective Service System in accordance with the Military Selective Service Act. Upon USCIS acceptance of my application, I authorize USCIS to transmit to the Selective Service System my name, current address, Social Security Number, date of birth, and the date I filed the application for the purpose of recording my Selective Service registration as of the filing date. If, however, USCIS does not accept my application, I further understand that, if so required, I am responsible for registering with the Selective Service by other means, provided I have not yet reached age 26."

Applicant's Certification

I certify, under penalty of perjury under the laws of the United States of America, that this application and the evidence submitted with it is all true and correct. I authorize the release of any information from my records that U.S. Citizenship and Immigration Services (USCIS) needs to determine eligibility for the benefit I am seeking.

Signature	*Print Your Name*	*Date*	**Daytime Phone Number** *(Include Area Code)*
	Emilia Rosalia Roberts	09/21/2009	+1 (303) 123-4567

NOTE: *If you do not completely fill out this form or fail to submit required documents listed in the instructions, you may not be found eligible for the requested document and this application may be denied.*

Part 5.   Signature of Person Preparing Form, If Other Than Above (Sign below)

I declare that I prepared this application at the request of the above person, and it is based on all information of which I have knowledge.

Signature	*Print Your Full Name*	*Date*	**Phone Number** *(Include Area Code)*

Firm Name and Address   *E-Mail Address (if any)*

Form I-485 (Rev. 12/16/08)Y Page 4

Both Christopher and Emilia were required to fill out Form G-325A: Biographic Information.

OMB No. 1615-0008; Expires 06/30/2011

Department of Homeland Security
U.S. Citizenship and Immigration Services

G-325A, Biographic Information

(Family Name)	(First Name)	(Middle Name)	[X] Male [ ] Female	Date of Birth (mm/dd/yyyy)	Citizenship/Nationality	File Number
Roberts	Christopher	John		02/12/1984	USA	A

All Other Names Used (include names by previous marriages)	City and Country of Birth	U.S. Social Security # (if any)
N/A	Royal Oak, MI, USA	111-11-1111

	Family Name	First Name	Date of Birth (mm/dd/yyyy)	City, and Country of Birth (if known)	City and Country of Residence
Father	Roberts	Anthony	02/09/1__	Royal Oak, MI, USA	Royal Oak, MI, USA
Mother (Maiden Name)	Miller	Judith	01/30/1__	Royal Oak, MI, USA	Royal Oak, MI, USA

Current Husband or Wife (If none, so state) Family Name (For wife, give maiden name)		First Name	Date of Birth (mm/dd/yyyy)	City and Country of Birth	Date of Marriage	Place of Marriage
Alvarez		Emilia	03/19/1986	LasCondes, Chile	05/15/20_	Denver, CO

Former Husbands or Wives (If none, so state) Family Name (For wife, give maiden name)	First Name	Date of Birth (mm/dd/yyyy)	Date and Place of Marriage	Date and Place of Termination of Marriage
None				

Applicant's residence last five years. List present address first.

Street and Number	City	Province or State	Country	From Month	From Year	To Month	To Year
1224 S. Gaylord St Apt. 462	Denver	CO	USA	05	2008	Present Time	
119 Farrington Ave.	Denver	CO	USA	02	2002	05	2008

Applicant's last address outside the United States of more than one year.

Street and Number	City	Province or State	Country	From Month	From Year	To Month	To Year
N/A							

Applicant's employment last five years. (If none, so state.) List present employment first.

Full Name and Address of Employer	Occupation (Specify)	From Month	From Year	To Month	To Year
Taylor Media Group	Marketing Manager	08	2006	Present Time	

Last occupation abroad if not shown above. (Include all information requested above.)

This form is submitted in connection with an application for: [ ] Naturalization [ ] Other (Specify): [X] Status as Permanent Resident	Signature of Applicant *Christopher J Roberts*	Date 09/22/20_

If your native alphabet is in other than Roman letters, write your name in your native alphabet below:

Penalties: Severe penalties are provided by law for knowingly and willfully falsifying or concealing a material fact.

Applicant: Print your name and Alien Registration Number in the box outlined by heavy border below.

Complete This Box (Family Name)	(Given Name)	(Middle Name)	(Alien Registration Number)
Roberts	Christopher	John	A

Form G-325A (Rev. 06/12/09)Y

Department of Homeland Security
U.S. Citizenship and Immigration Services

OMB No. 1615-0008; Expires 06/30/2011

G-325A, Biographic Information

(Family Name)	(First Name)	(Middle Name)	☐ Male ☒ Female	Date of Birth (mm/dd/yyyy)	Citizenship/Nationality	File Number
Roberts	Emilia	Rosalia		03/19/1986	Chile	A 000-000-000

All Other Names Used (include names by previous marriages)	City and Country of Birth	U.S. Social Security # (if any)
Emilia Rosalia Alvarez (maiden)	Las Condes, Chile	000-00-0000

	Family Name	First Name	Date of Birth (mm/dd/yyyy)	City, and Country of Birth (if known)	City and Country of Residence
Father	Alvarez	Carlos	11/22/19▓	Las Condes, Chile	Las Condes, Chile
Mother (Maiden Name)	Montes	Rene	09/12/19▓	Las Condes, Chile	Las Condes, Chile

Current Husband or Wife (If none, so state) Family Name (For wife, give maiden name)		First Name	Date of Birth (mm/dd/yyyy)	City and Country of Birth	Date of Marriage	Place of Marriage
Roberts		Christopher	02/12/1984	RoyalOak,MI,USA	05/15/20▓	Denver, CO

Former Husbands or Wives (If none, so state) Family Name (For wife, give maiden name)	First Name	Date of Birth (mm/dd/yyyy)	Date and Place of Marriage	Date and Place of Termination of Marriage
None				

Applicant's residence last five years. List present address first.

Street and Number	City	Province or State	Country	From Month	From Year	To Month	To Year
1224 S. Gaylord St Apt. 462	Denver	CO	USA	05	2008	Present Time	
1234 Dahlia St., Apt. 1-A	Denver	CO	USA	05	2003	05	2008

Applicant's last address outside the United States of more than one year.

Street and Number	City	Province or State	Country	From Month	From Year	To Month	To Year
Avenida Diego Bravo 12345	Las Condes	Santiago	Chile	03	1986	05	2003

Applicant's employment last five years. (If none, so state.) List present employment first.

Full Name and Address of Employer	Occupation (Specify)	From Month	From Year	To Month	To Year
none				Present Time	

Last occupation abroad if not shown above. (Include all information requested above.)

This form is submitted in connection with an application for:	Signature of Applicant	Date
☐ Naturalization ☐ Other (Specify): ☒ Status as Permanent Resident	*Emilia R. Roberts*	09/22/20▓

If your native alphabet is in other than Roman letters, write your name in your native alphabet below:

Penalties: Severe penalties are provided by law for knowingly and willfully falsifying or concealing a material fact.

Applicant: Print your name and Alien Registration Number in the box outlined by heavy border below.

Complete This Box (Family Name)	(Given Name)	(Middle Name)	(Alien Registration Number)
Roberts	Emilia	Rosalia	A 000-000-000

Form G-325A (Rev. 06/12/09)Y

Emilia also went to her doctor and had a complete physical examination. After the examination, her doctor filled out Form I-693: Report of Medical Examination and Vaccination Record (an example of this form can be found in Appendix A).

Christopher completed Form I-864: Affidavit of Support Under Section 213A of the Act and also enclosed a letter from his employer with his current salary, copies of his last three federal tax returns, copies of recent bank statements, and copies of his stock certificates and U.S. Savings Bonds.

Together, Emilia and Christopher compiled additional documents needed to complete the application package. They made a copy of Emilia's I-94 form, her passport, and the Approval Notice she received from the USCIS office when she previously changed her status from J-2 to F-1. They also included a copy of Emilia's birth certificate, which they had translated from Spanish to English and then notarized. Finally, Emilia and Christopher included the required passport-style photographs. (Photograph guidelines are contained in Form M-603, which is included in Appendix A.)

In addition to the information included in the Affidavit of Support, shown on the next page, Emilia and Christopher also provided a copy of their marriage certificate, a copy of Christopher's birth certificate, and all of the proofs required by the form.

Department of Homeland Security
U.S. Citizenship and Immigration Services

**I-864, Affidavit of Support
Under Section 213A of the Act**

Part 1. Basis for filing Affidavit of Support.

1. **I,** Christopher J. Roberts ,

am the sponsor submitting this affidavit of support because (Check only one box):

a. ☒ **I am the petitioner. I filed or am filing for the immigration of my relative.**

b. ☐ **I filed an alien worker petition on behalf of the intending immigrant, who is related to me as my** _____

c. ☐ **I have an ownership interest of at least 5 percent in** _____ , **which filed an alien worker petition on behalf of the intending immigrant, who is related to me as my** _____

d. ☐ **I am the only joint sponsor.**

e. ☐ **I am the** ☐ **first** ☐ **second of two joint sponsors.** *(Check appropriate box.)*

f. ☐ **The original petitioner is deceased. I am the substitute sponsor. I am the intending immigrant's** _____ .

**For Government
Use Only**

This I-864 is from:

☐ the Petitioner

☐ a Joint Sponsor # _____

☐ the Substitute Sponsor

☐ 5% Owner

This I-864:

☐ does not meet the requirements of section 213A.

☐ meets the requirements of section 213A.

_____ Reviewer

_____ Location

Date *(mm/dd/yyyy)*

Number of Affidavits of Support in file:

☐ 1   ☐ 2

Part 2. Information on the principal immigrant.

2. **Last Name** Roberts

First Name Emilia

Middle Name Rosalia

3. **Mailing Address Street Number and Name** *(Include Apartment Number)*

1224 S. Gaylord St., Apt. 462

City	State/Province	Zip/Postal Code	Country
Denver	CO	80231	USA

4. **Country of Citizenship** Chile

5. **Date of Birth** *(mm/dd/yyyy)* 03/19/1986

6. **Alien Registration Number** *(if any)* A- 00000000

7. **U.S. Social Security Number** *(if any)* 000-00-0000

Part 3. Information on the immigrant(s) you are sponsoring.

8. ☒ **I am sponsoring the principal immigrant named in Part 2 above.**

☒ Yes   ☐ No (Applicable only in cases with two joint sponsors)

9. ☐ **I am sponsoring the following family members immigrating at the same time or within six months of the principal immigrant named in Part 2 above. Do not include any relative listed on a separate visa petition.**

Name	Relationship to Sponsored Immigrant	Date of Birth *(mm/dd/yyyy)*	A-Number *(if any)*	U.S. Social Security Number *(if any)*
a. N/A				
b.				
c.				
d.				
e.				

10. **Enter the total number of immigrants you are sponsoring on this form from Part 3, Items 8 and 9.**   1

Form I-864 (Rev. 10/18/07)Y

Part 4. Information on the Sponsor.

			For Government Use Only
11. Name	Last Name Roberts		
	First Name Christopher	Middle Name John	
12. Mailing Address	Street Number and Name *(Include Apartment Number)* 1224 S. Gaylord St., Apt. 462		
	City Denver	State or Province CO	
	Country USA	Zip/Postal Code 80234	
13. Place of Residence *(if different from mailing address)*	Street Number and Name *(Include Apartment Number)*		
	City	State or Province	
	Country	Zip/Postal Code	

14. Telephone Number *(Include Area Code or Country and City Codes)*

303-123-4567

15. Country of Domicile

USA

16. Date of Birth *(mm/dd/yyyy)*

02/12/1984

17. Place of Birth *(City)*	State or Province	Country
Royal Oak	MI	USA

18. U.S. Social Security Number *(Required)*

111-11-1111

19. Citizenship/Residency

☒ I am a U.S. citizen.

☐ I am a U.S. national (for joint sponsors only).

☐ I am a lawful permanent resident. My alien registration number is A-_____

If you checked box (b), (c), (d), (e) or (f) in line 1 on Page 1, you must include proof of your citizen, national, or permanent resident status.

20. Military Service (To be completed by petitioner sponsors only.)

I am currently on active duty in the U.S. armed services.　☐ Yes　　☒ No

Part 5. Sponsor's household size.

21. Your Household Size - <u>DO NOT COUNT ANYONE TWICE</u>

    Persons you are sponsoring in this affidavit:

    a. Enter the number you entered on line 10. `☐` `1`

    Persons NOT sponsored in this affidavit:

    b. Yourself. `1`

    c. If you are currently married, enter "1" for your spouse. `1`

    d. If you have dependent children, enter the number here. `☐ ☐`

    e. If you have any other dependents, enter the number here. `☐ ☐`

    f. If you have sponsored any other persons on an I-864 or I-864 EZ who are now lawful permanent residents, enter the number here. `☐ ☐`

    g. OPTIONAL: If you have <u>siblings, parents, or adult children</u> with the same principal residence who are combining their income with yours by submitting Form I-864A, enter the number here. `☐ ☐`

    h. Add together lines and enter the number here. **Household Size:** `☐` `2`

For Government Use Only

Part 6. Sponsor's income and employment.

22. I am currently:

    a. ☒ Employed as a/an   Marketing Manager

    Name of Employer #1 *(if applicable)*   Taylor Media Group

    Name of Employer #2 *(if applicable)*   _____

    b. ☐ Self-employed as a/an   _____

    c. ☐ Retired from _____ since _____
        (Company Name)   *(Date)*

    d. ☐ Unemployed since _____
                        (Date)

23. **My current individual annual income is:** $ 65,000.00
                                    (See Step-by-Step Instructions)

Form I-864 (Rev. 10/18/07)Y Page 3

24. My current annual household income:

a. List your income from line 23 of this form. $ 65,000.00

b. Income you are using from any other person who was counted in your household size, including, in certain conditions, the intending immigrant. (See step-by-step instructions.) Please indicate name, relationship and income.

Name	Relationship	Current Income
_____	_____	$ _____
_____	_____	$ _____
_____	_____	$ _____
_____	_____	$ _____

c. **Total Household Income:** $ 65,000.00

(Total all lines from 24a and 24b. Will be Compared to Poverty Guidelines -- See Form I-864P.)

d. [X] The persons listed above have completed Form I-864A. I am filing along with this form all necessary Forms I-864A completed by these persons.

e. [ ] The person listed above, _____ does not need to
                                              (Name)
complete Form I-864A because he/she is the intending immigrant and has no accompanying dependents.

25. Federal income tax return information.

[X] I have filed a Federal tax return for each of the three most recent tax years. I have attached the required photocopy or transcript of my Federal tax return for only the most recent tax year.

My total income (adjusted gross income on IRS Form 1040EZ) as reported on my Federal tax returns for the most recent three years was:

Tax Year		Total Income
2008	*(most recent)*	$ 62,000.00
2007	*(2nd most recent)*	$ 55,000.00
2006	*(3rd most recent)*	$ 47,000.00

[ ] *(Optional)* I have attached photocopies or transcripts of my Federal tax returns for my second and third most recent tax years.

For Government Use Only

Household Size =

_____

Poverty line for year

_____ is:

$ _____

Part 7. Use of assets to supplement income. *(Optional)*

If your income, or the total income for you and your household, from line 24c exceeds the Federal Poverty Guidelines for your household size, YOU ARE NOT REQUIRED to complete this Part. Skip to Part 8.

26. **Your assets** *(Optional)*

    a. Enter the balance of all savings and checking accounts. $ 20,000.00

    b. Enter the net cash value of real-estate holdings. (Net means current assessed value minus mortgage debt.) $ 0.00

    c. Enter the net cash value of all stocks, bonds, certificates of deposit, and any other assets not already included in lines 26 (a) or (b). $ 10,000.00

    d. **Add together lines 26 a, b and c and enter the number here.**   **TOTAL:** $ 30,000.00

27. **Your household member's assets from Form I-864A.** *(Optional)*

    Assets from Form I-864A, line 12d for

N/A $ _____
_____
              (Name of Relative)

28. **Assets of the principal sponsored immigrant.** *(Optional)*

    The principal sponsored immigrant is the person listed in line 2.

    a. Enter the balance of the sponsored immigrant's savings and checking accounts. $ 0.00

    b. Enter the net cash value of all the sponsored immigrant's real estate holdings. (Net means investment value minus mortgage debt.) $ _____

    c. Enter the current cash value of the sponsored immigrant's stocks, bonds, certificates of deposit, and other assets not included on line a or b. $ 0.00

    d. **Add together lines 28a, b, and c, and enter the number here.** $ 0.00

29. **Total value of assets.**

    Add together lines 26d, 27 and 28d and enter the number here.   **TOTAL:** $ 30,000.00

For Government Use Only

Household Size =

_____

Poverty line for year

_____ is:

$ _____

The total value of all assests, line 29, must equal 5 times (3 times for spouses and children of USCs, or 1 time for orphans to be formally adopted in the U.S.) the difference between the poverty guidelines and the sponsor's household income, line 24c.

Form I-864 (Rev. 10/18/07)Y Page 5

What If I Do Not Fulfill My Obligations?

If you do not provide sufficient support to the person who becomes a permanent resident based on the Form I-864 that you signed, that person may sue you for this support.

If a Federal, State or local agency, or a private agency provides any covered means-tested public benefit to the person who becomes a permanent resident based on the Form I-864 that you signed, the agency may ask you to reimburse them for the amount of the benefits they provided. If you do not make the reimbursement, the agency may sue you for the amount that the agency believes you owe.

If you are sued, and the court enters a judgment against you, the person or agency that sued you may use any legally permitted procedures for enforcing or collecting the judgment. You may also be required to pay the costs of collection, including attorney fees.

If you do not file a properly completed Form I-865 within 30 days of any change of address, USCIS may impose a civil fine for your failing to do so.

When Will These Obligations End?

Your obligations under a Form I-864 will end if the person who becomes a permanent resident based on a Form I-864 that you signed:

- Becomes a U.S. citizen;
- Has worked, or can be credited with, 40 quarters of coverage under the Social Security Act;
- No longer has lawful permanent resident status, and has departed the United States;
- Becomes subject to removal, but applies for and obtains in removal proceedings a new grant of adjustment of status, based on a new affidavit of support, if one is required; or
- Dies.

Note that divorce **does not** terminate your obligations under this Form I-864.

Your obligations under a Form I-864 also end if you die. Therefore, if you die, your Estate will not be required to take responsibility for the person's support after your death. Your Estate may, however, be responsible for any support that you owed before you died.

30. I, Christopher J. Roberts

(Print Sponsor's Name)

certify under penalty of perjury under the laws of the United States that:

- **a.** I know the contents of this affidavit of support that I signed.

- **b.** All the factual statements in this affidavit of support are true and correct.

- **c.** I have read and I understand each of the obligations described in Part 8, and I agree, freely and without any mental reservation or purpose of evasion, to accept each of those obligations in order to make it possible for the immigrants indicated in Part 3 to become permanent residents of the United States;

- **d.** I agree to submit to the personal jurisdiction of any Federal or State court that has subject matter jurisdiction of a lawsuit against me to enforce my obligations under this Form I-864;

- **e.** Each of the Federal income tax returns submitted in support of this affidavit are true copies, or are unaltered tax transcripts, of the tax returns I filed with the U.S. Internal Revenue Service; and

Sign on following page.

Form I-864 (Rev. 10/18/07)Y Page 7

f. I authorize the Social Security Administration to release information about me in its records to the Department of State and U.S. Citizenship and Immigration Services.

g. Any and all other evidence submitted is true and correct.

31. _____   09/21/2009
      (Sponsor's Signature)   *(Date-- mm/dd/yyyy)*

Part 9. Information on Preparer, if prepared by someone other than the sponsor.

I certify under penalty of perjury under the laws of the United States that I prepared this affidavit of support at the sponsor's request and that this affidavit of support is based on all information of which I have knowledge.

Signature: _____   **Date:** _____

                                                                    (mm/dd/yyyy)

Printed Name: _____

Firm Name: _____

Address: _____

Telephone Number: _____

E-Mail Address : _____

Business State ID # *(if any)* _____

Form I-864 (Rev. 10/18/07)Y Page 8

Now that they were settled, Emilia wanted to get a job. Because she was still waiting to receive her green card, Emilia filled out Form I-765: Application for Employment Authorization. This way, she would be able to start working before the arrival of her green card.

OMB No. 1615-0040; Expires 09/30/11

Department of Homeland Security
U.S. Citizenship and Immigration Services

I-765, Application For Employment Authorization

Do not write in this block.

Remarks	Action Block	Fee Stamp
A#		
Applicant is filing under §274a.12 _____		

☐ Application Approved. Employment Authorized / Extended *(Circle One)*   until _____ (Date).
   _____ (Date).
   Subject to the following conditions: _____
   Application Denied.
   ☐ Failed to establish eligibility under 8 CFR 274a.12 (a) or (c).
   ☐ Failed to establish economic necessity as required in 8 CFR 274a.12(c)(14), (18) and 8 CFR 214.2(f)

I am applying for:
   ☒ Permission to accept employment.
   ☐ Replacement *(of lost employment authorization document)*
   ☐ Renewal of my permission to accept employment *(attach previous employment authorization document)*.

1. Name (Family Name in CAPS)   (First)   (Middle)
ROBERTS   Emilia   Rosalia

2. Other Names Used (Include Maiden Name)
Emilia Rosalia Alvarez (maiden)

3. Address in the United States (Number and Street)   (Apt. Number)
1224 S. Gaylord St.   462

(Town or City)   (State/Country)   (ZIP Code)
Denver   CO   80231

4. Country of Citizenship/Nationality
Chile

5. Place of Birth (Town or City)   (State/Province)   (Country)
Las Condes   Santiago   Chile

6. Date of Birth (mm/dd/yyyy)   **7.** Gender
03/19/1986   ☐ Male   ☒ Female

8. Marital Status   ☒ Married   ☐ Single
   ☐ Widowed   ☐ Divorced

9. Social Security Number (Include all numbers you have ever used) (if any)
000-00-0000

10. Alien Registration Number (A-Number) or I-94 Number (if any)
A00000000

11. Have you ever before applied for employment authorization from USCIS?
☐ Yes (If yes, complete below)   ☐ No

Which USCIS Office?   Date(s)

Results (Granted or Denied - attach all documentation)

12. Date of Last Entry into the U.S.   (mm/dd/yyyy)
05/07/2003

13. Place of Last Entry into the U.S.
Denver, CO

14. Manner of Last Entry (Visitor, Student, etc.)
J-2

15. Current Immigration Status (Visitor, Student, etc.)
F-1

16. Go to **Part 2** of the Instructions, Eligibility Categories. In the space below, place the letter and number of the category you selected from the instructions (For example, (a)(8), (c)(17)(iii), etc.).

Eligibility under 8 CFR 274a.12 (c) (9) ( )

17. If you entered the Eligibility Category, (c)(3)(C), in item 16 above, list your degree, your employer's name as listed in E-Verfy, and your employer's E-Verify Company Identification Number or a valid E-Verify Client Company Identification Number in the space below.

Degree: _____

Employer's Name as listed in E-Verify: _____

Employer's E-Verify Company Identification Number or a valid E-Verify Client Company Identification Number

Certification

Your Certification: I certify, under penalty of perjury under the laws of the United States of America, that the foregoing is true and correct. Furthermore, I authorize the release of any information that U.S. Citizenship and Immigration Services needs to determine eligibility for the benefit I am seeking. I have read the Instructions in **Part 2** and have identified the appropriate eligibility category in **Block 16**.

Signature   Telephone Number   Date
Emilia R. Roberts   303-123-4567   09/23/2009

Signature of person preparing form, if other than above: I declare that this document was prepared by me at the request of the applicant and is based on all information of which I have any knowledge.

Print Name   Address   Signature   Date

Remarks	Initial Receipt	Resubmitted	Relocated		Completed		
			Rec'd	Sent	Approved	Denied	Returned

Form I-765 (Rev. 10/30/08)Y

Emilia and Christopher made photocopies of their entire submission and then went to the local USCIS office to file it. They were given a receipt showing what documents they filed and the date they filed them.

Several months later, Emilia and Christopher were called to appear for an interview. They brought all of the original documents, their wedding folder, a photo album that included photos they had take since the wedding, and the video of their wedding day. At the interview, the examiner checked all of the forms and documentation Emilia and Christopher submitted.

Emilia and Christopher were questioned separately about their daily living habits, what they had eaten for dinner three nights ago, what activities they liked to do together, and where they met. They knew about this process, and so they were prepared and able to answer politely.

At the conclusion of the interview, Emilia and Christopher were told that Emilia would be granted Conditional Resident Alien (CRA) status. (Remember they had been married less than two years when they filed their papers.) To remove the conditional status, Emilia and Christopher waited almost two more years before filing Form I-751: Petition to Remove Conditions on Residence. This form should be filed ninety days before the second anniversary of being granted CRA status. Along with Form I-751, they submitted a copy of Emilia's conditional green card and documents proving that Emilia and Christopher entered into marriage in good faith and were still married. In addition, they submitted copies of their son's birth certificate, copies of their joint tax returns, insurance policies naming each other as beneficiaries, and joint loan agreements.

Emilia and Christopher's Form I-751 looked like this:

Department of Homeland Security
U.S. Citizenship and Immigration Services

I-751, Petition to Remove Conditions on Residence

START HERE - Please type or print in black ink.

For USCIS Use Only

Part 1. Information About You

Family Name (Last Name)	Given Name (First Name)	Full Middle Name
Roberts	Emilia	Rosalia

Address: (Street number and name) — Apt. #

1224 S. Gaylord Street — 462

C/O: (In care of)

City	State/Province
Denver	CO

Country	Zip/Postal Code
USA	80231

Mailing Address, if different than above (Street number and name):   Apt. #

C/O: (In care of)

City	State/Province

Country	Zip/Postal Code

Date of Birth (mm/dd/yyyy)	Country of Birth	Country of Citizenship
03/19/1986	Chile	Chile

Alien Registration Number (#A)	Social Security # (If any)
A00000000	000-00-0000

Conditional Residence Expires on (mm/dd/yyyy)	Daytime Phone # (Area/Country codes)
04/21/2013	303-123-4567

For USCIS Use Only

Returned

Date

Date

Resubmitted

Date

Date

Reloc Sent

Date

Date

Reloc Rec'd

Date

Date

☐ Petitioner Interviewed on _____

Receipt

Remarks

Part 2. Basis for Petition   *(Check one)*

a. ☒ My conditional residence is based on my marriage to a U.S. citizen or permanent resident, and we are filing this petition together.

b. ☐ I am a child who entered as a conditional permanent resident and I am unable to be included in a joint Petition to Remove the Conditions on Residence (Form I-751) filed by my parent(s)

OR

My conditional residence is based on my marriage to a U.S. citizen or permanent resident, but I am unable to file a joint petition and I request a waiver because: **(Check one)**

c. ☐ My spouse is deceased.

d. ☐ I entered into the marriage in good faith but the marriage was terminated through divorce or annulment.

e. ☐ I am a conditional resident spouse who entered a marriage in good faith, and during the marriage I was battered by or was the subject of extreme cruelty by my U.S. citizen or permanent resident spouse or parent.

f. ☐ I am a conditional resident child who was battered by or subjected to extreme cruelty by my U.S. citizen or conditional resident parent(s).

g. ☐ The termination of my status and removal from the United States would result in an extreme hardship.

Action Block

To Be Completed by
Attorney or Representative, if any.

☐ Fill in box if G-28 is attached to represent the applicant.

ATTY State License #

Part 3. Additional Information About You

1. Other Names Used *(including maiden name)*:

Emilia Rosalia Alvarez (maiden)

2. Date of Marriage *(mm/dd/yyyy)*   3. Place of Marriage   4. If your spouse is deceased, give the date of death *(mm/dd/yyyy)*

05/15/2008   Denver, CO   N/A

		Yes	No
5.	Are you in removal, deportation, or rescission proceedings?	☐	☒
6.	Was a fee paid to anyone other than an attorney in connection with this petition?	☐	☒
7.	Have you ever been arrested, detained, charged, indicted, fined, or imprisoned for breaking or violating any law or ordianance (excluding traffic regulations), or committed any crime which you were not arrested in the United States or abroad?	☐	☒
8.	If you are married, is this a different marriage than the one through which conditional residence status was obtained?	☐	☒
9.	Have you resided at any other address since you became a permanent resident? *(If yes, attach a list of all addresses and dates.)*	☐	☒
10.	Is your spouse currently serving with or employed by the U.S. government and serving outside the United States?	☐	☒

If you answered "Yes" to any of the above, provide a detailed explanation on a separate sheet(s) of paper and refer to "What Initial Evidence Is Required?" to determine what criminal history documentation to include with your petition. Place your name and Alien Registration Number (A#) at the top of each sheet and give the number of the item that refers to your response.

Part 4. Information About the Spouse or Parent Through Whom You Gained Your Conditional Residence

Family Name	First Name	Middle Name
Roberts	Christopher	John

Address

1224 S. Gaylord Street, Apt. 462, Denver, CO 80231

Date of Birth *(mm/dd/yyyy)*	Social Security # *(if any)*	A# *(if any)*
02/12/1984	111-11-1111	N/A

Part 5. Information About Your Children-List all your children *(Attach other sheet(s) if necessary)*

Name *(First/Middle/Last)*	Date of Birth *(mm/dd/yyyy)*	A # *(If any)*	If in U.S., give address/immigration status	Living with you?
none				☐ Yes ☐ No
				☐ Yes ☐ No
				☐ Yes ☐ No
				☐ Yes ☐ No
				☐ Yes ☐ No

Part 6. Signature.

Read the information on penalties in the instructions before completing this section. If you checked block "a" in Part 2, your spouse must also sign below.

I certify, under penalty of perjury of the laws of the United States of America, that this petition and the evidence submitted with it is all true and correct. If conditional residence was based on a marriage, I further certify that the marriage was entered in accordance with the laws of the place where the marriage took place and was not for the purpose of procuring an immigration benefit. I also authorize the release of any information from my records that the U.S. Citizenship and Immigration Services needs to determine eligibility for the benefit sought.

Signature	Print Name	Date *(mm/dd/yyyy)*
Emilia R. Roberts	Emilia R. Roberts	09/23/2009
Signature of Spouse	Print Name	Date *(mm/dd/yyyy)*
Christopher J. Roberts	Christopher J. Roberts	09/23/2009

NOTE: If you do not completely fill out this form or fail to submit any required documents listed in the instructions, you may not be found eligible for the requested benefit and this petition may be denied.

Part 7. Signature of Person Preparing Form, If Other than Above

I declare that I prepared this petition at the request of the above person and it is based on all information of which I have knowledge.

Signature	Print Name	Date *(mm/dd/yyyy)*

Firm Name and Address

Daytime Phone Number
(Area/Country codes)

E-Mail Address
(If any)

Emilia and Christopher made copies of all of their documentation and sent it by certified mail, return receipt requested, to the appropriate USCIS center and then waited.

Finally, the couple was summoned to appear for an interview. They again took with them the many documents that they had collected and submitted to the USCIS office. They also brought current photos and their son. Emilia and Christopher answered the examiners questions politely during the short interview. A short time later, Emilia received a green card.

CHAPTER 4

U.S. Immigration Laws

PAST U.S. IMMIGRATION LAWS

Immigration and Nationality Act

In 1952, the Immigration and Nationality Act (INA) was created. Although this act has been amended many times, it still forms the basis of U.S. immigration law. The INA is part of the United States Code, a collection of all U.S. laws. Title 8 of the U.S. Code addresses "Aliens and Nationality" and contains chapters and sections dealing with U.S. immigration law.

The 1996 Immigration Laws

In 1996, several important immigration laws were passed in the United States that had long-term effects on the immigration process and those wishing to become U.S. citizens. One of these laws was the Antiterrorism and Effective Death Penalty Act of 1996 (AEDPA). This law established a system in which the U.S. government could designate certain organizations as foreign terrorist organizations. After this law was passed, anyone associated with an international terrorist organization who wanted to stay in the United States could be denied asylum or deported.

Another law passed that year was the Illegal Immigration Reform and Immigrant Responsibility Act of 1996 (IIRIRA). Among other provisions, this law expanded the charge of aggravated felony to include non-violent crimes like shoplifting, theft, and driving while intoxicated. Not only were these laws more harsh, but they were also retroactive, meaning that those who had committed these types of crimes years ago could still be deported or denied citizenship.

The new laws also put an added burden on immigrant sponsors. Potential immigrants to the United States were now required to prove that they would not become a "public charge" (for example, they would not need food stamps, Medicaid, or other government aid) after obtaining their green cards. Furthermore, new restrictions for entering the United States were placed on people who had been living here unlawfully for six months or longer. Known as unlawful presence, those who had been living illegally in the United States before submitting their visa or naturalization applications could now be denied reentry into the country.

RECENT IMMIGRATION LEGISLATION

USA Patriot Act of 2001: Uniting and Strengthening America by Providing Appropriate Tools Required to Intercept and Obstruct Terrorism

Following the terrorist attacks on the United States on September 11, 2001, President George W. Bush signed the USA Patriot Act into law. This law added to the "bars of inadmissibility" outlined in previous laws by expanding the definition of terrorist activities and organizations. The new law barred those with associations to terrorist organizations from entering the United States, including immigrants with ties to these organizations who had already sought asylum in the United States.

In 2002, President Bush also signed the Enhanced Border Security and Visa Entry Reform Act. This legislation required the former Immigration and Naturalization Services (INS) to approve employment authorization documents with a photograph and fingerprint of those granted asylum in the United States.

Child Status Protection Act of 2002

The Child Status Protection Act (CSPA) was signed into law in 2002. This legislation amended sections of the Immigration and Nationality Act pertaining to children and the legal definition of a child. According to the new law, a child who reaches 21 years of age after his or her parents file an asylum application but before a decision is made on the parents' case may still be classified as a child. The child may also remain eligible for derivative asylum status. Children protected by this law must be unmarried and younger than 21 years old when their parents originally filed Form I-589: Application for Asylum and for Withholding of Removal. Even if the child was not listed as a dependent on the asylum application form, he or she may be included while the case is pending.

Establishment of U.S. Citizenship and Immigration Services (USCIS)

In 2002, the Homeland Security Act established the Department of Homeland Security (DHS) and led to the restructuring of the Immigration and Naturalization Service (INS). Before these changes, the INS administered immigration services, as well as U.S. border inspections and enforcement. Now, three separate bureaus within the DHS handle these responsibilities:

- U.S. Citizenship and Immigration Services (USCIS)
- Customs and Border Patrol (CBP)
- Immigration and Customs Enforcement (ICE)

The U.S. Citizenship and Immigration Services (USCIS) implements immigration laws in this country by overseeing the U.S. immigration process. It manages immigration services and policies and works to ensure that new immigrants do not pose a threat to public safety. The USCIS decides, or adjudicates, immigrant petitions and applications—including visa petitions, asylum and refugee applications, and naturalization petitions.

OBTAINING LEGAL ASSISTANCE

U.S. immigration laws can be complicated, especially with recent changes to existing legislation. Often, people wishing to work and live in the United States or to become naturalized citizens find the legal process a challenge and seek expert assistance. Those applying for immigration or naturalization have the option of being represented by an attorney or other accredited professionals from a recognized organization when filing applications or petitions with the USCIS. However, potential immigrants and citizens need to use caution and good judgment so that they do not become victims of fraud.

If you decide you'd like to have a lawyer or accredited representative assist you with your USCIS application or petition, this professional must file Form G-28: Notice of Entry of Appearance as Attorney or Representative along with your other documents. Only you or your attorney (or accredited representative) may receive information about your case from the USCIS. If you cannot afford legal assistance, you may qualify for free or reduced-cost services provided to potential immigrants. Attorneys, immigration lawyers' associations, state bar associations, and other organizations offer legal assistance to those who need help with immigration issues. If you decide to hire an attorney, he or she should be a member in good standing of a bar association for a U.S. state, possession, territory, or commonwealth or the District of Columbia.

The USCIS Web site at www.uscis.gov/legaladvice also provides legal advice. Here, you can find helpful tips for protecting yourself from immigration fraud. Among other precautions, the USCIS recommends that you do the following:

- Ask for copies of all forms and other documents prepared or submitted on your behalf.

- Make sure that any professional hired to represent you is legitimate. Ask your attorney for his or her current licensing document and admission number, and contact your State Bar Association to verify this information. Accredited representatives should be members of a recognized organization. Ask to see a copy of the Board of Immigration Appeals (BIA) official recognition of both the accredited representative and the recognized organization.

- Report any unlawful actions by an attorney or accredited representative to the USCIS, your State Bar Association, or a State Office of Attorney General.

In addition, the USCIS suggests that you take the following precautions to avoid becoming a victim:

- Do not pay for expensive services offered by non-attorneys.
- Do not sign any forms or documents containing incorrect information.
- Do not sign blank forms, petitions, or other documents.
- Do not pay service fees without obtaining a receipt.
- Do not sign any paperwork that you do not clearly understand.

PART II

The Naturalization Process

CHAPTER 5

Naturalization: From Application to Citizen

WHAT IS NATURALIZATION?

Naturalization is the process of becoming a citizen of the United States. Many U.S. citizens are born in this country or to parents who are U.S. citizens. The 14th Amendment of the U.S. Constitution grants citizenship to people who are born in the United States or one of its jurisdictions. Children who are born outside the United States are also guaranteed citizenship if their parents are U.S. citizens. Children under the age of 18 who are adopted by U.S. citizens and immigrate to this country immediately gain U.S. citizenship as well.

People from other countries may become U.S. citizens through the process of naturalization. The United States has a long history of welcoming immigrants and giving them an opportunity to create better lives for themselves and their children. Citizens of the United States are protected by many rights, including the right to vote in federal elections, serve on a jury, bring family members to the United States, travel abroad, run for federal office, and apply for federal grants and scholarships. They also are expected to uphold certain responsibilities, like respecting the rights of others; supporting the U.S. Constitution; obeying local, state, and federal laws; and serving the country if needed.

NATURALIZATION REQUIREMENTS

If you have lived in the United States as a permanent resident for at least five years, you may be eligible for naturalization. If you are married to a U.S. citizen and have lived together in the United States for the past three years, you may also be eligible. In addition to residency requirements, applicants for U.S. citizenship should meet the following criteria:

- Be 18 years of age or older when filing Form N-400: Application for Naturalization.
- Have been lawfully admitted to the United States for permanent residence by following immigration laws.
- Have demonstrated good moral character during the time in the United States as a lawful permanent resident. Applicants cannot meet this requirement if they have committed certain offenses involving crime, prostitution, gambling, substance abuse, polygamy, or lying under oath. Applicants who are convicted of murder or an aggravated felony are permanently barred from naturalization.
- Have been physically present in the United States for at least thirty months during the past five years and resided for at least three months in the USCIS district or state where the applicant's Form N-400 will be filed (continuous permanent residence).
- Be able to speak, write, and understand the English language.

- Demonstrate knowledge of U.S. civics (the history and government of the U.S.).
- Express loyalty to the U.S. Constitution.
- Take the oath of allegiance to the United States.

HOW TO PREPARE

As part of the naturalization process, applicants for U.S. citizenship undergo a naturalization interview. During this interview, a USCIS officer administers English and civics tests. One way you can prepare for these tests is by attending a school program.

School Programs

Younger U.S. immigrants may enroll in public elementary and secondary school. There are many advantages to attending public school, including mastery of English and civics, as well as obtaining a high school diploma (necessary for most jobs and for college admission).

Immigrants who are not of school age may still take classes to prepare for the English and civics tests. Many community colleges, public school systems, libraries, and community organizations offer GED (General Education Development) classes in which students may earn a high school equivalency diploma. You could also enroll in a U.S. citizenship class at similar institutions to prepare for the civics test, or an English as a Second Language (ESL) class to study for the English test.

The USCIS has developed materials for instructors, tutors, and program administrators who are helping immigrant students prepare for naturalization. One such resource is U.S. Civics and Citizenship Online: Resource Center for Instructors, a Web-based tool that combines ESL and civics instruction for adult students.

Studying on Your Own

You may also prepare for the naturalization tests by studying on your own. There are many types of study materials available to help you learn about the United States, its history and government, and the rights and responsibilities of citizenship. You may purchase study guides at bookstores or borrow them from your local library. The USCIS Web site (www.uscis.gov) also supplies numerous study aids to help you prepare for the naturalization interview, including the following:

- *Civics Flash Cards for the New Naturalization Test.* These flash cards help immigrants prepare for the naturalization test by learning about U.S. history and government.
- *Learn About the United States: Quick Civics Lessons for the New Naturalization Test.* This study guide contains short lessons to help immigrants with the civics and English sections of the naturalization interview.
- *Civics (History and Government) Questions for the Redesigned (New) Naturalization Test.* This guide helps to prepare students for the history and government questions that make up the civics test.
- *Vocabulary Flash Cards for the New Naturalization Test.* These flash cards help immigrants prepare for the English reading and writing sections of the naturalization test.

- *The Citizen's Almanac.* This booklet outlines the rights and responsibilities of U.S. citizenship and includes presidential speeches, founding documents, landmark decisions of the U.S. Supreme Court, and patriotic anthems and symbols.

- *Pocket Declaration of Independence and Constitution of the United States.* This booklet contains the complete text of these two important American documents.

- *A Promise of Freedom: An Introduction to U.S. History and Civics for Immigrants.* This 12-minute film spotlights the history and founding of the United States, citizenship, and the role of immigration in American history. Available on DVD.

- *Becoming a U.S. Citizen: An Overview of the Naturalization Process.* This 10-minute online video provides an overview of the naturalization process.

THE NEXT IMPORTANT STEP: ASSEMBLING YOUR N-400 PACKET

If you meet all the requirements for naturalization previously outlined, the next step is to assemble your N-400 packet. The packet will include:

- Form N-400: Application for Naturalization (to obtain a copy of Form N-400, visit www.uscis.gov and click on the "Forms" tab or call the USCIS Forms Line toll free at 800-870-3676)

- A photocopy of both sides of your green card

- Two identical color photographs of yourself with your name and your "A" number written on the back of each photo in pencil (be sure that all of your facial features are visible—remove eyeglasses, jewelry, or head coverings, if possible)

- A check or money order payable to the U.S. Department of Homeland Security for the application and biometric services fees (your "A" number should be written on the back of your check or money order)

The N-400 application fee is currently $595, and the biometrics service fee is $80. Fees may be combined into one check or money order.

Depending on your situation, you may also need to send copies of additional forms. For example, if you've changed your name because of marriage or divorce, you'll need to send a copy of the legal document recording your name change. For a complete list of documents that may be required for your N-400 packet, choose the link "Document Checklist for Form N-400, Application for Naturalization" on the USCIS Web site, www.uscis.gov.

A current fee schedule for the various forms you may be required to submit is included in Appendix B.

Your completed N-400 packet should be sent to one of these designated USCIS Service Centers:

- USCIS
  P.O. Box 21251
  Phoenix, Arizona 85036

(Residents of Alaska, Arizona, California, Colorado, Hawaii, Idaho, Illinois, Indiana, Iowa, Kansas, Michigan, Minnesota, Missouri, Montana, Nebraska, Nevada, North Dakota, Ohio, Oregon, South Dakota, Utah, Washington, Wisconsin, Wyoming, Guam, or the Commonwealth of the Northern Mariana Islands)

- USCIS
  P.O. Box 299026
  Lewisville, Texas 75029

(Residents of Alabama, Arkansas, Connecticut, Delaware, District of Columbia, Florida, Georgia, Kentucky, Louisiana, Maine, Maryland, Massachusetts, Mississippi, New Hampshire, New Jersey, New Mexico, New York, North Carolina, Oklahoma, Pennsylvania, Rhode Island, South Carolina, Tennessee, Texas, Vermont, Virginia, West Virginia, Puerto Rico, or the U.S. Virgin Islands)

- Nebraska Service Center
  P.O. Box 87426
  Lincoln, Nebraska 68501-7426

(Applicants for naturalization who are filing under military provisions)

Once You've Submitted Your N-400 Packet

After the USCIS receives your completed N-400 packet, you will receive notification about where you should go to be fingerprinted. Then you will be scheduled for your naturalization interview, but the wait time can be substantial. It currently takes between six and nine months to become a naturalized citizen, but the USCIS is constantly working to improve the timeliness of this process. You can check on the status of your naturalization application by clicking on the link to "Finding the Status of Your Case" at www.uscis.gov.

THE FINAL STEP: THE NATURALIZATION INTERVIEW

The final step in the naturalization process is the naturalization interview. Immigrants seeking U.S. citizenship will meet with a USCIS officer who will administer both an English test and a civics test. On October 1, 2008, a multi-year revision of these tests was completed. Applicants for naturalization who filed Form N-400: Application for Naturalization after this date will be given a new test. Those who filed before October 1, 2008, have their choice of either the old or new naturalization test.

It is highly recommended that you attend your scheduled interview because rescheduling can add several months to the naturalization process. If you absolutely cannot make the interview, you'll need to contact the USCIS office where your interview is scheduled as soon as possible, in writing. Your letter should explain why you are unable to attend your interview and request an alternate date. In an emergency, you may also call the National Customer Service Center at 800-375-5283 (toll-free) to request a last-minute rescheduling. In this case, your interview may or may not be rescheduled. If you miss your interview and do not notify the USCIS, your application for citizenship will be closed unless you schedule a new interview within one year.

The English Test

During the naturalization interview, a USCIS officer will test your English fluency, which will include an assessment of your basic skills in English reading, speaking, and writing. The USCIS officer will dictate up to three sentences in English and ask you to write each sentence. You will also be asked to read up to three sentences in English. During the course of your interview, your spoken English skills will be evaluated.

Depending on your age and how long you have lived in the United States as a permanent resident, you may be exempt from the English requirement for naturalization. Those who are 55 years of age or older and have lived in the United States as permanent residents for 15 years or more are exempt from the English test.

Similarly, immigrants who are 50 years of age or older and have lived in the United States legally for 20 years or more are also exempt. An immigrant is also exempted from the English requirement if he or she suffers from a physical or mental condition that prevents him or her from learning English.

The Civics Test

During the naturalization interview, applicants will also be expected to pass a civics test. Immigrants hoping to gain U.S. citizenship must show that they understand the principles of U.S. government. They must also demonstrate knowledge of U.S. history. As part of the newly designed naturalization test, the updated civics test is meant to encourage both civics learning and patriotism among potential U.S. citizens. For the civics test, a USCIS officer will ask up to ten questions (from a list of 100 approved questions) pertaining to U.S. history and government.

Just as with the English requirement, some applicants who have reached a certain age and have lived in the United States legally for a number of years may be exempt from this requirement. Exemptions may also be made for those who are physically or mentally impaired.

The Oath of Allegiance

LOYALTY

Some applicants for citizenship take the Oath of Allegiance on the same day as their naturalization interview. Others take the oath during a naturalization ceremony. The USCIS office handling your case will let you know the expected procedure and notify you, if applicable, of when your ceremony will take place. To become a citizen of the United States, an applicant takes an oath promising to:

- Obey all U.S. laws and support the Constitution
- Renounce any foreign titles or allegiances
- Perform services for the U.S. government and bear arms for the Armed Forces, if needed

During the naturalization interview, most applicants will recite the entire Oath of Allegiance, as follows:

"I hereby declare, on oath, that I absolutely and entirely renounce and abjure all allegiance and fidelity to any foreign prince, potentate, state, or sovereignty of whom or which I have heretofore been a subject or citizen; that I will support and defend the Constitution and laws of the United States of America against all enemies, foreign and domestic; that I will bear true faith and allegiance to the same; that I will bear arms on behalf of the United States when required by the law; that I will perform noncombatant service in the Armed Forces of the United States when required by the law; that I will perform work of national importance under civilian direction when required by the law; and that I take this obligation freely without any mental reservation or purpose of evasion; so help me God."

However, certain words or phrases from the Oath of Allegiance may be omitted for applicants with opposing religious beliefs. Those who are religiously opposed to all wars, for example, may leave out the clause pertaining to service in the U.S. Armed Forces. The phrase "so help me God" may also be removed from the oath for those with opposing religious beliefs.

EMILIA'S STORY: PART 3

Let's check in once again with Emilia and see where she is on her path to citizenship.

Emilia adjusted well to married life with her husband, Christopher, and life as a lawful, permanent resident. She stayed in touch with her family—especially with her mother, Rene, who had to move back to Chile because of the requirements of her J-1 visa. In their phone conversations, Rene commented often about how much she would like to move back to the United States to be close to her daughter and grandson.

Emilia knew that the easiest way for her mother to immigrate would be for her to come as the immediate family member of a U.S. citizen. So, Emilia began the final steps for attaining her own citizenship. When she had held her permanent, unconditional green card for a full nine months (after having a conditional green card for two years), Emilia filed Form N-400 along with the supporting documents and filing fee with her Regional Service Center.

Department of Homeland Security
U.S Citizenship and Immigration Services

**N-400 Application
for Naturalization**

Print clearly or type your answers using **CAPITAL** letters. Failure to print clearly may delay your application. Use black ink.

Part 1. Your Name *(Person applying for naturalization)*

Write your USCIS A-Number here:
A 00000000

A. Your current legal name.

Family Name *(Last Name)*

Roberts

Given Name *(First Name)*	Full Middle Name *(If applicable)*
Emilia	Rosalia

B. Your name **exactly** as it appears on your Permanent Resident Card.

Family Name *(Last Name)*

Roberts

Given Name *(First Name)*	Full Middle Name *(If applicable)*
Emilia	Rosalia

C. If you have ever used other names, provide them below.

Family Name *(Last Name)*	Given Name *(First Name)*	Middle Name
Alvarez	Emilia	Rosalia

For USCIS Use Only

Bar Code	Date Stamp
	Remarks

D. Name change *(optional)*

Read the Instructions before you decide whether to change your name.

1. Would you like to legally change your name?   ☐ Yes   ☒ No

2. If "Yes," print the new name you would like to use. Do not use initials or abbreviations when writing your new name.

Family Name *(Last Name)*

Given Name *(First Name)*	Full Middle Name

Action Block

Part 2. Information About Your Eligibility *(Check only one)*

I am at least 18 years old **AND**

A. ☐ I have been a lawful permanent resident of the United States for at least five years.

B. ☒ I have been a lawful permanent resident of the United States for at least three years, **and** I have been married to and living with the same U.S. citizen for the last three years, **and** my spouse has been a U.S. citizen for the last three years.

C. ☐ I am applying on the basis of qualifying military service.

D. ☐ Other *(Explain)* _____

Part 3. Information About You

Write your USCIS A-Number here:
A 00000000

A. U.S. Social Security Number

000-00-0000

B. Date of Birth *(mm/dd/yyyy)*

03/19/1986

C. Date You Became a Permanent Resident *(mm/dd/yyyy)*

08/15/2004

D. Country of Birth

Chile

E. Country of Nationality

Chile

F. Are either of your parents U.S. citizens? *(If yes, see instructions)* ☐ Yes ☒ No

G. What is your current marital status? ☐ Single, Never Married ☒ Married ☐ Divorced ☐ Widowed

☐ Marriage Annulled or Other *(Explain)* _____

H. Are you requesting a waiver of the English and/or U.S. History and Government requirements based on a disability or impairment and attaching Form N-648 with your application? ☐ Yes ☒ No

I. Are you requesting an accommodation to the naturalization process because of a disability or impairment? *(See instructions for some examples of accommodations.)* ☐ Yes ☒ No

If you answered "Yes," check the box below that applies:

☐ I am deaf or hearing impaired and need a sign language interpreter who uses the following language: _____

☐ I use a wheelchair.

☐ I am blind or sight impaired.

☐ I will need another type of accommodation. Explain: _____

_____

Part 4. Addresses and Telephone Numbers

A. Home Address - Street Number and Name *(Do **not** write a P.O. Box in this space.)*

1224 S. Gaylord Street

Apartment Number

Apt. 1-A

City	County	State	ZIP Code	Country
Denver	Denver	CO	80231	USA

B. Care of

Mailing Address - Street Number and Name *(If different from home address)*

Apartment Number

City	State	ZIP Code	Country

C. Daytime Phone Number *(If any)*

(303) 123-4567

Evening Phone Number *(If any)*

( )

E-Mail Address *(If any)*

| Part 5. Information for Criminal Records Search | Write your USCIS A-Number here: A 00000000 |

NOTE: The categories below are those required by the FBI. See instructions for more information.

A. Gender
☐ Male   ☒ Female

B. Height
5 Feet 9 Inches

C. Weight
130 Pounds

D. Are you Hispanic or Latino? ☒ Yes ☐ No

E. Race *(Select one or more)*
☒ White ☐ Asian ☐ Black or African American ☐ American Indian or Alaskan Native ☐ Native Hawaiian or Other Pacific Islander

F. Hair color
☐ Black ☒ Brown ☐ Blonde ☐ Gray ☐ White ☐ Red ☐ Sandy ☐ Bald (No Hair)

G. Eye color
☐ Brown ☒ Blue ☐ Green ☐ Hazel ☐ Gray ☐ Black ☐ Pink ☐ Maroon ☐ Other

Part 6. Information About Your Residence and Employment

A. Where have you lived during the last five years? Begin with where you live now and then list every place you lived for the last five years. If you need more space, use a separate sheet of paper.

Street Number and Name, Apartment Number, City, State, Zip Code, and Country	Dates (mm/dd/yyyy) From	To
Current Home Address - Same as Part 4.A	05/15/2008	Present
1234 Dahlia Street, Apt. 1-A, Denver, CO 80224	05/07/2003	05/15/2008

B. Where have you worked (or, if you were a student, what schools did you attend) during the last five years? Include military service. Begin with your current or latest employer and then list every place you have worked or studied for the last five years. If you need more space, use a separate sheet of paper.

Employer or School Name	Employer or School Address (Street, City, and State)	Dates (mm/dd/yyyy) From	To	Your Occupation
Knowledge University	123 Knowledge Street, Denver, CO	05/07/2004	05/20/2008	student

Write your USCIS A-Number here:
A 00000000

A. How many total days did you spend outside of the United States during the past five years? ⟶ | 0 | days

B. How many trips of 24 hours or more have you taken outside of the United States during the past five years? ⟶ | 0 | trips

C. List below all the trips of 24 hours or more that you have taken outside of the United States since becoming a lawful permanent resident. Begin with your most recent trip. If you need more space, use a separate sheet of paper.

Date You Left the United States *(mm/dd/yyyy)*	Date You Returned to the United States *(mm/dd/yyyy)*	Did Trip Last Six Months or More?	Countries to Which You Traveled	Total Days Out of the United States
		☐ Yes ☐ No		
		☐ Yes ☐ No		
		☐ Yes ☐ No		
		☐ Yes ☐ No		
		☐ Yes ☐ No		
		☐ Yes ☐ No		
		☐ Yes ☐ No		
		☐ Yes ☐ No		
		☐ Yes ☐ No		
		☐ Yes ☐ No		

Part 8. Information About Your Marital History

A. How many times have you been married (including annulled marriages)? | 1 | If you have **never** been married, go to Part 9.

B. If you are now married, give the following information about your spouse:

1. Spouse's Family Name *(Last Name)*
Roberts

Given Name *(First Name)*
Christopher

Full Middle Name *(If applicable)*
John

2. Date of Birth *(mm/dd/yyyy)*
02/12/1984

3. Date of Marriage *(mm/dd/yyyy)*
05/15/2008

4. Spouse's U.S. Social Security #
111-11-1111

5. Home Address - Street Number and Name
1224 S. Gaylord Street

Apartment Number
462

City
Denver

State
CO

Zip Code
80231

Part 8. Information About Your Marital History *(Continued)*

Write your USCIS A-Number here:
A 00000000

C. Is your spouse a U.S. citizen? ☒ Yes ☐ No

D. If your spouse is a U.S. citizen, give the following information:

1. When did your spouse become a U.S. citizen? ☒ At Birth ☐ Other

If "Other," give the following information:

2. Date your spouse became a U.S. citizen

3. Place your spouse became a U.S. citizen (See *instructions*)

City and State

E. If your spouse is **not** a U.S. citizen, give the following information :

1. Spouse's Country of Citizenship

2. Spouse's USCIS A- Number *(If applicable)*

A

3. Spouse's Immigration Status

☐ Lawful Permanent Resident ☐ Other

F. If you were married before, provide the following information about your prior spouse. If you have more than one previous marriage, use a separate sheet of paper to provide the information requested in Questions 1-5 below.

1. Prior Spouse's Family Name *(Last Name)*   Given Name *(First Name)*   Full Middle Name *(If applicable)*

2. Prior Spouse's Immigration Status

☐ U.S. Citizen

☐ Lawful Permanent Resident

☐ Other

3. Date of Marriage *(mm/dd/yyyy)*

4. Date Marriage Ended *(mm/dd/yyyy)*

5. How Marriage Ended

☐ Divorce ☐ Spouse Died ☐ Other

G. How many times has your current spouse been married (including annulled marriages)? | 1 |

If your spouse has **ever** been married before, give the following information about **your spouse's** prior marriage.
If your spouse has more than one previous marriage, use a separate sheet(s) of paper to provide the information requested in Questions 1 - 5 below.

1. Prior Spouse's Family Name *(Last Name)*   Given Name *(First Name)*   Full Middle Name *(If applicable)*

2. Prior Spouse's Immigration Status

☐ U.S. Citizen

☐ Lawful Permanent Resident

☐ Other

3. Date of Marriage *(mm/dd/yyyy)*

4. Date Marriage Ended *(mm/dd/yyyy)*

5. How Marriage Ended

☐ Divorce ☐ Spouse Died ☐ Other

www.facebook.com/become.citizen

Part 9. Information About Your Children	Write your USCIS A-Number here: A 00000000

A. How many sons and daughters have you had? For more information on which sons and daughters you should include and how to complete this section, see the Instructions.

`0`

B. Provide the following information about all of your sons and daughters. If you need more space, use a separate sheet of paper.

Full Name of Son or Daughter	Date of Birth *(mm/dd/yyyy)*	USCIS A- number *(if child has one)*	Country of Birth	Current Address *(Street, City, State and Country)*
		A		
		A		
		A		
		A		
		A		
		A		
		A		
		A		

[Add Children]   [Go to continuation page]

Part 10. Additional Questions

Answer Questions 1 through 14. If you answer "Yes" to any of these questions, include a written explanation with this form. Your written explanation should (1) explain why your answer was "Yes" and (2) provide any additional information that helps to explain your answer.

A. General Questions.

1. Have you **ever** claimed to be a U.S. citizen *(in writing or any other way)*? ☐ Yes ☒ No

2. Have you **ever** registered to vote in any Federal, State, or local election in the United States? ☐ Yes ☒ No

3. Have you **ever** voted in any Federal, State, or local election in the United States? ☐ Yes ☒ No

4. Since becoming a lawful permanent resident, have you **ever** failed to file a required Federal, State, or local tax return? ☐ Yes ☒ No

5. Do you owe any Federal, State, or local taxes that are overdue? ☐ Yes ☒ No

6. Do you have any title of nobility in any foreign country? ☐ Yes ☒ No

7. Have you ever been declared legally incompetent or been confined to a mental institution within the last five years? ☐ Yes ☒ No

Form N-400 (Rev. 01/22/09) Y Page 6

Part 10. Additional Questions *(Continued)*

Write your USCIS A-Number here:
A 00000000

B. Affiliations.

8. a Have you **ever** been a member of or associated with any organization, association, fund foundation, party, club, society, or similar group in the United States or in any other place?   ☐ Yes ☒ No

  b. If you answered "Yes," list the name of each group below. If you need more space, attach the names of the other group(s) on a separate sheet of paper.

Name of Group	Name of Group
1.	6.
2.	7.
3.	8.
4.	9.
5.	10.

9. Have you **ever** been a member of or in any way associated *(either directly or indirectly)* with:

  a. The Communist Party?   ☐ Yes ☒ No

  b. Any other totalitarian party?   ☐ Yes ☒ No

  c. A terrorist organization?   ☐ Yes ☒ No

10. Have you **ever** advocated *(either directly or indirectly)* the overthrow of any government by force or violence?   ☐ Yes ☒ No

11. Have you **ever** persecuted *(either directly or indirectly)* any person because of race, religion, national origin, membership in a particular social group, or political opinion?   ☐ Yes ☒ No

12. Between March 23, 1933, and May 8, 1945, did you work for or associate in any way *(either directly or indirectly)* with:

  a. The Nazi government of Germany?   ☐ Yes ☒ No

  b. Any government in any area (1) occupied by, (2) allied with, or (3) established with the help of the Nazi government of Germany?   ☐ Yes ☒ No

  c. Any German, Nazi, or S.S. military unit, paramilitary unit, self-defense unit, vigilante unit, citizen unit, police unit, government agency or office, extermination camp, concentration camp, prisoner of war camp, prison, labor camp, or transit camp?   ☐ Yes ☒ No

C. Continuous Residence.

Since becoming a lawful permanent resident of the United States:

13. Have you **ever** called yourself a "nonresident" on a Federal, State, or local tax return?   ☐ Yes ☒ No

14. Have you **ever** failed to file a Federal, State, or local tax return because you considered yourself to be a "nonresident"?   ☐ Yes ☒ No

Form N-400 (Rev. 01/22/09) Y Page 7

Part 10. Additional Questions *(continued)*

Write your USCIS A-Number here:
A 00000000

D. Good Moral Character.

For the purposes of this application, you must answer "Yes" to the following questions, if applicable, even if your records were sealed or otherwise cleared or if anyone, including a judge, law enforcement officer, or attorney, told you that you no longer have a record.

15. Have you **ever** committed a crime or offense for which you were **not** arrested? ☐ Yes ☒ No

16. Have you **ever** been arrested, cited, or detained by any law enforcement officer (including USCIS or former INS and military officers) for any reason? ☐ Yes ☒ No

17. Have you **ever** been charged with committing any crime or offense? ☐ Yes ☒ No

18. Have you **ever** been convicted of a crime or offense? ☐ Yes ☒ No

19. Have you **ever** been placed in an alternative sentencing or a rehabilitative program (for example: diversion, deferred prosecution, withheld adjudication, deferred adjudication)? ☐ Yes ☒ No

20. Have you **ever** received a suspended sentence, been placed on probation, or been paroled? ☐ Yes ☒ No

21. Have you **ever** been in jail or prison? ☐ Yes ☒ No

If you answered "Yes" to any of Questions 15 through 21, complete the following table. If you need more space, use a separate sheet of paper to give the same information.

Why were you arrested, cited, detained, or charged?	Date arrested, cited, detained, or charged? *(mm/dd/yyyy)*	Where were you arrested, cited, detained, or charged? *(City, State, Country)*	Outcome or disposition of the arrest, citation, detention, or charge *(No charges filed, charges dismissed, jail, probation, etc.)*

Answer Questions 22 through 33. If you answer "Yes" to any of these questions, attach (1) your written explanation why your answer was "Yes" and (2) any additional information or documentation that helps explain your answer.

22. Have you **ever**:

    a. Been a habitual drunkard? ☐ Yes ☒ No

    b. Been a prostitute, or procured anyone for prostitution? ☐ Yes ☒ No

    c. Sold or smuggled controlled substances, illegal drugs, or narcotics? ☐ Yes ☒ No

    d. Been married to more than one person at the same time? ☐ Yes ☒ No

    e. Helped anyone enter or try to enter the United States illegally? ☐ Yes ☒ No

    f. Gambled illegally or received income from illegal gambling? ☐ Yes ☒ No

    g. Failed to support your dependents or to pay alimony? ☐ Yes ☒ No

23. Have you **ever** given false or misleading information to any U.S. Government official while applying for any immigration benefit or to prevent deportation, exclusion, or removal? ☐ Yes ☒ No

24. Have you **ever** lied to any U.S. Government official to gain entry or admission into the United States? ☐ Yes ☒ No

Form N-400 (Rev. 01/22/09) Y Page 8

Part 10. Additional Questions *(Continued)*	Write your USCIS A-Number here: A 00000000

E. Removal, Exclusion, and Deportation Proceedings.

25. Are removal, exclusion, rescission, or deportation proceedings pending against you? ☐ Yes ☒ No

26. Have you **ever** been removed, excluded, or deported from the United States? ☐ Yes ☒ No

27. Have you **ever** been ordered to be removed, excluded, or deported from the United States? ☐ Yes ☒ No

28. Have you **ever** applied for any kind of relief from removal, exclusion, or deportation? ☐ Yes ☒ No

F. Military Service.

29. Have you **ever** served in the U.S. Armed Forces? ☐ Yes ☒ No

30. Have you **ever** left the United States to avoid being drafted into the U.S. Armed Forces? ☐ Yes ☒ No

31. Have you **ever** applied for any kind of exemption from military service in the U.S. Armed Forces? ☐ Yes ☒ No

32. Have you **ever** deserted from the U.S. Armed Forces? ☐ Yes ☒ No

G. Selective Service Registration.

33. Are you a male who lived in the United States at any time between your 18th and 26th birthdays in any status except as a lawful nonimmigrant? ☐ Yes ☒ No

If you answered "NO," go on to question 34.

If you answered "YES," provide the information below.

If you answered "YES," but you did not register with the Selective Service System and are still under 26 years of age, you must register before you apply for naturalization, so that you can complete the information below:

Date Registered (mm/dd/yyyy) [   ] Selective Service Number [   ]

If you answered "YES," but you did not register with the Selective Service and you are now 26 years old or older, attach a statement explaining why you did not register.

H. Oath Requirements. *(See Part 14 for the text of the oath)*

Answer Questions 34 through 39. If you answer "No" to any of these questions, attach (1) your written explanation why the answer was "No" and (2) any additional information or documentation that helps to explain your answer.

34. Do you support the Constitution and form of government of the United States? ☒ Yes ☐ No

35. Do you understand the full Oath of Allegiance to the United States? ☒ Yes ☐ No

36. Are you willing to take the full Oath of Allegiance to the United States? ☒ Yes ☐ No

37. If the law requires it, are you willing to bear arms on behalf of the United States? ☒ Yes ☐ No

38. If the law requires it, are you willing to perform noncombatant services in the U.S. Armed Forces? ☒ Yes ☐ No

39. If the law requires it, are you willing to perform work of national importance under civilian direction? ☒ Yes ☐ No

Form N-400 (Rev. 01/22/09) Y Page 9

Part 11. Your Signature

Write your USCIS A-Number here:
A 00000000

I certify, under penalty of perjury under the laws of the United States of America, that this application, and the evidence submitted with it, are all true and correct. I authorize the release of any information that the USCIS needs to determine my eligibility for naturalization.

Your Signature

Emilia R. Roberts

Date *(mm/dd/yyyy)*
09/21/2009

Part 12. Signature of Person Who Prepared This Application for You *(If applicable)*

I declare under penalty of perjury that I prepared this application at the request of the above person. The answers provided are based on information of which I have personal knowledge and/or were provided to me by the above named person in response to the *exact questions* contained on this form.

Preparer's Printed Name

Preparer's Signature

Date *(mm/dd/yyyy)*

Preparer's Firm or Organization Name *(If applicable)*

Preparer's Daytime Phone Number

Preparer's Address - Street Number and Name

City

State

Zip Code

NOTE: Do not complete Parts 13 and 14 until a USCIS Officer instructs you to do so.

Part 13. Signature at Interview

I swear (affirm) and certify under penalty of perjury under the laws of the United States of America that I know that the contents of this application for naturalization subscribed by me, including corrections numbered 1 through _____ and the evidence submitted by me numbered pages 1 through _____ , are true and correct to the best of my knowledge and belief.

Subscribed to and sworn to (affirmed) before me

Officer's Printed Name or Stamp

Date *(mm/dd/yyyy)*

Complete Signature of Applicant

Officer's Signature

Part 14. Oath of Allegiance

If your application is approved, you will be scheduled for a public oath ceremony at which time you will be required to take the following Oath of Allegiance immediately prior to becoming a naturalized citizen. By signing, you acknowledge your willingness and ability to take this oath:

I hereby declare, on oath, that I absolutely and entirely renounce and abjure all allegiance and fidelity to any foreign prince, potentate, state, or sovereignty, of whom or which I have heretofore been a subject or citizen;

that I will support and defend the Constitution and laws of the United States of America against all enemies, foreign and domestic;

that I will bear true faith and allegiance to the same;

that I will bear arms on behalf of the United States when required by the law;

that I will perform noncombatant service in the Armed Forces of the United States when required by the law;

that I will perform work of national importance under civilian direction when required by the law; and

that I take this obligation freely, without any mental reservation or purpose of evasion, so help me God.

Printed Name of Applicant

Complete Signature of Applicant

Form N-400 (Rev. 01/22/09) Y Page 10

After a short time, Emilia was contacted by the INS, and she made an appointment to have her fingerprints taken. Several months later, Emilia received an appointment letter in the mail scheduling her interview. Emilia was very excited and realized that all of her hard work and attention to the details of attaining citizenship were finally going to pay off. On the appointed day, she dressed in her best outfit and arrived for her interview 15 minutes early. The office was crowded and the examiner was running behind schedule, but Emilia patiently waited until she was called.

The examiner finally called Emilia in and began the interview. He asked her what it was in particular that she liked about the United States and why she wanted to become a citizen. Emilia replied that she appreciated the many opportunities that were available to have a better life and improve her circumstances and those of her family. Emilia was also asked about the times she had left the country, the different places she had lived, her job, and her willingness to take the Oath of Allegiance. The examiner also administered the civics and English tests, which Emilia passed. After she had answered all of the questions and met all of the requirements, the examiner signed Emilia's N-400 form.

Almost two months later, Emilia received an invitation to a ceremony to take the Oath of Allegiance. On the day of the ceremony, Emilia, Christopher, their son, and several friends and members of Christopher's family attended the ceremony. At its conclusion, Emilia was presented with her Certificate of Naturalization.

A short time later, Emilia went to the local INS office and picked up a Form I-130, Petition for Alien Relative, and began the process of applying for a green card on behalf of her mother. She entered her naturalization certificate number on the form and prepared it to be filed. With the usual precautions of making a full set of copies for her own records, and using certified mail, Emilia sent in the completed I-130 form along with a copy of her Certificate of Naturalization, a copy of her birth certificate to prove her relationship to her mother, a form G-325A for herself and another one completed by her mother, photos of herself and her mother, and the required fee. (A blank copy of these forms can be found in Appendix A.)

If you have studied the preceding material carefully you should have all of the information you need to come to the United States legally, adjust your status from nonimmigrant to immigrant, and apply for naturalization. Practice forms can be found in Appendix A.

The next chapters will help you prepare to take the English and civics tests. If you feel uncertain about whether you will be able to fulfill the requirements, as they have been explained, on your own, you can seek the advice of an attorney who specializes in immigration law. There are also many groups—ethnic clubs, fraternal organizations, unions, and churches and synagogues, for example—that can assist you in your quest to become a U.S. citizen.

CHAPTER 6

The English and Civics Tests

As you know by now, one of the requirements for attaining U.S. citizenship through the naturalization process is a test to show that you can read, write, and speak basic English, and that you have a basic knowledge of U.S. history and government—also known as civics.

Once you have completed and submitted your Form N-400: Application for Naturalization and have had your fingerprints taken at a USCIS facility, you will receive an appointment for an interview. At your interview, you will be asked to answer questions about your application and background. You will also take an English and civics test.

You will have two chances to take the English and civics tests and to answer all questions relating to your naturalization application in English. If you fail any of the tests at your first interview, you will have another chance to take the portion of the test you didn't pass between sixty and ninety days after your first interview.

READING AND WRITING ENGLISH

To pass the English portion of the test, you will be asked to correctly read one sentence—out of three sentences—and to correctly write one of the three sentences as well. Your grasp of spoken English will largely be assessed during the interview itself; you will need to show the USCIS officer that you understand what you have just read.

Vocabulary Words You Need to Know

The following are some of the more common words used in the English reading and writing portions of the naturalization test. You can make your own flash cards to practice writing the vocabulary word(s) in English as well as writing a sentence that uses each word, name, or phrase.

Reading Vocabulary for the Naturalization Test

People
Abraham Lincoln
George Washington

Civics
American flag
Bill of Rights
capital
citizen
Congress

country
Father of Our Country
government
President
right
Senators
state/states
White House

Places
America
U.S.
United States

Holidays
Presidents' Day
Memorial Day
Flag Day
Independence Day

Labor Day
Columbus Day
Thanksgiving

Question Words
How
What
When
Where
Who
Why

Verbs
can
come
do/does
elects

have/has
is/are/was/be
lives/lived
meet
name
pay
vote
want

Other (function)
a
for
here
in
of
on

the
to
we

Other (content)
colors
dollar bill
first
largest
many
most
north
one
people
second
south

Writing Vocabulary for the Naturalization Test

People
John Adams
Abraham Lincoln
George Washington

Civics
American Indians
capital
citizens
Civil War
Congress
Father of Our Country
flag
free
freedom of speech
President
right
Senators
state/states
White House

Places
Alaska
California
Canada
Delaware
Mexico
New York City
United States
Washington
Washington, D.C.

Months
February
May
June
July
September
October
November

Holidays
Presidents' Day
Memorial Day
Flag Day
Independence Day
Labor Day
Columbus Day
Thanksgiving

Verbs
can
come
elect
have/has
is/was/be
lives/lived
meets
pay
vote
want

Other (function)
and
during
for
here
in
of
on
the
to
we

Other (content)
blue
dollar bill
fifty (50)
first
largest
most
north
one
one hundred (100)
people
red
second
south
taxes
white

THE CIVICS PORTION OF THE NATURALIZATION TEST

On the USCIS Web site, you'll find a short historical overview of the United States (click on "Learn about the United States: Quick Civics Lessons for the New Naturalization Test") and sample questions that are asked on the civics test, along with their answers. To help you further prepare for the civics test, check out Chapter 8: Practice Tests. Here, you'll find five practice tests, with the answers to each question—as well as 100 of the actual civics test questions and answers.

Common Words and Terms for the Civics Test

The following are some of the more common words used in the civics portion of the naturalization test.

People
John Adams
Susan B. Anthony
Benjamin Franklin
Alexander Hamilton
John Jay
Thomas Jefferson
Martin Luther King Jr.
Abraham Lincoln
James Madison
Barack Obama
Franklin D. Roosevelt
George Washington
Woodrow Wilson

Civics
American flag
American Indians
Bill of Rights
capital/the Capitol
checks and balances
citizen
city
Civil War
Congress
Constitution

Country
Declaration of Independence
Father of Our Country
federal
flag
free
freedom of speech
government
judicial
President
Representative
right
Senator
state/states
Supreme Court
White House

Places
Alaska
America
Atlantic Ocean
California
Canada
Delaware
Ellis Island
Florida

Hudson River
Louisiana
Mexico
Missouri River
Mississippi River
New York City
Pacific Ocean
Statue of Liberty
United States
Washington, D.C.

Holidays
New Year's Day
Martin Luther King Jr. Day
Presidents' Day
Memorial Day
Flag Day
Independence Day
Labor Day
Columbus Day
Veterans Day
Thanksgiving Day
Christmas

STUDYING FOR THE NATURALIZATION TEST

On the USCIS Web site, www.uscis.gov, there are a variety of materials that are designed to help you pass the English and civics portions of the naturalization test. Follow the link "Study Materials for the Naturalization Test," and you will find flash cards, booklets, and video and audio items that can be downloaded to your computer or MP3 player.

In addition to the study aids that are provided on the USCIS Web site, a tremendous amount of information designed specifically for people who are learning English as a second language (ESL) is available on the

Internet—for free. Keep in mind that the test you will be taking is geared toward correctly speaking and writing basic English, so the most helpful information for you will offer lessons in such topics as the correct use of punctuation, grammar, sentence structure, and the basic parts of speech, such as prepositions, verbs, pronouns, and nouns.

English Language Resources

The Community Writing and Education Station (http://owl.english.purdue.edu/engagement/index.php?category_id=3) is an online resource in conjunction with Purdue University that offers a variety of lessons to ESL students.

The Writing Center at the University of North Carolina at Chapel Hill (http://www.unc.edu/depts/wcweb/) also has an extensive ESL resources page. You will find links to documents and handouts that cover such topics as "Understanding the Assignment" and "Developing Paragraphs" and other helpful information on writing and the writing process at http://www.unc.edu/depts/wcweb/handouts/index.html and http://www.unc.edu/depts/wcweb/esl/esl.html.

Although not geared specifically toward people who are learning English as a second language, The Writing Center at the University of Wisconsin–Madison has some helpful information about writing "clear, concise, and direct sentences." This information may be accessed at http://writing.wisc.edu/Handbook/ClearConciseSentences.html.

The Writing Center at George Mason University provides an abundance of helpful information about ESL assistance and guidance, grammar resources, information regarding different aspects of the writing process, and links to other credible and very useful sites. Find these resources by going to http://writingcenter.gmu.edu/writing-resources.php.

Civics Resources

The **Library of Congress** is the nation's oldest federal cultural institution and serves as the research arm of Congress. It is also the largest library in the world with millions of books, recordings, photographs, maps, and manuscripts in its collections—and many are now available online. If you take some time to explore the amazing wealth of information that is available through the Library's Web site, you will find information about everything you need to know to pass the civics portion of your naturalization test.

In particular, the Library's "American Memory" collection provides free and open access to historic maps, photos, documents, audio, and video. Here, you will find entire collections of information dedicated to such topics as government and law, culture and folklife, immigration and American expansion, women's history, war and the military, and Native American history, to name just a few. The main Web address for the Library of Congress is http://www.loc.gov/index.html. To access the American Memory pages, start at http://memory.loc.gov/ammem/index.html.

The **National Archives and Records Administration** is known as the nation's record keeper. Of all of the documents and materials that are created in the course of the nation's business, only a very small portion (1 to 3 percent) is considered important enough to be kept forever. These documents are preserved and available to everyone in the National Archives. The main Web address for the Archive is http://archives.gov.

An especially good resource for your civics studies is the Archives' "Charters of Freedom" online collection, which may be accessed at http://archives.gov/exhibits/charters/charters.html. This collection of documents will take you chronologically through the events that established the United States. Starting in 1761 with the history surrounding what were initially English colonies, this historical overview progresses through the events of the American Revolution, presents the texts of the Declaration of Independence and the U.S. Constitution, explains the Louisiana Purchase, provides an overview of the Civil War, discusses the landmark case that established the Supreme Court's fundamental function of judicial review, and examines the end of slavery, the country's history of welcoming immigrants, and the establishment of voting rights. Even if you weren't studying to pass a test, this is a fascinating overview of many of the most important events in U.S. history.

As you study to become a U.S. citizen, you should take advantage of the many other sources that provide free and easily accessible information. Your local library and school district are good places to continue your search for information and to find classes that may be offered to help you establish a solid grasp of the English language and understanding of the historic events that have made the United States the great country it is today.

AMERICA'S FOUNDATION: THE DECLARATION OF INDEPENDENCE, THE CONSTITUTION, AND THE BILL OF RIGHTS

Citizens of the United States enjoy tremendous freedoms and protections, which represent many of the basic ideals and principles upon which this country was founded. These principles are spelled out and preserved in documents that were written when the United States became an independent nation and continue to provide guidance to the men and women who govern U.S. citizens. Although these historic documents may have been amended or slightly altered, they are still the cornerstone of how current laws are made, interpreted, and enforced.

Two of the most well-known of these documents are the Declaration of Independence and the U.S. Constitution. The Bill of Rights, which represents the first ten amendments to the Constitution, is another important document often referred to in U.S. history. The text of the Declaration of Independence, the U.S. Constitution, the Bill of Rights, and the succeeding seventeen amendments to the Constitution is included here. Reading these documents will provide you with much of the information you will need to know to pass the civics test. It will also help you practice the English language.

Reading these documents and understanding the events and history surrounding the time in which they were written will provide you with valuable information about the country of which you are seeking to become a citizen. Two excellent resources that provide comprehensive and accurate information about U.S. history and that put into context the historical significance of many of our country's events are The National Archives and the Library of Congress.

The Declaration of Independence

When in the Course of human events, it becomes necessary for one people to dissolve the political bands which have connected them with another, and to assume among the powers of the earth, the separate and equal station to which the Laws of Nature and of Nature's God entitle them, a decent respect to the opinions of mankind requires that they should declare the causes which impel them to the separation.

We hold these truths to be self-evident, that all men are created equal, that they are endowed by their Creator with certain unalienable Rights, that among these are Life, Liberty and the pursuit of Happiness.–That to secure these rights, Governments are instituted among Men, deriving their just powers from the consent of the governed, –That whenever any Form of Government becomes destructive of these ends, it is the Right of the People to alter or to abolish it, and to institute new Government, laying its foundation on such principles and organizing its powers in such form, as to them shall seem most likely to effect their Safety and Happiness. Prudence, indeed, will dictate that Governments long established should not be changed for light and transient causes; and accordingly all experience hath shown, that mankind are more disposed to suffer, while evils are sufferable, than to right themselves by abolishing the forms to which they are accustomed. But when a long train of abuses and usurpations, pursuing invariably the same Object evinces a design to reduce them under absolute Despotism, it is their right, it is their duty, to throw off such Government, and to provide new Guards for their future security.–Such has been the patient sufferance of these Colonies; and such is now the necessity which constrains them to alter their former Systems of Government. The history of the present King of Great Britain is a history of repeated injuries and usurpations, all having in direct object the establishment of an absolute Tyranny over these States. To prove this, let Facts be submitted to a candid world.

He has refused his Assent to Laws, the most wholesome and necessary for the public good.

He has forbidden his Governors to pass Laws of immediate and pressing importance, unless suspended in their operation till his Assent should be obtained; and when so suspended, he has utterly neglected to attend to them.

He has refused to pass other Laws for the accommodation of large districts of people, unless those people would relinquish the right of Representation in the Legislature, a right inestimable to them and formidable to tyrants only.

He has called together legislative bodies at places unusual, uncomfortable, and distant from the depository of their public Records, for the sole purpose of fatiguing them into compliance with his measures.

He has dissolved Representative Houses repeatedly, for opposing with manly firmness his invasions on the rights of the people.

He has refused for a long time, after such dissolutions, to cause others to be elected; whereby the Legislative powers, incapable of Annihilation, have returned to the People at large for their exercise; the State remaining in the mean time exposed to all the dangers of invasion from without, and convulsions within.

He has endeavored to prevent the population of these States; for that purpose obstructing the Laws for Naturalization of Foreigners; refusing to pass others to encourage their migrations hither, and raising the conditions of new Appropriations of Lands.

He has obstructed the Administration of Justice, by refusing his Assent to Laws for establishing Judiciary powers.

He has made Judges dependent on his Will alone, for the tenure of their offices, and the amount and payment of their salaries.

He has erected a multitude of New Offices, and sent hither Swarms of Officers to harass our people, and eat out their Substance.

He has kept among us, in times of peace, Standing Armies without the Consent of our legislatures.

He has affected to render the Military independent of and superior to the Civil power.

He has combined with others to subject us to a jurisdiction foreign to our constitution, and unacknowledged by our laws; giving his Assent to their Acts of pretended Legislation:

For Quartering large bodies of armed troops among us:

For protecting them, by a mock Trial, from punishment for any Murders which they should commit on the Inhabitants of these States:

For cutting off our Trade with all parts of the world:

For imposing Taxes on us without our Consent:

For depriving us in many cases, of the benefits of Trial by Jury:

For transporting us beyond Seas to be tried for pretended offences

For abolishing the free System of English Laws in a neighboring Province, establishing therein an Arbitrary government, and enlarging its Boundaries so as to render it at once an example and fit instrument for introducing the same absolute rule into these Colonies:

For taking away our Charters, abolishing our most valuable Laws, and altering fundamentally the Forms of our Governments:

For suspending our own Legislatures, and declaring themselves invested with power to legislate for us in all cases whatsoever.

He has abdicated Government here, by declaring us out of his Protection and waging War against us.

He has plundered our seas, ravaged our Coasts, burnt our towns, and destroyed the lives of our people.

He is at this time transporting large Armies of foreign Mercenaries to complete the works of death, desolation and tyranny, already begun with circumstances of Cruelty and Perfidy scarcely paralleled in the most barbarous ages, and totally unworthy the Head of a civilized nation.

He has constrained our fellow Citizens taken Captive on the high Seas to bear Arms against their Country, to become the executioners of their friends and Brethren, or to fall themselves by their Hands.

He has excited domestic insurrections amongst us, and has endeavored to bring on the inhabitants of our frontiers, the merciless Indian Savages, whose known rule of warfare, is an undistinguished destruction of all ages, sexes and conditions.

In every stage of these Oppressions We have Petitioned for Redress in the most humble terms: Our repeated Petitions have been answered only by repeated injury. A Prince whose character is thus marked by every act which may define a Tyrant, is unfit to be the ruler of a free people.

Nor have We been wanting in attentions to our British brethren. We have warned them from time to time of attempts by their legislature to extend an unwarrantable jurisdiction over us. We have reminded them of the circumstances of our emigration and settlement here. We have appealed to their native justice and magnanimity, and we have conjured them by the ties of our common kindred to disavow these usurpations, which, would inevitably interrupt our connections and correspondence. They too have been deaf to the voice of justice and of consanguinity. We must, therefore, acquiesce in the necessity, which denounces our Separation, and hold them, as we hold the rest of mankind, Enemies in War, in Peace Friends.

We, therefore, the Representatives of the UNITED STATES OF AMERICA, in General Congress, Assembled, appealing to the Supreme Judge of the world for the rectitude of our intentions, do, in the Name, and by Authority of the good People of these Colonies, solemnly publish and declare, That these United Colonies are, and of Right ought to be Free and Independent States; that they are Absolved from all Allegiance to the British Crown, and that all political connection between them and the State of Great Britain, is and ought to be totally dissolved; and that as Free and Independent States, they have full Power to levy War, conclude Peace, contract Alliances, establish Commerce, and to do all other Acts and Things which Independent States may of right do. And for the support of this Declaration, with a firm reliance on the protection of divine Providence, we mutually pledge to each other our Lives, our Fortunes, and our sacred Honor.

(here follow the signatures)

The Constitution of the United States

We, the People of the United States, in Order to form a more perfect Union, establish Justice, insure domestic Tranquility, provide for the common defense, promote the general Welfare, and secure the Blessings of Liberty to ourselves and our Posterity, do ordain and establish this Constitution for the United States of America.

Article I.

Section 1.

All legislative Powers herein granted shall be vested in a Congress of the United States, which shall consist of a Senate and House of Representatives.

Section 2.

The House of Representatives shall be composed of Members chosen every second Year by the People of the several States, and the Electors in each State shall have the Qualifications requisite for Electors of the most numerous Branch of the State Legislature.

No Person shall be a Representative who shall not have attained to the Age of twenty five Years, and been seven Years a Citizen of the United States, and who shall not, when elected, be an Inhabitant of that State in which he shall be chosen.

Representatives and direct Taxes shall be apportioned among the several States which may be included within this Union, according to their respective Numbers, which shall be determined by adding to the whole Number of free Persons, including those bound to Service for a Term of Years, and excluding Indians not taxed, three fifths of all other Persons. The actual Enumeration shall be made within three Years after the first Meeting of the Congress of the United States, and within every subsequent Term of ten Years, in such Manner as they shall by Law direct. The Number of Representatives shall not exceed one for every thirty Thousand, but each State shall have at Least one Representative; and until such enumeration shall be made, the State of New Hampshire shall be entitled to choose three, Massachusetts eight, Rhode-Island and Providence Plantations one, Connecticut five, New-York six, New Jersey four, Pennsylvania eight, Delaware one, Maryland six, Virginia ten, North Carolina five, South Carolina five, and Georgia three.

When vacancies happen in the Representation from any State, the Executive Authority thereof shall issue Writs of Election to fill such Vacancies.

The House of Representatives shall choose their Speaker and other Officers; and shall have the sole Power of Impeachment.

Section 3.

The Senate of the United States shall be composed of two Senators from each State, chosen by the Legislature thereof for six Years; and each Senator shall have one Vote.

Immediately after they shall be assembled in Consequence of the first Election, they shall be divided as equally as may be into three Classes. The Seats of the Senators of the first Class shall be vacated at the Expiration of the second Year, of the second Class at the Expiration of the fourth Year, and of the third Class at the Expiration of the sixth Year, so that one third may be chosen every second Year; and if Vacancies happen by Resignation, or otherwise, during the Recess of the Legislature of any State, the Executive thereof may make temporary Appointments until the next Meeting of the Legislature, which shall then fill such Vacancies.

No Person shall be a Senator who shall not have attained to the Age of thirty Years, and been nine Years a Citizen of the United States, and who shall not, when elected, be an Inhabitant of that State for which he shall be chosen.

The Vice President of the United States shall be President of the Senate, but shall have no Vote, unless they be equally divided.

The Senate shall choose their other Officers, and also a President pro tempore, in the Absence of the Vice President, or when he shall exercise the Office of President of the United States.

The Senate shall have the sole Power to try all Impeachments. When sitting for that Purpose, they shall be on Oath or Affirmation. When the President of the United States is tried, the Chief Justice shall preside: And no Person shall be convicted without the Concurrence of two thirds of the Members present.

Judgment in Cases of Impeachment shall not extend further than to removal from Office, and disqualification to hold and enjoy any Office of honor, Trust or Profit under the United States: but the Party convicted shall nevertheless be liable and subject to Indictment, Trial, Judgment and Punishment, according to Law.

Section 4.

The Times, Places and Manner of holding Elections for Senators and Representatives, shall be prescribed in each State by the Legislature thereof; but the Congress may at any time by Law make or alter such Regulations, except as to the Places of choosing Senators.

The Congress shall assemble at least once in every Year, and such Meeting shall be on the first Monday in December, unless they shall by Law appoint a different Day.

Section 5.

Each House shall be the Judge of the Elections, Returns and Qualifications of its own Members, and a Majority of each shall constitute a Quorum to do Business; but a smaller Number may adjourn from day to day, and may be authorized to compel the Attendance of absent Members, in such Manner, and under such Penalties as each House may provide.

Each House may determine the Rules of its Proceedings, punish its Members for disorderly Behavior, and, with the Concurrence of two thirds, expel a Member.

Each House shall keep a Journal of its Proceedings, and from time to time publish the same, excepting such Parts as may in their Judgment require Secrecy; and the Yeas and Nays of the Members of either House on any question shall, at the Desire of one fifth of those Present, be entered on the Journal.

Neither House, during the Session of Congress, shall, without the Consent of the other, adjourn for more than three days, nor to any other Place than that in which the two Houses shall be sitting.

Section 6.

The Senators and Representatives shall receive a Compensation for their Services, to be ascertained by Law, and paid out of the Treasury of the United States. They shall in all Cases, except Treason, Felony and Breach of the Peace, be privileged from Arrest during their Attendance at the Session of their respective Houses, and in going to and returning from the same; and for any Speech or Debate in either House, they shall not be questioned in any other Place.

No Senator or Representative shall, during the Time for which he was elected, be appointed to any civil Office under the Authority of the United States, which shall have been created, or the Emoluments whereof shall have been increased during such time; and no Person holding any Office under the United States, shall be a Member of either House during his Continuance in Office.

Section 7.

All Bills for raising Revenue shall originate in the House of Representatives; but the Senate may propose or concur with Amendments as on other Bills.

Every Bill which shall have passed the House of Representatives and the Senate, shall, before it become a Law, be presented to the President of the United States: If he approve he shall sign it, but if not he shall return it, with his Objections to that House in which it shall have originated, who shall enter the Objections at large on their Journal, and proceed to reconsider it. If after such Reconsideration two thirds of that House shall agree to pass the Bill, it shall be sent, together with the Objections, to the other House, by which it shall likewise be reconsidered, and if approved by two thirds of that House, it shall become a Law. But in all such Cases the Votes of both Houses shall be determined by yeas and Nays, and the Names of the Persons voting for and against the Bill shall be entered on the Journal of each House respectively. If any Bill shall not be returned by the President within ten Days (Sundays excepted) after it shall have been presented to him, the Same shall be a Law, in like Manner as if he had signed it, unless the Congress by their Adjournment prevent its Return, in which Case it shall not be a Law.

Every Order, Resolution, or Vote to which the Concurrence of the Senate and House of Representatives may be necessary (except on a question of Adjournment) shall be presented to the President of the United States; and before the Same shall take Effect, shall be approved by him, or being disapproved by him, shall be re-passed by two thirds of the Senate and House of Representatives, according to the Rules and Limitations prescribed in the Case of a Bill.

Section 8.

The Congress shall have Power To lay and collect Taxes, Duties, Imposts and Excises, to pay the Debts and provide for the common Defense and general Welfare of the United States; but all Duties, Imposts and Excises shall be uniform throughout the United States;

To borrow Money on the credit of the United States;

To regulate Commerce with foreign Nations, and among the several States, and with the Indian Tribes;

To establish an uniform Rule of Naturalization, and uniform Laws on the subject of Bankruptcies throughout the United States;

To coin Money, regulate the Value thereof, and of foreign Coin, and fix the Standard of Weights and Measures;

To provide for the Punishment of counterfeiting the Securities and current Coin of the United States;

To establish Post Offices and post Roads;

To promote the Progress of Science and useful Arts, by securing for limited Times to Authors and Inventors the exclusive Right to their respective Writings and Discoveries;

To constitute Tribunals inferior to the supreme Court;

To define and punish Piracies and Felonies committed on the high Seas, and Offences against the Law of Nations;

To declare War, grant Letters of Marque and Reprisal, and make Rules concerning Captures on Land and Water;

To raise and support Armies, but no Appropriation of Money to that Use shall be for a longer Term than two Years;

To provide and maintain a Navy;

To make Rules for the Government and Regulation of the land and naval Forces;

To provide for calling forth the Militia to execute the Laws of the Union, suppress Insurrections and repel Invasions;

To provide for organizing, arming, and disciplining, the Militia, and for governing such Part of them as may be employed in the Service of the United States, reserving to the States respectively, the Appointment of the Officers, and the Authority of training the Militia according to the discipline prescribed by Congress;

To exercise exclusive Legislation in all Cases whatsoever, over such District (not exceeding ten Miles square) as may, by Cession of particular States, and the Acceptance of Congress, become the Seat of the Government of the United States, and to exercise like Authority over all Places purchased by the Consent of the Legislature of the State in which the Same shall be, for the Erection of Forts, Magazines, Arsenals, dock-Yards, and other needful Buildings;–And

To make all Laws which shall be necessary and proper for carrying into Execution the foregoing Powers, and all other Powers vested by this Constitution in the Government of the United States, or in any Department or Officer thereof.

Section 9.

The Migration or Importation of such Persons as any of the States now existing shall think proper to admit, shall not be prohibited by the Congress prior to the Year one thousand eight hundred and eight, but a Tax or duty may be imposed on such Importation, not exceeding ten dollars for each Person.

The Privilege of the Writ of Habeas Corpus shall not be suspended, unless when in Cases of Rebellion or Invasion the public Safety may require it.

No Bill of Attainder or ex post facto Law shall be passed.

No Capitation, or other direct, Tax shall be laid, unless in Proportion to the Census or enumeration herein before directed to be taken.

No Tax or Duty shall be laid on Articles exported from any State.

No Preference shall be given by any Regulation of Commerce or Revenue to the Ports of one State over those of another; nor shall Vessels bound to, or from, one State, be obliged to enter, clear, or pay Duties in another.

No Money shall be drawn from the Treasury, but in Consequence of Appropriations made by Law; and a regular Statement and Account of the Receipts and Expenditures of all public Money shall be published from time to time.

No Title of Nobility shall be granted by the United States: And no Person holding any Office of Profit or Trust under them, shall, without the Consent of the Congress, accept of any present, Emolument, Office, or Title, of any kind whatever, from any King, Prince, or foreign State.

Section 10.

No State shall enter into any Treaty, Alliance, or Confederation; grant Letters of Marque and Reprisal; coin Money; emit Bills of Credit; make any Thing but gold and silver Coin a Tender in Payment of

Debts; pass any Bill of Attainder, ex post facto Law, or Law impairing the Obligation of Contracts, or grant any Title of Nobility.

No State shall, without the Consent of the Congress, lay any Imposts or Duties on Imports or Exports, except what may be absolutely necessary for executing it's inspection Laws: and the net Produce of all Duties and Imposts, laid by any State on Imports or Exports, shall be for the Use of the Treasury of the United States; and all such Laws shall be subject to the Revision and Control of the Congress.

No State shall, without the Consent of Congress, lay any Duty of Tonnage, keep Troops, or Ships of War in time of Peace, enter into any Agreement or Compact with another State, or with a foreign Power, or engage in War, unless actually invaded, or in such imminent Danger as will not admit of delay.

Article II.

Section 1.

The executive Power shall be vested in a President of the United States of America. He shall hold his Office during the Term of four Years, and, together with the Vice President, chosen for the same Term, be elected, as follows:

Each State shall appoint, in such Manner as the Legislature thereof may direct, a Number of Electors, equal to the whole Number of Senators and Representatives to which the State may be entitled in the Congress: but no Senator or Representative, or Person holding an Office of Trust or Profit under the United States, shall be appointed an Elector.

The Electors shall meet in their respective States, and vote by Ballot for two Persons, of whom one at least shall not be an Inhabitant of the same State with themselves. And they shall make a List of all the Persons voted for, and of the Number of Votes for each; which List they shall sign and certify, and transmit sealed to the Seat of the Government of the United States, directed to the President of the Senate. The President of the Senate shall, in the Presence of the Senate and House of Representatives, open all the Certificates, and the Votes shall then be counted. The Person having the greatest Number of Votes shall be the President, if such Number be a Majority of the whole Number of Electors appointed; and if there be more than one who have such Majority, and have an equal Number of Votes, then the House of Representatives shall immediately choose by Ballot one of them for President; and if no Person have a Majority, then from the five highest on the List the said House shall in like Manner choose the President. But in choosing the President, the Votes shall be taken by States, the Representation from each State having one Vote; A quorum for this purpose shall consist of a Member or Members from two thirds of the States, and a Majority of all the States shall be necessary to a Choice. In every Case, after the Choice of the President, the Person having the greatest Number of Votes of the Electors shall be the Vice President. But if there should remain two or more who have equal Votes, the Senate shall choose from them by Ballot the Vice President.

The Congress may determine the Time of choosing the Electors, and the Day on which they shall give their Votes; which Day shall be the same throughout the United States.

No Person except a natural born Citizen, or a Citizen of the United States, at the time of the Adoption of this Constitution, shall be eligible to the Office of President; neither shall any Person be eligible to that Office who shall not have attained to the Age of thirty five Years, and been fourteen Years a Resident within the United States.

In Case of the Removal of the President from Office, or of his Death, Resignation, or Inability to discharge the Powers and Duties of the said Office, the Same shall devolve on the Vice President, and the Congress may by Law provide for the Case of Removal, Death, Resignation or Inability, both of the President and Vice President, declaring what Officer shall then act as President, and such Officer shall act accordingly, until the Disability be removed, or a President shall be elected.

The President shall, at stated Times, receive for his Services, a Compensation, which shall neither be increased nor diminished during the Period for which he shall have been elected, and he shall not receive within that Period any other Emolument from the United States, or any of them.

Before he enter on the Execution of his Office, he shall take the following Oath or Affirmation:–"I do solemnly swear (or affirm) that I will faithfully execute the Office of President of the United States, and will to the best of my Ability, preserve, protect and defend the Constitution of the United States."

Section 2.

The President shall be Commander in Chief of the Army and Navy of the United States, and of the Militia of the several States, when called into the actual Service of the United States; he may require the Opinion, in writing, of the principal Officer in each of the executive Departments, upon any Subject relating to the Duties of their respective Offices, and he shall have Power to grant Reprieves and Pardons for Offences against the United States, except in Cases of Impeachment.

He shall have Power, by and with the Advice and Consent of the Senate, to make Treaties, provided two thirds of the Senators present concur; and he shall nominate, and by and with the Advice and Consent of the Senate, shall appoint Ambassadors, other public Ministers and Consuls, Judges of the supreme Court, and all other Officers of the United States, whose Appointments are not herein otherwise provided for, and which shall be established by Law: but the Congress may by Law vest the Appointment of such inferior Officers, as they think proper, in the President alone, in the Courts of Law, or in the Heads of Departments.

The President shall have Power to fill up all Vacancies that may happen during the Recess of the Senate, by granting Commissions which shall expire at the End of their next Session.

Section 3.

He shall from time to time give to the Congress Information of the State of the Union, and recommend to their Consideration such Measures as he shall judge necessary and expedient; he may, on extraordinary Occasions, convene both Houses, or either of them, and in Case of Disagreement between them, with Respect to the Time of Adjournment, he may adjourn them to such Time as he shall think proper; he shall receive Ambassadors and other public Ministers; he shall take Care that the Laws be faithfully executed, and shall Commission all the Officers of the United States.

Section 4.

The President, Vice President and all civil Officers of the United States, shall be removed from Office on Impeachment for, and Conviction of, Treason, Bribery, or other high Crimes and Misdemeanors.

Article III.

Section 1.

The judicial Power of the United States shall be vested in one supreme Court, and in such inferior Courts as the Congress may from time to time ordain and establish. The Judges, both of the supreme and inferior Courts, shall hold their Offices during good Behaviour, and shall, at stated Times, receive for their Services a Compensation, which shall not be diminished during their Continuance in Office.

Section 2.

The judicial Power shall extend to all Cases, in Law and Equity, arising under this Constitution, the Laws of the United States, and Treaties made, or which shall be made, under their Authority;–to all Cases affecting Ambassadors, other public Ministers and Consuls;–to all Cases of admiralty and maritime Jurisdiction;–to Controversies to which the United States shall be a Party;–to Controversies between two or more States;– between a State and Citizens of another State,–between Citizens of different States,–between Citizens of the same State claiming Lands under Grants of different States, and between a State, or the Citizens thereof, and foreign States, Citizens or Subjects.

In all Cases affecting Ambassadors, other public Ministers and Consuls, and those in which a State shall be Party, the supreme Court shall have original Jurisdiction. In all the other Cases before mentioned, the supreme Court shall have appellate Jurisdiction, both as to Law and Fact, with such Exceptions, and under such Regulations as the Congress shall make.

The Trial of all Crimes, except in Cases of Impeachment, shall be by Jury; and such Trial shall be held in the State where the said Crimes shall have been committed; but when not committed within any State, the Trial shall be at such Place or Places as the Congress may by Law have directed.

Section 3.

Treason against the United States, shall consist only in levying War against them, or in adhering to their Enemies, giving them Aid and Comfort. No Person shall be convicted of Treason unless on the Testimony of two Witnesses to the same overt Act, or on Confession in open Court.

The Congress shall have Power to declare the Punishment of Treason, but no Attainder of Treason shall work Corruption of Blood, or Forfeiture except during the Life of the Person attainted.

Article IV.

Section 1.

Full Faith and Credit shall be given in each State to the public Acts, Records, and judicial Proceedings of every other State. And the Congress may by general Laws prescribe the Manner in which such Acts, Records and Proceedings shall be proved, and the Effect thereof.

Section 2.

The Citizens of each State shall be entitled to all Privileges and Immunities of Citizens in the several States.

A Person charged in any State with Treason, Felony, or other Crime, who shall flee from Justice, and be found in another State, shall on Demand of the executive Authority of the State from which he fled, be delivered up, to be removed to the State having Jurisdiction of the Crime.

No Person held to Service or Labor in one State, under the Laws thereof, escaping into another, shall, in Consequence of any Law or Regulation therein, be discharged from such Service or Labor, but shall be delivered up on Claim of the Party to whom such Service or Labor may be due.

Section 3.

New States may be admitted by the Congress into this Union; but no new State shall be formed or erected within the Jurisdiction of any other State; nor any State be formed by the Junction of two or more States, or Parts of States, without the Consent of the Legislatures of the States concerned as well as of the Congress.

The Congress shall have Power to dispose of and make all needful Rules and Regulations respecting the Territory or other Property belonging to the United States; and nothing in this Constitution shall be so construed as to Prejudice any Claims of the United States, or of any particular State.

Section 4.

The United States shall guarantee to every State in this Union a Republican Form of Government, and shall protect each of them against Invasion; and on Application of the Legislature, or of the Executive (when the Legislature cannot be convened), against domestic Violence.

Article V.

The Congress, whenever two thirds of both Houses shall deem it necessary, shall propose Amendments to this Constitution, or, on the Application of the Legislatures of two thirds of the several States, shall call a Convention for proposing Amendments, which, in either Case, shall be valid to all Intents and Purposes, as Part of this Constitution, when ratified by the Legislatures of three fourths of the several States, or by Conventions in three fourths thereof, as the one or the other Mode of Ratification may be proposed by the Congress; Provided that no Amendment which may be made prior to the Year One thousand eight hundred and eight shall in any Manner affect the first and fourth Clauses in the Ninth Section of the first Article; and that no State, without its Consent, shall be deprived of its equal Suffrage in the Senate.

Article VI.

All Debts contracted and Engagements entered into, before the Adoption of this Constitution, shall be as valid against the United States under this Constitution, as under the Confederation.

This Constitution, and the Laws of the United States which shall be made in Pursuance thereof; and all Treaties made, or which shall be made, under the Authority of the United States, shall be the supreme Law of the Land; and the Judges in every State shall be bound thereby, any Thing in the Constitution or Laws of any State to the Contrary notwithstanding.

The Senators and Representatives before mentioned, and the Members of the several State Legislatures, and all executive and judicial Officers, both of the United States and of the several States, shall be bound by Oath or Affirmation, to support this Constitution; but no religious Test shall ever be required as a Qualification to any Office or public Trust under the United States.

Article VII.

The Ratification of the Conventions of nine States, shall be sufficient for the Establishment of this Constitution between the States so ratifying the Same.

The Word, "the," being interlined between the seventh and eighth Lines of the first Page, the Word "Thirty" being partly written on an Erasure in the fifteenth Line of the first Page, The Words "is tried" being interlined between the thirty second and thirty third Lines of the first Page and the Word "the" being interlined between the forty third and forty fourth Lines of the second Page.

Attest William Jackson Secretary

Done in Convention by the Unanimous Consent of the States present the Seventeenth Day of September in the Year of our Lord one thousand seven hundred and Eighty seven and of the Independence of the United States of America the Twelfth.

In witness whereof We have hereunto subscribed our Names,

(here follow the signatures)

The Bill of Rights

The First 10 Amendments to the Constitution as Ratified by the States

The Preamble to The Bill of Rights

Congress of the United States

begun and held at the City of New York, on Wednesday the fourth of March, one thousand seven hundred and eighty nine.

THE Conventions of a number of the States, having at the time of their adopting the Constitution, expressed a desire, in order to prevent misconstruction or abuse of its powers, that further declaratory and restrictive clauses should be added: And as extending the ground of public confidence in the Government, will best ensure the beneficent ends of its institution.

RESOLVED by the Senate and House of Representatives of the United States of America, in Congress assembled, two thirds of both Houses concurring, that the following Articles be proposed to the Legislatures of the several States, as amendments to the Constitution of the United States, all, or any of which Articles, when ratified by three fourths of the said Legislatures, to be valid to all intents and purposes, as part of the said Constitution; viz.

ARTICLES in addition to, and Amendment of the Constitution of the United States of America, proposed by Congress, and ratified by the Legislatures of the several States, pursuant to the fifth Article of the original Constitution.

Amendment I

Congress shall make no law respecting an establishment of religion, or prohibiting the free exercise thereof; or abridging the freedom of speech, or of the press; or the right of the people peaceably to assemble, and to petition the Government for a redress of grievances.

Amendment II

A well regulated Militia, being necessary to the security of a free State, the right of the people to keep and bear Arms, shall not be infringed.

Amendment III

No Soldier shall, in time of peace be quartered in any house, without the consent of the Owner, nor in time of war, but in a manner to be prescribed by law.

Amendment IV

The right of the people to be secure in their persons, houses, papers, and effects, against unreasonable searches and seizures, shall not be violated, and no Warrants shall issue, but upon probable cause, supported by Oath or affirmation, and particularly describing the place to be searched, and the persons or things to be seized.

Amendment V

No person shall be held to answer for a capital, or otherwise infamous crime, unless on a presentment or indictment of a Grand Jury, except in cases arising in the land or naval forces, or in the Militia, when in actual service in time of War or public danger; nor shall any person be subject for the same offence to be twice put in jeopardy of life or limb; nor shall be compelled in any criminal case to be a witness against himself, nor be deprived of life, liberty, or property, without due process of law; nor shall private property be taken for public use, without just compensation.

Amendment VI

In all criminal prosecutions, the accused shall enjoy the right to a speedy and public trial, by an impartial jury of the State and district wherein the crime shall have been committed, which district shall have been previously ascertained by law, and to be informed of the nature and cause of the accusation; to be confronted with the witnesses against him; to have compulsory process for obtaining witnesses in his favor, and to have the Assistance of Counsel for his defense.

Amendment VII

In Suits at common law, where the value in controversy shall exceed twenty dollars, the right of trial by jury shall be preserved, and no fact tried by a jury, shall be otherwise re-examined in any Court of the United States, than according to the rules of the common law.

Amendment VIII

Excessive bail shall not be required, nor excessive fines imposed, nor cruel and unusual punishments inflicted.

Amendment IX

The enumeration in the Constitution, of certain rights, shall not be construed to deny or disparage others retained by the people.

Amendment X

The powers not delegated to the United States by the Constitution, nor prohibited by it to the States, are reserved to the States respectively, or to the people.

AMENDMENT XI

Passed by Congress March 4, 1794. Ratified February 7, 1795.

Note: Article III, section 2, of the Constitution was modified by amendment 11.

The Judicial power of the United States shall not be construed to extend to any suit in law or equity, commenced or prosecuted against one of the United States by Citizens of another State, or by Citizens or Subjects of any Foreign State.

AMENDMENT XII

Passed by Congress December 9, 1803. Ratified June 15, 1804.

Note: A portion of Article II, section 1 of the Constitution was superseded by the 12th amendment.

The Electors shall meet in their respective states and vote by ballot for President and Vice-President, one of whom, at least, shall not be an inhabitant of the same state with themselves; they shall name in their ballots the person voted for as President, and in distinct ballots the person voted for as Vice-President, and they shall make distinct lists of all persons voted for as President, and of all persons voted for as Vice-President, and of the number of votes for each, which lists they shall sign and certify, and transmit sealed to the seat of the government of the United States, directed to the President of the Senate; – the President of the Senate shall, in the presence of the Senate and House of Representatives, open all the certificates and the votes shall then be counted; – The person having the greatest number of votes for President, shall be the President, if such number be a majority of the whole number of Electors appointed; and if no person have such majority, then from the persons having the highest numbers not exceeding three on the list of those voted for as President, the House of Representatives shall choose immediately, by ballot, the President. But in choosing the President, the votes shall be taken by states, the representation from each state having one vote; a quorum for this purpose shall consist of a member or members from two-thirds of the states, and a majority of all the states shall be necessary to a choice. [And if the House of Representatives shall not choose a President whenever the right of choice shall devolve upon them, before the fourth day of March next following, then the Vice-President shall act as President, as in case of the death or other constitutional disability of the President. –]* The person having the greatest number of votes as Vice-President, shall be the Vice-President, if such number be a majority of the whole number of Electors appointed, and if no person have a majority, then from the two highest numbers on the list, the Senate shall choose the Vice-President; a quorum for the purpose shall consist of two-thirds of the whole number of Senators, and a majority of the whole number shall be necessary to a choice. But no person constitutionally ineligible to the office of President shall be eligible to that of Vice-President of the United States.

*Superseded by section 3 of the 20th amendment.

AMENDMENT XIII

Passed by Congress January 31, 1865. Ratified December 6, 1865.

Note: A portion of Article IV, section 2, of the Constitution was superseded by the 13th amendment.

Section 1.

Neither slavery nor involuntary servitude, except as a punishment for crime whereof the party shall have been duly convicted, shall exist within the United States, or any place subject to their jurisdiction.

Section 2.

Congress shall have power to enforce this article by appropriate legislation.

AMENDMENT XIV

Passed by Congress June 13, 1866. Ratified July 9, 1868.

Note: Article I, section 2, of the Constitution was modified by section 2 of the 14th amendment.

Section 1.

All persons born or naturalized in the United States, and subject to the jurisdiction thereof, are citizens of the United States and of the State wherein they reside. No State shall make or enforce any law which shall abridge the privileges or immunities of citizens of the United States; nor shall any State deprive any person of life, liberty, or property, without due process of law; nor deny to any person within its jurisdiction the equal protection of the laws.

Section 2.

Representatives shall be apportioned among the several States according to their respective numbers, counting the whole number of persons in each State, excluding Indians not taxed. But when the right to vote at any election for the choice of electors for President and Vice-President of the United States, Representatives in Congress, the Executive and Judicial officers of a State, or the members of the Legislature thereof, is denied to any of the male inhabitants of such State, being twenty-one years of age,* and citizens of the United States, or in any way abridged, except for participation in rebellion, or other crime, the basis of representation therein shall be reduced in the proportion which the number of such male citizens shall bear to the whole number of male citizens twenty-one years of age in such State.

Section 3.

No person shall be a Senator or Representative in Congress, or elector of President and Vice-President, or hold any office, civil or military, under the United States, or under any State, who, having previously taken an oath, as a member of Congress, or as an officer of the United States, or as a member of any State legislature, or as an executive or judicial officer of any State, to support the Constitution of the United States, shall have engaged in insurrection or rebellion against the same, or given aid or comfort to the enemies thereof. But Congress may by a vote of two-thirds of each House, remove such disability.

Section 4.

The validity of the public debt of the United States, authorized by law, including debts incurred for payment of pensions and bounties for services in suppressing insurrection or rebellion, shall not be questioned. But neither the United States nor any State shall assume or pay any debt or obligation incurred in aid of insurrection or rebellion against the United States, or any claim for the loss or emancipation of any slave; but all such debts, obligations and claims shall be held illegal and void.

Section 5.

The Congress shall have the power to enforce, by appropriate legislation, the provisions of this article.

*Changed by section 1 of the 26th amendment.

AMENDMENT XV

Passed by Congress February 26, 1869. Ratified February 3, 1870.

Section 1.

The right of citizens of the United States to vote shall not be denied or abridged by the United States or by any State on account of race, color, or previous condition of servitude–

Section 2.

The Congress shall have the power to enforce this article by appropriate legislation.

AMENDMENT XVI

Passed by Congress July 2, 1909. Ratified February 3, 1913.

Note: Article I, section 9, of the Constitution was modified by amendment 16.

The Congress shall have power to lay and collect taxes on incomes, from whatever source derived, without apportionment among the several States, and without regard to any census or enumeration.

AMENDMENT XVII

Passed by Congress May 13, 1912. Ratified April 8, 1913.

Note: Article I, section 3, of the Constitution was modified by the 17th amendment.

The Senate of the United States shall be composed of two Senators from each State, elected by the people thereof, for six years; and each Senator shall have one vote. The electors in each State shall have the qualifications requisite for electors of the most numerous branch of the State legislatures.

When vacancies happen in the representation of any State in the Senate, the executive authority of such State shall issue writs of election to fill such vacancies: Provided, That the legislature of any State may empower the executive thereof to make temporary appointments until the people fill the vacancies by election as the legislature may direct.

This amendment shall not be so construed as to affect the election or term of any Senator chosen before it becomes valid as part of the Constitution.

AMENDMENT XVIII

Passed by Congress December 18, 1917. Ratified January 16, 1919. Repealed by amendment 21.

Section 1.

After one year from the ratification of this article the manufacture, sale, or transportation of intoxicating liquors within, the importation thereof into, or the exportation thereof from the United States and all territory subject to the jurisdiction thereof for beverage purposes is hereby prohibited.

Section 2.

The Congress and the several States shall have concurrent power to enforce this article by appropriate legislation.

Section 3.

This article shall be inoperative unless it shall have been ratified as an amendment to the Constitution by the legislatures of the several States, as provided in the Constitution, within seven years from the date of the submission hereof to the States by the Congress.

AMENDMENT XIX

Passed by Congress June 4, 1919. Ratified August 18, 1920.

The right of citizens of the United States to vote shall not be denied or abridged by the United States or by any State on account of sex.

Congress shall have power to enforce this article by appropriate legislation.

AMENDMENT XX

Passed by Congress March 2, 1932. Ratified January 23, 1933.

Note: Article I, section 4, of the Constitution was modified by section 2 of this amendment. In addition, a portion of the 12th amendment was superseded by section 3.

Section 1.

The terms of the President and the Vice President shall end at noon on the 20th day of January, and the terms of Senators and Representatives at noon on the 3d day of January, of the years in which such terms would have ended if this article had not been ratified; and the terms of their successors shall then begin.

Section 2.

The Congress shall assemble at least once in every year, and such meeting shall begin at noon on the 3d day of January, unless they shall by law appoint a different day.

Section 3.

If, at the time fixed for the beginning of the term of the President, the President elect shall have died, the Vice President elect shall become President. If a President shall not have been chosen before the time fixed for the beginning of his term, or if the President elect shall have failed to qualify, then the Vice President elect shall act as President until a President shall have qualified; and the Congress may by law provide for the case wherein neither a President elect nor a Vice President shall have qualified, declaring who shall then act as President, or the manner in which one who is to act shall be selected, and such person shall act accordingly until a President or Vice President shall have qualified.

Section 4.

The Congress may by law provide for the case of the death of any of the persons from whom the House of Representatives may choose a President whenever the right of choice shall have devolved upon them, and for the case of the death of any of the persons from whom the Senate may choose a Vice President whenever the right of choice shall have devolved upon them.

Section 5.

Sections 1 and 2 shall take effect on the 15th day of October following the ratification of this article.

Section 6.

This article shall be inoperative unless it shall have been ratified as an amendment to the Constitution by the legislatures of three-fourths of the several States within seven years from the date of its submission.

AMENDMENT XXI

Passed by Congress February 20, 1933. Ratified December 5, 1933.

Section 1.

The eighteenth article of amendment to the Constitution of the United States is hereby repealed.

Section 2.

The transportation or importation into any State, Territory, or Possession of the United States for delivery or use therein of intoxicating liquors, in violation of the laws thereof, is hereby prohibited.

Section 3.

This article shall be inoperative unless it shall have been ratified as an amendment to the Constitution by conventions in the several States, as provided in the Constitution, within seven years from the date of the submission hereof to the States by the Congress.

AMENDMENT XXII

Passed by Congress March 21, 1947. Ratified February 27, 1951.

Section 1.

No person shall be elected to the office of the President more than twice, and no person who has held the office of President, or acted as President, for more than two years of a term to which some other person was elected President shall be elected to the office of President more than once. But this Article shall not apply to any person holding the office of President when this Article was proposed by Congress, and shall not prevent any person who may be holding the office of President, or acting as President, during the term within which this Article becomes operative from holding the office of President or acting as President during the remainder of such term.

Section 2.

This article shall be inoperative unless it shall have been ratified as an amendment to the Constitution by the legislatures of three-fourths of the several States within seven years from the date of its submission to the States by the Congress.

AMENDMENT XXIII

Passed by Congress June 16, 1960. Ratified March 29, 1961.

Section 1.

The District constituting the seat of Government of the United States shall appoint in such manner as Congress may direct:

A number of electors of President and Vice President equal to the whole number of Senators and Representatives in Congress to which the District would be entitled if it were a State, but in no event more than the least populous State; they shall be in addition to those appointed by the States, but they shall be considered, for the purposes of the election of President and Vice President, to be electors appointed by a State; and they shall meet in the District and perform such duties as provided by the twelfth article of amendment.

Section 2.

The Congress shall have power to enforce this article by appropriate legislation.

AMENDMENT XXIV

Passed by Congress August 27, 1962. Ratified January 23, 1964.

Section 1.

The right of citizens of the United States to vote in any primary or other election for President or Vice President, for electors for President or Vice President, or for Senator or Representative in Congress, shall not be denied or abridged by the United States or any State by reason of failure to pay poll tax or other tax.

Section 2.

The Congress shall have power to enforce this article by appropriate legislation.

AMENDMENT XXV

Passed by Congress July 6, 1965. Ratified February 10, 1967.

Note: Article II, section 1, of the Constitution was affected by the 25th amendment.

Section 1.

In case of the removal of the President from office or of his death or resignation, the Vice President shall become President.

Section 2.

Whenever there is a vacancy in the office of the Vice President, the President shall nominate a Vice President who shall take office upon confirmation by a majority vote of both Houses of Congress.

Section 3.

Whenever the President transmits to the President pro tempore of the Senate and the Speaker of the House of Representatives his written declaration that he is unable to discharge the powers and duties of his office, and until he transmits to them a written declaration to the contrary, such powers and duties shall be discharged by the Vice President as Acting President.

Section 4.

Whenever the Vice President and a majority of either the principal officers of the executive departments or of such other body as Congress may by law provide, transmit to the President pro tempore of the Senate and the Speaker of the House of Representatives their written declaration that the President is unable to discharge the powers and duties of his office, the Vice President shall immediately assume the powers and duties of the office as Acting President.

Thereafter, when the President transmits to the President pro tempore of the Senate and the Speaker of the House of Representatives his written declaration that no inability exists, he shall resume the powers and duties of his office unless the Vice President and a majority of either the principal officers of the executive department or of such other body as Congress may by law provide, transmit within four days to the President pro tempore of the Senate and the Speaker of the House of Representatives their written declaration that the President is unable to discharge the powers and duties of his office. Thereupon Congress shall decide the issue, assembling within forty-eight hours for that purpose if not in session. If the Congress, within twenty-one days after receipt of the latter written declaration, or, if Congress is not in session, within twenty-one days after Congress is required to assemble, determines by two-thirds vote of both Houses that the President is unable to discharge the powers and duties of his office, the Vice President shall continue to discharge the same as Acting President; otherwise, the President shall resume the powers and duties of his office.

AMENDMENT XXVI

Passed by Congress March 23, 1971. Ratified July 1, 1971.

Note: Amendment 14, section 2, of the Constitution was modified by section 1 of the 26th amendment.

Section 1.

The right of citizens of the United States, who are eighteen years of age or older, to vote shall not be denied or abridged by the United States or by any State on account of age.

Section 2.

The Congress shall have power to enforce this article by appropriate legislation.

AMENDMENT XXVII

Originally proposed Sept. 25, 1789. Ratified May 7, 1992.

No law, varying the compensation for the services of the Senators and Representatives, shall take effect, until an election of representatives shall have intervened.

PART III

5 Practice Tests

CHAPTER 7

Practice Tests for the Naturalization Interview

WHAT TO EXPECT

During your naturalization eligibility interview, you will be given a civics test in English to test your knowledge and understanding of the history of the United States and how the U.S. government works. You will be asked ten questions. You must answer six of them correctly to pass the test.

The next pages contain five practice tests of ten questions each. These are followed by the correct answers. These are questions from the actual test. If you practice, you should be well-prepared to successfully pass the civics test portion of your naturalization interview.

Although you will have to speak your answers to the questions, for the practice tests you should write your answer choice on a piece of paper so you can easily see which questions you answered correctly and which ones you need to study more. Good luck!

PRACTICE TEST 1

1. What is the supreme law of the land?
   (A) The Declaration of Independence
   (B) The Constitution
   (C) The Emancipation Proclamation
   (D) The Bill of Rights

2. What stops one branch of government from becoming too powerful?
   (A) The right to vote
   (B) The market economy
   (C) Checks and balances
   (D) The states' governors

3. Who is in charge of the executive branch?
   (A) The president
   (B) The Supreme Court
   (C) The Speaker of the House
   (D) The governor of Washington, D.C.

4. How many U.S. senators are there?
   (A) 435
   (B) 100
   (C) 50
   (D) 25

5. How many justices are on the Supreme Court?
   (A) 4
   (B) 5
   (C) 9
   (D) 10

6. What is one responsibility that is only for U.S. citizens?
   (A) Driving the speed limit
   (B) Reporting criminal activity
   (C) Serving on a jury
   (D) Paying taxes

7. When was the Constitution written?
   (A) 1787
   (B) 1612
   (C) 1814
   (D) 1492

8. Who is the "Father of Our Country"?
   (A) John Adams
   (B) Benjamin Franklin
   (C) Thomas Jefferson
   (D) George Washington

9. What did Susan B. Anthony do?
   (A) Invent money
   (B) Fought in the Civil War
   (C) Flew a fighter plane in World War I
   (D) Fought for women's rights

10. What ocean is on the West Coast of the United States?
    (A) The Pacific Ocean
    (B) The Indian Ocean
    (C) The Atlantic Ocean
    (D) The Bering Sea

The Answer Key to Practice Test 1 can be found after Practice Test 5. Check your answers against the correct answers for each question. If you got six or more correct, try another practice test. If you didn't do well or had to guess at most of the answers, spend some more time studying, and then try again.

PRACTICE TEST 2

1. What is one right or freedom from the First Amendment?
   (A) The right to vote
   (B) The right to drive
   (C) The right to an education
   (D) The right of free speech

2. We elect a U.S. senator for how many years?
   (A) Two
   (B) Four
   (C) Six
   (D) Eight

3. Who does a U.S. senator represent?
   (A) Everyone in the United States
   (B) All of the people who voted for him or her
   (C) Everyone who lives in Washington, D.C.
   (D) All of the people of the state he was elected in

4. Who vetoes bills?
   (A) All members of Congress
   (B) The president
   (C) All members of the state legislature
   (D) The Supreme Court

5. What is the highest court in the United States?
   (A) The Court of Appeals
   (B) The 10th Circuit Court
   (C) The Supreme Court
   (D) The Judicial Court

6. What do we show loyalty to when we say the Pledge of Allegiance?
   (A) The United States
   (B) The president
   (C) The Constitution
   (D) Washington, D.C.

7. What is one promise you make when you become a U.S. citizen?
   (A) To vote
   (B) To serve in the U.S. military if needed
   (C) To graduate from college
   (D) To run for public office

8. What happened at the Constitutional Convention?
   (A) The Constitution was written.
   (B) Benjamin Franklin was elected president.
   (C) The Founding Fathers established states' rights.
   (D) The Civil War was ended.

9. During the Cold War, what was the main concern of the United States?
   (A) The Nazis
   (B) Communism
   (C) Anarchy
   (D) The economy

10. Name one state that borders Canada.
    (A) Florida
    (B) Colorado
    (C) Oregon
    (D) North Dakota

PRACTICE TEST 3

1. What is an amendment?
   (A) A change to the Oath of Office
   (B) A change to the Constitution
   (C) A change to the Declaration of Independence
   (D) A change to the Pledge of Allegiance

2. What are two rights in the Declaration of Independence?
   (A) Life and freedom of religion
   (B) Liberty and the pursuit of happiness
   (C) Liberty and the right to bear arms
   (D) Freedom of speech and the pursuit of happiness

3. We elect a president for how many years?
   (A) Three
   (B) Four
   (C) Six
   (D) Ten

4. If both the president and the vice president can no longer serve, who becomes president?
   (A) The attorney general
   (B) The Chief Justice of the Supreme Court
   (C) The secretary of state
   (D) The Speaker of the House

5. Under our Constitution, some powers belong to the states. What is one power of the states?
   (A) To print money
   (B) To make treaties
   (C) To grant a driver's license
   (D) To declare war

6. When is the last day you can send in federal income tax forms?
   (A) April 15
   (B) January 1
   (C) July 4
   (D) September 15

7. Who lived in America before the Europeans arrived?
   (A) Alaskans
   (B) Nobody
   (C) American Indians
   (D) Canadians

8. There were thirteen original states. Name three.
   (A) West Virginia, Delaware, Florida
   (B) New Hampshire, Connecticut, Arkansas
   (C) Massachusetts, Rhode Island, Pennsylvania
   (D) New Jersey, New York, Louisiana

9. Who was the first president?
   (A) Alexander Hamilton
   (B) Thomas Jefferson
   (C) Theodore Roosevelt
   (D) George Washington

10. What did the Emancipation Proclamation do?
    (A) Gave women the right to vote
    (B) Declared freedom from England
    (C) Abolished taxation without representation
    (D) Freed the slaves

PRACTICE TEST 4

1. What do we call the first ten amendments to the Constitution?
   (A) The Bill of Rights
   (B) The Declaration of Independence
   (C) The Federalist Papers
   (D) The Emancipation Proclamation

2. How many amendments does the Constitution have?
   (A) Fifteen
   (B) Twenty-one
   (C) Twenty-seven
   (D) Thirty-five

3. What is the economic system in the United States?
   (A) The stock market
   (B) A libertarian economy
   (C) A capitalist economy
   (D) A Marxist economy

4. Who makes federal laws?
   (A) The state legislature
   (B) Congress
   (C) The president
   (D) The Supreme Court

5. The House of Representatives has how many voting members?
   (A) 100
   (B) 215
   (C) 322
   (D) 435

6. In what month do we vote for president?
   (A) January
   (B) March
   (C) July
   (D) November

7. Who wrote the Declaration of Independence?
   (A) George Washington
   (B) Thomas Jefferson
   (C) Thomas Edison
   (D) Alexander Hamilton

8. What territory did the United States buy from France in 1803?
   (A) Louisiana
   (B) Alaska
   (C) The great west territory
   (D) Long Island

9. Who did the United States fight in World War II?
   (A) Russia, Japan, and Italy
   (B) Japan, China, and Germany
   (C) Japan, Germany, and Italy
   (D) France, Germany, and Italy

10. Name one of the two longest rivers in the United States.
    (A) The Everglades
    (B) The Colorado
    (C) The Michigan
    (D) The Missouri

PRACTICE TEST 5

1. What are the two parts of the U.S. Congress?
   - (A) The House of Representatives and the Executive branch
   - (B) The Executive and Judicial branches
   - (C) The Senate and the Legislature
   - (D) The Senate and House of Representatives

2. We elect a U.S. representative for how many years?
   - (A) Two
   - (B) Four
   - (C) Five
   - (D) Seven

3. Why do some states have more representatives than other states?
   - (A) Because they have been states longer
   - (B) Because they are larger
   - (C) Because they have more people
   - (D) Because they have more money

4. When must all men register for the selective service?
   - (A) It is no longer required.
   - (B) Between the ages of 18 and 26
   - (C) By the age of 28
   - (D) Men and women must both register.

5. Name one problem that led to the Civil War.
   - (A) The gold rush
   - (B) Religious oppression
   - (C) Slavery
   - (D) Unfair taxation

6. Name one war fought by the United States in the 1900s.
   - (A) The Civil War
   - (B) The Vietnam War
   - (C) The Spanish-American War
   - (D) The Turkish War

7. Who was president during the Great Depression and World War II?
   - (A) Andrew Jackson
   - (B) Woodrow Wilson
   - (C) Theodore Roosevelt
   - (D) Franklin Roosevelt

8. Name one state that borders Mexico.
   - (A) Colorado
   - (B) Arizona
   - (C) Arkansas
   - (D) Utah

9. What is the capital of the United States?
   - (A) Los Angeles, California
   - (B) New York, New York
   - (C) Washington, D.C.
   - (D) Boston, Massachusetts

10. What is the name of the national anthem?
    - (A) "The Star-Spangled Banner"
    - (B) "America the Beautiful"
    - (C) "Battle Hymn of the Republic"
    - (D) "God Bless America"

ANSWER KEY FOR PRACTICE TESTS

Practice Test 1

1. The correct answer is (B).
2. The correct answer is (C).
3. The correct answer is (A).
4. The correct answer is (B).
5. The correct answer is (C).
6. The correct answer is (C).
7. The correct answer is (A).
8. The correct answer is (D).
9. The correct answer is (D).
10. The correct answer is (A).

Practice Test 2

1. The correct answer is (D).
2. The correct answer is (C).
3. The correct answer is (D).
4. The correct answer is (B).
5. The correct answer is (C).
6. The correct answer is (A).
7. The correct answer is (B).
8. The correct answer is (A).
9. The correct answer is (B).
10. The correct answer is (D).

Practice Test 3

1. The correct answer is (B).
2. The correct answer is (B).
3. The correct answer is (B).
4. The correct answer is (D).
5. The correct answer is (C).
6. The correct answer is (A).
7. The correct answer is (C).
8. The correct answer is (C).
9. The correct answer is (D).
10. The correct answer is (D).

Practice Test 4

1. The correct answer is (A).
2. The correct answer is (C).
3. The correct answer is (C).
4. The correct answer is (B).
5. The correct answer is (D).
6. The correct answer is (D).
7. The correct answer is (B).
8. The correct answer is (A).
9. The correct answer is (C).
10. The correct answer is (D).

Practice Test 5

1. The correct answer is (D).
2. The correct answer is (A).
3. The correct answer is (C).
4. The correct answer is (B).
5. The correct answer is (C).
6. The correct answer is (B).
7. The correct answer is (D).
8. The correct answer is (B).
9. The correct answer is (C).
10. The correct answer is (A).

OFFICIAL USCIS INTERVIEW QUESTIONS

Now that you have had a chance to practice, you should have a look at the actual questions and answers for the civics test portion of your naturalization interview.

As mentioned previously, the civics test is an oral test. A USCIS officer will ask you ten questions from the 100 questions listed here. You must answer six questions correctly to pass this portion of the naturalization test. Although there may be additional correct answers to these questions, you are encouraged to respond using the answers provided. You will find the answers following these 100 questions. Some questions have more than one acceptable answer.

If you are 65 years of age or older and have been a legal permanent resident of the United States for twenty or more years, you may study just the questions that have been marked with an asterisk.

American Government

Principles of American Democracy

1. What is the supreme law of the land?

2. What does the Constitution do?

3. The idea of self-government is in the first three words of the Constitution. What are these words?

4. What is an amendment?

5. What do we call the first ten amendments to the Constitution?

6. What is one right or freedom from the First Amendment?*

7. How many amendments does the Constitution have?

8. What did the Declaration of Independence do?

9. What are two rights in the Declaration of Independence?

10. What is freedom of religion?

11. What is the economic system in the United States?*

12. What is the "rule of law"?

System of Government

13. Name one branch or part of the government.*

14. What stops one branch of government from becoming too powerful?

15. Who is in charge of the executive branch?

16. Who makes federal laws?

17. What are the two parts of the U.S. Congress?*

18. How many U.S. senators are there?

19. We elect a U.S. senator for how many years?

20. Who is one of your state's U.S. senators now?*

21. The House of Representatives has how many voting members?

22. We elect a U.S. representative for how many years?

23. Name your U.S. representative.

24. Who does a U.S. senator represent?

25. Why do some states have more representatives than other states?

26. We elect a president for how many years?

27. In what month do we vote for president?*

28. What is the name of the president of the United States now?*

29. What is the name of the vice president of the United States now?

30. If the president can no longer serve, who becomes president?

31. If both the president and the vice president can no longer serve, who becomes president?

32. Who is the commander in chief of the military?

33. Who signs bills to become laws?

34. Who vetoes bills?

35. What does the president's Cabinet do?

36. What are two Cabinet-level positions?

37. What does the judicial branch do?

38. What is the highest court in the United States?

39. How many justices are on the Supreme Court?

40. Who is the chief justice of the United States now?

41. Under our Constitution, some powers belong to the federal government. What is one power of the federal government?

42. Under our Constitution, some powers belong to the states. What is one power of the states?

43. Who is the governor of your state now?

44. What is the capital of your state?*

45. What are the two major political parties in the United States?*

46. What is the political party of the president now?

47. What is the name of the Speaker of the House of Representatives now?

Rights and Responsibilities

48. There are four amendments to the Constitution about who can vote. Describe one of them.

49. What is one responsibility that is only for United States citizens?*

50. Name one right only for United States citizens?

51. What are two rights of everyone living in the United States?

52. What do we show loyalty to when we say the Pledge of Allegiance?

53. What is one promise you make when you become a United States citizen?

54. How old do citizens have to be to vote for president?*

55. What are two ways that Americans can participate in their democracy?

56. When is the last day you can send in federal income tax forms?*

57. When must all men register for the Selective Service?

American History

Colonial Period and Independence

58. What is one reason colonists came to America?

59. Who lived in America before the Europeans arrived?

60. What group of people was taken to America and sold as slaves?

61. Why did the colonists fight the British?

62. Who wrote the Declaration of Independence?

63. When was the Declaration of Independence adopted?

64. There were thirteen original states. Name three.

65. What happened at the Constitutional Convention?

66. When was the Constitution written?

67. The Federalist Papers supported the passage of the U.S. Constitution. Name one of the writers.

68. What is one thing Benjamin Franklin is famous for?

69. Who is the "Father of Our Country"?

70. Who was the first president?*

The 1800s

71. What territory did the United States buy from France in 1803?

72. Name one war fought by the United States in the 1800s.

73. Name the U.S. war between the North and the South.

74. Name one problem that led to the Civil War.

75. What was one important thing that Abraham Lincoln did?*

76. What did the Emancipation Proclamation do?

77. What did Susan B. Anthony do?

Recent American History and Other Important Historical Information

78. Name one war fought by the United States in the 1900s.*

79. Who was president during World War I?

80. Who was president during the Great Depression and World War II?

81. Who did the United States fight in World War II?

82. Before he was president, Eisenhower was a general. What war was he in?

83. During the Cold War, what was the main concern of the United States?

84. What movement tried to end racial discrimination?

85. What did Martin Luther King Jr. do?*

86. What major event happened on September 11, 2001, in the United States?

87. Name one American Indian tribe in the United States.

Integrated Civics

Geography

88. Name one of the two longest rivers in the United States.

89. What ocean is on the West Coast of the United States?

90. What ocean is on the East Coast of the United States?

91. Name one U.S. territory.

92. Name one state that borders Canada.

93. Name one state that borders Mexico.

94. What is the capital of the United States?*

95. Where is the Statue of Liberty?*

Symbols

96. Why does the flag have 13 stripes?

97. Why does the flag have 50 stars?*

98. What is the name of the national anthem?

Holidays

99. When do we celebrate Independence Day?*

100. Name two national U.S. holidays.

ANSWERS TO THE INTERVIEW QUESTIONS

(For some questions, several acceptable answers have been provided.)

1. The Constitution

2. Sets up the government
   Defines the government
   Protects basic rights of Americans

3. We the People

4. A change (to the Constitution)
   An addition (to the Constitution)

5. The Bill of Rights

6. Speech
   Religion
   Assembly
   The press
   To petition the government

7. Twenty-seven (27)

8. Announced our independence (from Great
     Britain)
   Declared our independence (from Great
     Britain)
   Said that the United States is free (from
     Great Britain)

9. Life
   Liberty
   Pursuit of happiness

10. You can practice any religion, or not practice
    a religion.

11. Capitalist economy
    Market economy

12. Everyone must follow the law.
    Leaders must obey the law.
    Government must obey the law.
    No one is above the law.

13. Congress
    Legislative
    President
    Executive
    The courts
    Judicial

14. Checks and balances
    Separation of powers

15. The president

16. Congress
    Senate and House of Representatives
    U.S. or national legislature

17. The Senate and House of Representatives

18. One hundred (100)

19. Six (6)

20. Answers will vary. District of Columbia resi-
    dents and residents of U.S. territories should
    answer that D.C. (or the territory where the
    applicant lives) has no U.S. Senators.

21. Four hundred thirty-five (435)

22. Two (2)

23. Answers will vary. Residents of territo-
    ries with nonvoting Delegates or Resident
    Commissioners may provide the name of that
    Delegate or Commissioner. Also acceptable
    is any statement that the territory has no
    (voting) representatives in Congress.

24. All people of the state

25. (Because of) the state's population
    (Because) they have more people
    (Because) some states have more people

26. Four (4)

27. November

28. Barack Obama
    Obama

29. Joseph R. Biden Jr.
    Joe Biden
    Biden

30. The vice president

31. The Speaker of the House

32. The president

33. The president

34. The president

35. Advises the president

36. Attorney General
    Secretary of Agriculture
    Secretary of Commerce
    Secretary of Defense
    Secretary of Education
    Secretary of Energy
    Secretary of Health and Human Services
    Secretary of Homeland Security
    Secretary of Housing and Urban Development
    Secretary of the Interior
    Secretary of Labor
    Secretary of State
    Secretary of Transportation
    Secretary of the Treasury
    Secretary of Veterans Affairs
    Vice President

37. Reviews laws
    Explains laws
    Resolves disputes (disagreements)
    Decides if a law goes against the Constitution

38. The Supreme Court

39. Nine (9)

40. John Roberts (John G. Roberts Jr.)

41. To print money
    To declare war
    To create an army
    To make treaties

42. Provide schooling and education
    Provide protection (police)
    Provide safety (fire departments)
    Grant a driver's license
    Approve zoning and land use

43. Answers will vary. District of Columbia residents should answer that D.C. does not have a Governor.

44. Answers will vary. District of Columbia residents should answer that D.C. is not a state and does not have a capital. Residents of U.S. territories should name the capital of the territory.

45. Democratic and Republican

46. Democratic (Party)

47. (Nancy) Pelosi *(at the time this book was published)*

48. Citizens 18 years and older (can vote).
    You don't have to pay (a poll tax) to vote.
    Any citizen can vote. (Women and men can vote.)
    A male citizen of any race (can vote).

49. Serve on a jury
    Vote in a federal election

50. Vote in a federal election
    Run for federal office

51. Freedom of expression
    Freedom of speech
    Freedom of assembly
    Freedom to petition the government
    Freedom of worship
    The right to bear arms

52. The United States
    The flag

53. Give up loyalty to other countries
    Defend the Constitution and laws of the United States
    Obey the laws of the United States
    Serve in the U.S. military (if needed)
    Serve (do important work for) the nation (if needed)
    Be loyal to the United States

54. Eighteen (18) years and older

55. Vote
    Join a political party
    Help with a campaign
    Join a civic group
    Join a community group
    Express your opinion to an elected official
    Call senators and representatives
    Publicly support or oppose an issue or policy
    Run for office
    Write to a newspaper

56. April 15

57. At age eighteen (18)
    Between eighteen (18) and twenty-six (26)

58. Freedom
    Political liberty
    Religious freedom
    Economic opportunity
    Practice their religion
    Escape persecution

59. American Indians
Native Americans

60. Africans
People from Africa

61. Because of high taxes (taxation without
representation)
Because the British army stayed in their
houses (boarding, quartering)
Because they didn't have self-government

62. (Thomas) Jefferson

63. July 4, 1776

64. Connecticut
Delaware
Georgia
Maryland
Massachusetts
New Hampshire
New Jersey
New York
North Carolina
Pennsylvania
Rhode Island
South Carolina
Virginia

65. The Constitution was written.
The Founding Fathers wrote the
Constitution.

66. 1787

67. (James) Madison
(Alexander) Hamilton
(John) Jay
Publius [Collective pseudonym adopted by
James Madison, Alexander Hamilton,
and John Jay as authors of The Federalist
Papers (1787–1788)]

68. U.S. diplomat
Oldest member of the Constitutional
Convention
First Postmaster General of the United
States
Writer of "Poor Richard's Almanack"
Started the first free libraries

69. (George) Washington

70. (George) Washington

71. The Louisiana Territory
Louisiana

72. Civil War
Mexican-American War
Spanish-American War
War of 1812

73. The Civil War
The War Between the States

74. Slavery
Economic reasons
States' rights

75. Freed the slaves (Emancipation
Proclamation)
Saved (or preserved) the Union
Led the United States during the Civil War

76. Freed the slaves
Freed slaves in the Confederacy
Freed slaves in the Confederate states
Freed slaves in most Southern states

77. Fought for women's rights
Fought for civil rights

78. World War I
World War II
Korean War
Vietnam War
(Persian) Gulf War

79. (Woodrow) Wilson

80. (Franklin) Roosevelt

81. Japan, Germany, and Italy

82. World War II

83. Communism

84. Civil rights (movement)

85. Fought for civil rights
Worked for equality for all Americans

86. Terrorists attacked the United States.

87. (Note: USCIS Officers will be supplied with a
list of federally recognized American Indian
tribes.)
Apache
Arawak
Blackfeet
Cherokee
Cheyenne
Chippewa
Choctaw
Creek
Crow

Hopi
Huron
Inuit
Iroquois
Lakota
Mohegan
Navajo
Oneida
Pueblo
Seminole
Shawnee
Sioux
Teton

88. Missouri (River)
Mississippi (River)

89. Pacific (Ocean)

90. Atlantic (Ocean)

91. American Samoa
Guam
Northern Mariana Islands
Puerto Rico
U.S. Virgin Islands

92. Alaska
Idaho
Maine
Michigan
Minnesota
Montana
New Hampshire
New York
North Dakota
Ohio
Pennsylvania
Vermont
Washington

93. Arizona
California
New Mexico
Texas

94. Washington, D.C.

95. New York (Harbor)
Liberty Island
(Also acceptable are New Jersey, near New
York City, and on the Hudson [River].)

96. Because there were thirteen (13) original
colonies
Because the stripes represent the original
colonies

97. Because there is one star for each state
Because each star represents a state
Because there are fifty (50) states

98. "The Star-Spangled Banner"

99. July 4

100. In order from January through December:
New Year's Day
Martin Luther King Jr. Day
Presidents' Day
Memorial Day
Independence Day
Labor Day
Columbus Day
Veterans Day
Thanksgiving Day
Christmas

PART IV

Appendixes

APPENDIX A

USCIS Instructions and Blank Practice Forms

Below is a list of forms, many of which were shown filled out in previous chapters. On the pages that follow are instructions for filling out each of the forms and then a blank copy of the form. Take the time to carefully read the instructions, and then fill out the blank forms for practice.

Although you cannot use these forms to file, the practice will help you understand exactly what information is required, what information you still might need to gather, and exactly what you will need to do to file the forms.

When you are ready to fill out and submit the actual forms, the easiest way to get copies, instructions, and fee schedules is by downloading them from the USCIS Web site at http://www.uscis.gov/portal/site/uscis. You can also obtain information and help from your local USCIS office or by calling the USCIS National Customer Service Center at 800-375-5283 (toll-free). Many additional forms plus a great deal of helpful information can also be found on the USCIS Web site.

G-325A   Biographic Information

I-20   Certificate of Eligibility for Nonimmigrant (F-1) Student Status

I-94   Departure Records

I-129F   Petition for Alien Fiancé(e)

I-130   Petition for Alien Relative

I-134   Affidavit of Support

I-140   Petition for Alien Worker

I-485   Application to Register Permanent Residence or Adjust Status

I-539   Application to Extend/change Nonimmigrant Status

I-693   Medical Examination Sheet

I-751   Petition to Remove Conditions on Residence

I-765   Application for Employment Authorization

I-864   Affidavit of Support Under Section 213A of the Act

I-865   Sponsor's Notice of Change of Address

M-603   Photo Requirements

N-400   Application for Naturalization

Department of Homeland Security
U.S. Citizenship and Immigration Services

OMB No. 1615-0008; Expires 06/30/2011

G-325A, Biographic Information

(Family Name)	(First Name)	(Middle Name)	☐ Male ☐ Female	Date of Birth (mm/dd/yyyy)	Citizenship/Nationality	File Number A

All Other Names Used (include names by previous marriages)	City and Country of Birth	U.S. Social Security # *(if any)*

	Family Name	First Name	Date of Birth (mm/dd/yyyy)	City, and Country of Birth (if known)	City and Country of Residence
Father					
Mother (Maiden Name)					

Current Husband or Wife (If none, so state) Family Name (For wife, give maiden name)	First Name	Date of Birth (mm/dd/yyyy)	City and Country of Birth	Date of Marriage	Place of Marriage

Former Husbands or Wives (If none, so state) Family Name (For wife, give maiden name)	First Name	Date of Birth (mm/dd/yyyy)	Date and Place of Marriage	Date and Place of Termination of Marriage

Applicant's residence last five years. List present address first.

Street and Number	City	Province or State	Country	From Month	From Year	To Month	To Year
						Present Time	

Applicant's last address outside the United States of more than one year.

Street and Number	City	Province or State	Country	From Month	From Year	To Month	To Year

Applicant's employment last five years. (If none, so state.) List present employment first.

Full Name and Address of Employer	Occupation (Specify)	From Month	From Year	To Month	To Year
				Present Time	

Last occupation abroad if not shown above. (Include all information requested above.)

This form is submitted in connection with an application for: ☐ Naturalization ☐ Other (Specify): ☐ Status as Permanent Resident	Signature of Applicant	Date

If your native alphabet is in other than Roman letters, write your name in your native alphabet below:

Penalties: Severe penalties are provided by law for knowingly and willfully falsifying or concealing a material fact.

Applicant: Print your name and Alien Registration Number in the box outlined by heavy border below.

Complete This Box (Family Name)	(Given Name)	(Middle Name)	(Alien Registration Number) A

Form G-325A (Rev. 06/12/09)Y

S. Department of Justice
nigration and Naturalization Service
ase Read Instructions on Page 2

Certificate of Eligibility for Nonimmigrant (F-1) Student Status - For Academic and Language Students

OMB No. 1115-0051

Page 1

s page must be completed and signed in the U.S. by a designated school official.

Family Name (surname)

First (given) name (do not enter middle name)

Country of birth

Date of birth (mo./day/year)

Country of citizenship

Admission number (Complete if known)

School (school district) name

School official to be notified of student's arrival in U.S. (Name and Title)

School address (include zip code)

School code (including 3-digit suffix, if any) and approval date

_____ 214F _____ approved on _____

For Immigration Official Use

Visa issuing post | Date Visa issued

Reinstated, extension granted to:

. This certificate is issued to the student named above for:
(Check and fill out as appropriate)
a. ☐ Initial attendance at this school
b. ☐ Continued attendance at this school
c. ☐ School transfer. Transferred from _____
d. ☐ Use by dependents for entering the United States.
e. ☐ Other _____

. Level of education the student is pursuing or will pursue in the United States:
(check only one)
a. ☐ Primary   e. ☐ Master's
b. ☐ Secondary   f. ☐ Doctorate
c. ☐ Associate   g. ☐ Language training
d. ☐ Bachelor's   h. ☐ Other

. The student named above has been accepted for a full course of study at this school, majoring in _____
The student is expected to report to the school no later than (date) _____ and complete studies not later than (date) _____
The normal length of study is _____

. ☐ English proficiency is required:
☐ The student has the required English proficiency
☐ The student is not yet proficient, English instructions will be given at the school.
☐ English proficiency is not required because _____

7. This school estimates the student's average costs for an academic term of _____ (up to 12) months to be:
a. Tuition and fees $_____
b. Living expenses $_____
c. Expenses of dependents $_____
d. Other(specify): $_____
Total $_____

8. This school has information showing the following as the students means of support, estimated for an academic term of _____ months (Use the same number of months given in item 7).
a. Student's personal funds $_____
b. Funds from this school $_____
(specify type)   _____
c. Funds from another source $_____
(specify type and source)   _____
d. On-campus employment (if any) $_____
Total $_____

9 Remarks: _____

I-20 SCHOOL

0. School Certification: I certify under penalty of perjury that all information provided above in items 1 through 8 was completed before I signed this form and is true and correct; I executed this form in the United States after review and evaluation in the United States by me or other officials of the school of the student's application, transcripts or other records of courses taken and proof of financial responsibility, which were received at the school prior to the execution of this form; the school has determined that the above named student's qualifications meet all standards for admission to the school; the student will be required to pursue a full course of study as defined by 8 CFR 214.2(f)(6); I am a designated official of the above named school and I am authorized to issue this form.

Signature of designated school official | Name of school official (print or type) | Title | Date issued | Place issued (city and state)

1. Student Certification: I have read and agreed to comply with the terms and conditions of my admission and those of any extension of stay as specified on page 2. I certify that all information provided on this form refers specifically to me and is true and correct to the best of my knowledge. I certify that I seek to enter or remain in the United States temporarily, and solely for the purpose of pursuing a full course of study at the school named on page 1 of this form. I also authorize the named school to release any information from my records which is needed by the INS pursuant to 8 CFR 214.3(g) to determine my nonimmigrant status.

Signature of student | Name of student | Date

Signature of parent or guardian if student is under 18 | Name of parent/guardian (Print or type) | Address(city) | (State or province) | (Country) | (Date)

For official use only
Microfilm Index Number

I20 A-B/I20ID(Rev 04-27-88)N

DEPARTMENT OF HOMELAND SECURITY
U.S. Customs and Border Protection

OMB No. 1651-0111

Admission Number

Welcome to the United States

I-94 Arrival/Departure Record - Instructions

This form must be completed by all persons except U.S.Citizens, returning resident aliens, aliens with immigrant visas, and Canadian Citizens visiting or in transit.

Type or print legibly with pen in ALL CAPITAL LETTERS. Use English. Do not write on the back of this form.

This form is in two parts. Please complete both the Arrival Record (Items 1 through 13) and the Departure Record (Items 14 through 17).

When all items are completed, present this form to the CBP Officer.

Item 7 - If you are entering the United States by land, enter **LAND** in this space. If you are entering the United States by ship, enter **SEA** in this space.

CBP Form I-94 (10/04)

Admission Number

OMB No. 1651-0111

Arrival Record

1. Family Name

2. First (Given) Name

3. Birth Date (Day/Mo/Yr)

4. Country of Citizenship

5. Sex (Male or Female)

6. Passport Number

7. Airline and Flight Number

8. Country Where You Live

9. City Where You Boarded

10. City Where Visa was Issued

11. Date Issued (Day/Mo/Yr)

12. Address While in the United States (Number and Street)

13. City and State

CBP Form I-94 (10/04)

Departure Number

OMB No. 1651-0111

I-94
Departure Record

14. Family Name

15. First (Given) Name

16. Birth Date (Day/Mo/Yr)

17. Country of Citizenship

CBP Form I-94 (10/04)

See Other Side

STAPLE HERE

Department of Homeland Security
U.S. Citizenship and Immigration Services

**Instructions for Form I-129F,
Petition for Alien Fiancé(e)**

Instructions

Please read these instructions carefully to properly complete this form. If you need more space to complete an answer, use a separate sheet(s) of paper. Write your name and Alien Registration Number (A #), if any, at the top of each sheet of paper and indicate the part and number of the item to which the answer refers.

The filing addresses provided on this form reflect the most current information as of the date this form was last printed. If you are filing Form I-129F more than 30 days after the latest edition date shown in the lower right-hand corner, please visit our website online at www.uscis.gov before you file, and check the Immigration Forms page to confirm the correct filing address and version currently in use. Check the edition date located in the lower right-hand corner of the form. If the edition date on your Form I-129F matches the edition date listed for Form I-129F on the online Immigration Forms page, your version is current and will be accepted by USCIS. If the edition date on the online version is later, download a copy and use the online version. If you do not have internet access, call the National Customer Service Center at 1-800-375-5283 to verify the current filing address and edition date. **Improperly filed forms will be rejected, and the fee returned, with instructions to resubmit the entire filing using the current form instructions.**

What Is the Purpose of This Form.

This form is used to petition to bring your fiancé(e) and that person's children to the United States for marriage to you or to bring your spouse and that person's children (K-3 and K-4 visas, respectively) to the United States to complete processing for permanent resident status (under the LIFE Act and Amendments of 2000).

Who May File This Form I-129F.

You may file this petition if:

1. You are a U.S. citizen, and

2. You and your fiancé(e) intend to marry within 90 days of your fiancé(e) entering the United States, and are both free to marry, and have met in person within two years before your filing of this petition unless:

   A. The requirement to meet your fiancé(e) in person would violate strict and long-established customs of your or your fiancé(e)'s foreign culture or social practice; or

   B. It is established that the requirement to personally meet your fiancé(e) would result in extreme hardship to you.

   OR

   C. You wish to have your spouse enter as a nonimmigrant. **See Item 8, How Do You Use This Form for Your Spouse Seeking Entry Using a K-3 Visa, on Page 4.**

NOTE: Unmarried children of your fiancé(e) or spouse who are under 21 years of age and listed on this form will be eligible to apply to accompany your fiancé(e) or spouse.

General Instructions.

Step 1. Fill Out the Form I-129.

1. Type or print legibly in black ink.

2. If extra space is needed to complete any item, attach a continuation sheet, indicate the item number, and date and sign each sheet.

3. Answer all questions fully and accurately. State that an item is not applicable with "N/A." If the answer is none, write "none."

Step 2. General requirements

1. **Compliance with the International Marriage Broker Regulation Act (IMBRA).**

   If you met your fiancé(e) or spouse through the services of an international marriage broker, you must notify USCIS of that fact by answering Question 19 on this form. The term "international marriage broker" means a corporation, partnership, business, individual, or other legal entity, whether or not organized under any law of the United States, that charges fees for providing dating, matrimonial, matchmaking services, or social referrals between United States citizens or nationals or aliens lawfully admitted to the United States as lawful permanent residents and foreign national clients by providing personal contact information or otherwise facilitating communication between individuals.

   The term "international marriage broker" does not include:

   A. Traditional matchmaking organizations of a cultural or religious nature that operate on a non-profit basis and in compliance with the laws of the countries in which it operates, including the laws of the United States; or

B. Entities that provide dating services if their principal business is not to provide international dating services between United States citizens or United States residents and foreign nationals and charge comparable rates and offers comparable services to all individuals it serves regardless of the individual's gender or country of citizenship.

For additional IMBRA requirements, see **Items 7** and **9** of these instructions

2. Filing Limitations on K Nonimmigrant Petitioners.

If you have filed two or more K-1 visa petitions at any time in the past or previously had a K-1 visa petition approved within two years prior to the filing of this petition, you must apply for a waiver. To request a waiver you must submit a written request with this petition accompanied by documentation of your claim to the waiver.

If you have committed a violent offense against a person or persons, USCIS may not grant such a waiver unless you can demonstrate that extraordinary circumstances exist. For details regarding those circumstances, see **Item 7.B.** of these instructions.

3. What Documents Do You Need to Show That You Are a U.S. Citizen?

A. If you were born in the United States, give USCIS a copy, front and back, of your birth certificate.

B. If you were naturalized, give USCIS a copy, front and back, of your original Certificate of Naturalization.

C. If you were born outside the United States and you are a U.S. citizen through your parents, give USCIS:

    1. Your original Certificate of Citizenship, or

    2. Your Form FS-240 (Report of Birth Abroad of a United States Citizen).

D. In place of any of the above, you may give USCIS a copy of your valid, unexpired U.S. passport issued with a validity period of at least five years. You must submit copies of all pages in the passport.

E. If you do not have any of the above and were born in the United States, see **Item 4, What If a Document Is Not Available.**

4. What If a Document Is Not Available?

If the documents needed above are not available, you can instead give USCIS the following secondary evidence. However, USCIS may request in writing that you obtain a statement from the appropriate civil authority certifying that the needed document is not available. Any evidence submitted must contain enough information, such as a birth date, to establish the event you are trying to prove.

A. *Baptismal certificate.* A copy, front and back, of the certificate under the seal of the church, synagogue or other religious entity showing where the baptism, dedication or comparable rite occurred, as well as the date and place of the child's birth, date of baptism and names of the child's parents. The baptism must have occurred within two months after the birth of the child.

B. *Census record.* State or Federal census records showing the name(s), date(s) and place(s) of birth or age(s) of the person(s) listed.

C. *School record.* A letter from the school authority (preferably from the first school attended), showing the date of admission to the school, child's date or age at that time, place of birth and the names of the parents.

D. *Affidavits.* If a required document cannot be obtained, you must submit either an original written statement from the governmental agency that should have the record, verifying that the record does not exist or a citation to the Department of State Foreign Affairs Manual indicating that such records are generally not available. Only then may you submit written affidavits sworn to or affirmed by two persons who were living at the time and who have personal knowledge of the event. Each affidavit must contain the affiant's full name, address, date and place of birth, and signature. The affidavit must also explain the affiant's relationship to you, full information concerning event and complete details of how the affiant acquired the information.

5. What Documents Do You Need to Prove That You Can Legally Marry?

A. Provide copies of evidence that you and your fiancé(e) have personally met within the last two years; or if you have never met within the last two years, provide a detailed explanation and evidence of the extreme hardship or customary, cultural or social practices that have prohibited your meeting; and

B. Provide original statements from you and your fiancé(e) whom you plan to marry within 90 days of his or her admission, and copies of any evidence you wish to submit to establish your mutual intent; and

C. If either of you is of an age that requires special consent or permission for you to marry in the jurisdiction where your marriage will occur, give proof of that consent or permission; and

D. If either you or your fiancé(e) were married before, give copies of documents showing that each prior marriage was legally terminated.

6. What Other Documents Do You Need?

A. Submit a completed and signed Form G-325A (Biographic Information) for you and a completed and signed Form G-325A for your fiancé(e). Except for name and signature, you do not have to repeat on the Biographic Information form the information given on your Form I-129F.

B. Give USCIS a passport-style color photograph of yourself and a passport-style color photograph of your fiancé(e), with both photos taken within 30 days of the date of filing this petition. The photos must have a white background, be glossy, un-retouched and not mounted. The dimension of the full frontal facial image of you and your fiancé(e) in separate photos should be about one inch from your chin to the top of your hair. Using a pencil or felt pen, lightly print the name (and Alien Registration Number, if known) on the back of each photograph.

C. If either you or the person you are filing for is using a name other than that shown on the relevant documents, you must give USCIS copies of the legal documents that made the change, such as a marriage certificate, adoption decree or court order.

7. What Documents Do You Need to Comply With the International Marriage Broker Regulation Act?

A. If you have ever been convicted of any of the following crimes, submit certified copies of all court and police records showing the charges and dispositions for every such conviction. This is required even if your records were sealed or otherwise cleared or if anyone, including a judge, law enforcement officer, or attorney, told you that you no longer have a record.

1. Domestic violence, sexual assault, child abuse and neglect, dating violence, elder abuse, and stalking.

The term "domestic violence" includes felony or misdemeanor crimes of violence committed by a current or former spouse of the victim, by a person with whom the victim shares a child in common, by a person who is cohabitating with or has cohabitated with the victim as a spouse, by a person similarly situated to a spouse of the victim under the domestic or family violence laws of the jurisdiction receiving grant monies, or by any other person against an adult or youth victim who is protected from that person's acts under the domestic or family violence laws of the jurisdiction.

2. Homicide, murder, manslaughter, rape, abusive sexual contact, sexual exploitation, incest, torture, trafficking, peonage, holding hostage, involuntary servitude, slave trade, kidnapping, abduction, unlawful criminal restraint, false imprisonment, or an attempt to commit any of these crimes.

3. Crimes relating to a controlled substance or alcohol on three or more occasions, and such crimes did not arise from a single act.

NOTE: If your petition is approved, a copy of your petition, including the information you submit regarding your criminal convictions, will be provided to the Department of State for dissemination to the beneficiary of your petition pursuant to section 833(a)(5)(A)(ii) of IMBRA. In addition, pursuant to section 833(a)(5)(A)(iii) of IMBRA, any criminal background information pertaining to you that USCIS may discover independently in adjudicating this petition will also be provided to the Department of State for disclosure to the beneficiary of your petition. You should also note that under section 833(c) of IMBRA, the name and contact information of any person who was granted a protection or restraining order against you, or of any victim of a crime of violence perpetrated by the petitioner, will remain confidential but that the relationship of the petitioner of such person or victim (i.e., spouse, child, etc.) will be disclosed.

B. If you are seeking a waiver of the filing limitations imposed by IMBRA, you must attach a signed and dated request for the waiver, explaining why a waiver would be appropriate in your case, together with any evidence in support of your request. Examples of such evidence include, but are not limited to: a death certificate, police reports, news articles, or medical reports from a licensed medical professional, regarding the death of an alien approved for a prior K visa.

If you have committed a violent offense and seek a waiver, you must attach a signed and dated request for the waiver, together with evidence that extraordinary circumstances exist in your case, i.e., that you were being battered or subjected to extreme cruelty by your spouse, parent, or adult child at the time you committed your violent offense(s), you were not the primary perpetrator of violence in the relationship, and:

1. You were acting in self-defense;

2. You violated a protection order intended for your protection; or

3. You committed, were arrested for, were convicted of, or plead guilty to committing a crime that did not result in serious bodily injury and where there was a connection between the crime committed and your having been battered or subjected to extreme cruelty.

Examples of such evidence include, but are not limited to:

Police reports;

Court records;

News articles;

Trial transcripts.

Applicants may submit any credible evidence that is relevant to the request for such a waiver.

8. How Do You Use This Form for Your Spouse Seeking Entry With a K-3 Visa?

This form may be used to obtain a K-3 visa for your alien spouse. Fill out the form as directed, except assume that "fiancé" or "fiancé(e)" means "spouse." Answer Questions **B.17** and **B.18** by stating "N/A." Note that filing this form is only necessary to facilitate the entry of your spouse as a **nonimmigrant**.

You must submit the documents required in **Items 1, 2** and **4** of the instructions, but may omit the documents required in **Item 3**. In addition, U.S. citizens petitioning for K-3 visas for their alien spouses must also include evidence that they have filed Form I-130, Petition for Alien Relative, on behalf of the alien spouse listed on this form, and a marriage certificate evidencing the legal marriage between the citizen and alien.

The LIFE Act requires applicants to apply for a K-3 visa in the country where their marriage to the U.S. citizen petitioner occurred. Petitioners should make sure to identify the appropriate consulate, in the same country where they married the alien for whom they are petitioning, in **Block 20** to avoid lengthy delays. In the event the petitioner and alien were married in the United States, they should list the country of the alien's current residence. See U.S. Department of State regulations at 21 CFR 41.81.

9. Mandatory Tracking of Multiple Petitions and Dissemination of Information Pamphlet.

The International Marriage Broker Regulation Act requires USCIS to maintain a database to track repeated petitions for K visas. Upon approval of a second petition for a K-1 or K-3 visa filed by the same U.S. citizen petitioner, USCIS will notify the petitioner that information concerning the petitioner has been entered into a multiple visa petition tracking database. USCIS will enter all subsequent K-1 or K-3 petitions filed by that petitioner into the database. When a subsequent petition for a K-1 or K-3 visa petition has been filed less than ten years after the date the first petition was filed, USCIS will notify both the petitioner and the beneficiary of the number of previously approved petitions listed in the database. USCIS will also send the beneficiary a pamphlet containing information on legal rights and resources for immigrant victims of domestic violence.

Translations. Any document containing foreign language submitted to the Service shall be accompanied by a full English language translation which the translator has certified as complete and accurate, and by the translator's certification that he or she is competent to translate from the foreign language into English.

Copies. Unless specifically required that an original document be filed with an application or petition, an ordinary legible photocopy may be submitted. Original documents submitted when not required will remain a part of the record, even if the submission was not required.

Where To File.

Before you file Form I-129F for your K-3 spouse or K-1 fiancé(e) please note the different filing addresses. Failure to follow these instructions may result in your application or petition being rejected, delayed or denied.

A. Form I-129F Filing Locations for K-1 Fiancé(e)

If you live in the United States:

File Form I-129F at the service center listed below based on where you live.

If you are filing abroad:

File Form I-129F with the service center listed below based on the last place you lived in the United States.

NOTE: Your petition cannot be adjudicated at a USCIS office abroad.

California Service Center Filings

File Form I-129F with the California Service Center if you live in:

Alaska, Arizona, California, Colorado, Guam, Hawaii, Idaho, Illinois, Indiana, Iowa, Kansas, Michigan, Minnesota, Missouri, Montana, Nebraska, Nevada, North Dakota, Ohio, Oregon, South Dakota, Utah, Washington, Wisconsin, or Wyoming.

Mail your Form I-129F package to:

> **USCIS**
> **California Service Center**
> **P.O. Box 10130**
> **Laguna Niguel, CA 92607-0130**

Vermont Service Center Filings

File form I-129F with the Vermont Service Center if you live in:

Alabama, Arkansas, Connecticut, Delaware, Florida, Georgia, Kentucky, Louisiana, Maine, Maryland, Massachusetts, Mississippi, New Hampshire, New Jersey, New Mexico, New York, North Carolina, Oklahoma, Pennsylvania, Puerto Rico, Rhode Island, South Carolina, Tennessee, Texas, Vermont, Virginia, U.S. Virgin Islands, West Virginia and the District of Columbia.

Mail your Form I-129F package to:

> **USCIS**
> **Vermont Service Center**
> **Attn: I-129F**
> **75 Lower Welden Street**
> **St. Albans, VT 05479-0001**

B. Form I-129F Filing Locations for K-3 Spouse

If you are filing an I-129F petition for your spouse, mail your petition to the Service Center where the underlying I-130 petition is currently pending. Use the address listed on your most recent receipt notice or transfer notice and include a copy of that notice with your Form I-129F.

Questions Regarding Form I-129F

For additional information about Form I-129F, including how to file your application or filing locations not mentioned, call the USCIS National Customer Service Center at **1-800-375-5283** or visit our website at **www.uscis.gov.**

What Is the Filing Fee.

The filing fee for a Form I-129F is **$455.00.**

Use the following guidelines when you prepare your check or money order for the Form I-129F fee:

1. The check or money order must be drawn on a bank or other financial institution located in the United States and must be payable in U.S. currency; and

2. Make the check or money order payable to **U.S. Department of Homeland Security**, unless:

   A. If you live in Guam and are filing your petition there, make it payable to **Treasurer, Guam**.

   B. If you live in the U.S. Virgin Islands and are filing your petition there, make it payable to **Commissioner of Finance of the Virgin Islands**.

   C. If you live outside the United States, Guam, or the U.S. Virgin Islands, contact the nearest U.S. consulate or embassy for instructions on the method of payment.

NOTE: Please spell out U.S. Department of Homeland Security; do not use the initials "USDHS" or "DHS."

Notice to Those Making Payment by Check. If you send us a check, it will be converted into an electronic funds transfer (EFT). This means we will copy your check and use the account information on it to electronically debit your account for the amount of the check. The debit from your account will usually take 24 hours, and will be shown on your regular account statement.

You will not receive your original check back. We will destroy your original check, but we will keep a copy of it. If the EFT cannot be processed for technical reasons, you authorize us to process the copy in place of your original check. If the EFT cannot be completed because of insufficient funds, we may try to make the transfer up to two times.

How to Check If the Fees Are Correct.

The form fee on this form is current as of the edition date appearing in the lower right corner of this page.

However, because USCIS fees change periodically, you can verify if the fees are correct by following one of the steps below:

1. Visit our website at **www.uscis.gov**, select "Immigration Forms" check the appropriate fee;

2. Review the Fee Schedule included in your form package, if you called us to request the form; or

3. Telephone our National Customer Service Center at **1-800-375-5283** and ask for the fee information.

Address Changes.

If you change your address and you have an application or petition pending with USCIS, you may change your address on-line at **www.uscis.gov**, click on "Change your address with USCIS" and follow the prompts or by completing and mailing Form AR-11, Alien's Change of Address Card, to:

**U.S. Citizenship and Immigration Services
Change of Address
P.O. Box 7134
London, KY 40742-7134**

For commercial overnight or fast freight services only, mail to:

**U.S. Citizenship and Immigration Services
Change of Address
1084-I South Laurel Road
London, KY 40744**

Processing Information.

How Does Your Alien Fiancé(e) Obtain Permanent Resident Status?

Your alien fiancé(e) may apply for conditional permanent resident status after you have entered into a valid marriage to each other within 90 days of your fiancé(e)'s entry into the United States. Your alien spouse should then apply promptly to USCIS for adjustment of status to conditional permanent resident, using Form I-485, Application to Register or Adjust Status.

How Does Your Spouse Become a Permanent Resident Without Conditions?

Both you and your conditional permanent resident spouse are required to file a petition, Form I-751, Petition to Remove the Conditions on Residence, during the 90-day period immediately before the second anniversary of the date your alien spouse was granted conditional permanent residence. Children who were admitted as conditional permanent residents with your spouse may be included in the joint petition to remove the conditions.

The rights, privileges, responsibilities and duties that apply to all other permanent residents apply equally to a conditional permanent resident to file petitions on behalf of qualifying relatives, or to reside permanently in the United States as an immigrant in accordance with the immigration laws.

Notice

Failure to file Form I-751, Petition to Remove the Conditions on Residence, will result in termination of permanent residence status and initiation of removal proceedings.

What Are the Penalties for Marriage Fraud or Giving False Information?

Title 18, United States Code, Section 100 states that whoever willfully and knowingly falsifies a material fact, makes a false statement or makes use of a false document will be fined up to $10,000 or imprisoned up to five years, or both.

Title 8, United States Code, Section 1325 states that any person who knowingly enters into a marriage contract for the purpose of evading any provision of the immigration laws shall be imprisoned for not more than five years or fined not more than $250,000, or both.

Any Form I-129F that is not signed or accompanied by the correct fee, will be rejected with a notice that the Form I-129F is deficient. You may correct the deficiency and resubmit the Form I-129F. An application or petition is not considered properly filed until accepted by USCIS.

Initial processing. Once a Form I-129F has been accepted, it will be checked for completeness, including submission of the required initial evidence. If you do not completely fill out the form, or file it without required initial evidence, you will not establish a basis for eligibility and we may deny your Form I-129F.

Requests for more information or interview. We may request more information or evidence, or we may request that you appear at a USCIS office for an interview. We may also request that you submit the originals of any copy. We will return these originals when they are no longer required.

Decision. The decision on a Form I-129F involves a determination of whether you have established eligiblity for the requested benefit. You will be notified of the decision in writing.

USCIS Forms and Information.

To order USCIS forms, call our toll-free number at **1-800-870-3676**. You can also get USCIS forms and information on immigration laws, regulations and procedures by telephoning our National Customer Service Center at **1-800-375-5283** or visiting our internet website at **www.uscis.gov**.

As an altenative to waiting in line for assistance at your local USCIS office, you can now schedule an appointment through our internet-based system, **InfoPass**. To access the system, visit our website. Use the **InfoPass** appointment scheduler and follow the screen prompts to set up your appointment. **InfoPass** generates an electronic appointment notice that appears on the screen.

Penalties.

If you knowingly and willfully falsify or conceal a material fact or submit a false document with this Form I-129F, we will deny the Form I-129F and may deny any other immigration benefit.

In addition, you will face severe penalties provided by law and may be subject to criminal prosecution.

Privacy Act Notice.

We ask for the information on this form, and associated evidence, to determine if you have established eligibility for the immigration benefit for which you are filing. Our legal right to ask for this information can be found in the Immigration and Nationality Act, as amended. We may provide this information to other government agencies. Failure to provide this information, and any requested evidence, may delay a final decision or result in denial of your Form I-129F.

Paperwork Reduction Act.

An agency may not conduct or sponsor an information collection and a person is not required to respond to a collection of information unless it displays a currently valid OMB control number. The public reporting burden for this collection of information is estimated at 1 hour, 30 minutes per response, including the time for reviewing instructions, completing and submitting the form. Send comments regarding this burden estimate or any other aspect of this collection of information, including suggestions for reducing this burden, to: U.S. Citizenship and Immigration Services, Regulatory Management Division, 111 Massachusetts Avenue, N.W., 3rd Floor, Suite 3008, Washington, DC 20529. OMB No. 1615-0001. **Do not mail your application to this address.**

Department of Homeland Security
U.S. Citizenship and Immigration Services

**I-129F, Petition
for Alien Fiancé(e)**

Do not write in these blocks. For USCIS Use Only

Case ID #	Action Block	Fee Stamp
A #		
G-28 #		
The petition is approved for status under Section 101(a)(5)(k). It is valid for four months from the date of action. _____		**AMCON:** _____

AMCON:
- [ ] Personal Interview
- [ ] Previously Forwarded
- [ ] Document Check
- [ ] Field Investigation

Remarks:

Part A. Start Here. Information about you.

1. Name *(Family name in CAPS) (First) (Middle)*

2. Address *(Number and Street)* Apt. #

(Town or City) (State or Country) (Zip/Postal Code)

3. Place of Birth *(Town or City) (State/Country)*

4. Date of Birth *(mm/dd/yyyy)* **5. Gender**
- [ ] Male [ ] Female

6. Marital Status
- [ ] Married [ ] Single [ ] Widowed [ ] Divorced

7. Other Names Used *(including maiden name)*

8a. U.S. Social Security Number 8b. A# *(if any)*

9. Names of Prior Spouses   Date(s) Marriage(s) Ended

10. My citizenship was acquired through *(check one)*
- [ ] Birth in the U.S. [ ] Naturalization

Give number of certificate, date and place it was issued.

- [ ] Parents

Have you obtained a certificate of citizenship in your name?
- [ ] Yes [ ] No

If "Yes," give certificate number, date and place it was issued.

11. Have you ever filed for this or any other alien fiancé(e) or husband/wife before?
- [ ] Yes [ ] No

If "Yes," give name of all aliens, place and date of filing, A# and result. *(Attached additional sheets as necessary.)*

Part B. Information about your alien fiancé(e).

1. Name *(Family name in CAPS) (First) (Middle)*

2. Address *(Number and Street)* Apt. #

(Town or City) (State or Country) (Zip/Postal Code)

3a. Place of Birth *(Town or City) (State/Country)*

3b. Country of Citizenship

4. Date of Birth *(mm/dd/yyyy)* **5. Gender**
- [ ] Male [ ] Female

6. Marital Status
- [ ] Married [ ] Single [ ] Widowed [ ] Divorced

7. Other Names Used *(including maiden name)*

8. U.S. Social Security #   9. A# *(if any)*

10. Names of Prior Spouses   Date(s) Marriage(s) Ended

11. Has your fiancé(e) ever been in the U.S.?
- [ ] Yes [ ] No

12. If your fiancé(e) is currently in the U.S., complete the following:

He or she last arrived as a:*(visitor, student, exchange alien, crewman, stowaway, temporary worker, without inspection, etc.)*

Arrival/Departure Record (I-94) Number

				—								

Date of Arrival *(mm/dd/yy)*   **Date authorized stay expired, or will expire as shown on I-94 or I-95**

INITIAL RECEIPT _____ RESUBMITTED _____ RELOCATED: Rec'd _____ Sent _____ COMPLETED: Appv'd. _____ Denied _____ Ret'd. _____

Part B.   Information about your alien fiancé(e).   *(Continued.)*

13. List all children of your alien fiancé(e) *(if any)*

Name *(First/Middle/Last)*	Date of Birth *(mm/dd/yyyy)*	Country of Birth	Present Address

14. Address in the United States where your fiancé(e) intends to live.

(Number and Street)   (Town or City)   (State)

15. Your fiancé(e)'s address abroad.

(Number and Street)   (Town or City)   (State or Province)

(Country)   (Phone Number; Include Country, City and Area Codes)

16. If your fiancé(e)'s native alphabet uses other than Roman letters, write his or her name and address abroad in the native alphabet.

(Name)   (Number and Street)

(Town or City)   (State or Province)   (Country)

17. Is your fiancé(e) related to you?   ☐ Yes   ☐ No

If you are related, state the nature and degree of relationship, e.g., third cousin or maternal uncle, etc.

18. Has your fiancé(e) met and seen you within the two-year period immediately receding the filing of this petition?

☐ Yes   ☐ No

Describe the circumstances under which you met. If you have not personally met each other, explain how the relationship was established. If you met your fiancé(e) or spouse though an international marriage broker, please explain those circumstances in Question 19 below. Explain also in detail any reasons you may have for requesting that the requirement that you and your fiancé(e) must have met should not apply to you.

19. Did you meet your fiancé(e) or spouse through the services of an international marriage broker?

☐ Yes   ☐ No

If you answered yes, please provide the name and any contact information you may have (including internet or street address) of the international marriage broker and where the international marriage broker is located. Attach additional sheets of paper if necessary.

20. Your fiancé(e) will apply for a visa abroad at the American embassy or consulate at:

(City)   (Country)

NOTE: (Designation of a U.S. embassy or consulate outside the country of your fiancé(e)'s last residence does not guarantee acceptance for processing by that foreign post. Acceptance is at the discretion of the designated embassy or consulate.)

Part C. Other information.

1. If you are serving overseas in the Armed Forces of the United States, please answer the following:

I presently reside or am stationed overseas and my current mailing address is:

2. Have you ever been convicted by a court of law (civil or criminal) or court martialed by a military tribunal for any of the following crimes:

- Domestic violence, sexual assault, child abuse and neglect, dating violence, elder abuse or stalking. (Please refer to page 3 of the instructions for the full definition of the term "domestic violence.)

- Homicide, murder, manslaughter, rape, abusive sexual contact, sexual exploitation, incest, torture, trafficking, peonage, holding hostage, involuntary servitude, slave trade, kidnapping, abduction, unlawful criminal restraint, false imprisonment or an attempt to commit any of these crimes, or

- Three or more convictions for crimes relating to a controlled substance or alcohol not arising from a single act.

☐ Yes   ☐ No

Answering this question is required even if your records were sealed or otherwise cleared or if anyone, including a judge, law enforcement officer, or attorney, told you that you no longer have a record. Using a separate sheet(s) of paper, attach information relating to the conviction(s), such as crime involved, date of conviction and sentence.

3. If you have provided information about a conviction for a crime listed above and you were being battered or subjected to extreme cruelty by your spouse, parent, or adult child at the time of your conviction, check all of the following that apply to you:

☐ I was acting in self-defense.

☐ I violated a protection order issued for my own protection.

☐ I committed, was arrested for, was convicted of, or plead guilty to committing a crime that did not result in serious bodily injury, and there was a connection between the crime committed and my having been battered or subjected to extreme cruelty.

Part D. Penalties, certification and petitioner's signature.

PENALTIES: You may by law be imprisoned for not more than five years, or fined $250,000, or both, for entering into a marriage contract for the purpose of evading any provision of the immigration laws, and you may be fined up to $10,000 or imprisoned up to five years, or both, for knowingly and willfully falsifying or concealing a material fact or using any false document in submitting this petition.

YOUR CERTIFICATION: I am legally able to and intend to marry my alien fiancé(e) within 90 days of his or her arrival in the United States. I certify, under penalty of perjury under the laws of the United States of America, that the foregoing is true and correct. Furthermore, I authorize the release of any information from my records that U.S. Citizenship and Immigration Services needs to determine eligibility for the benefit that I am seeking.

Moreover, I understand that this petition, including any criminal conviction information that I am required to provide with this petition, as well as any related criminal background information pertaining to me that U.S. Citizenship and Immigration Services may discover independently in adjudicating this petition will be disclosed to the beneficiary of this petition.

Signature	Date (mm/dd/yyyy)	Daytime Telephone Number (with area code)

E-Mail Address (if any)

Part E. Signature of person preparing form, if other than above. *(Sign below.)*

I declare that I prepared this application at the request of the petitioner and it is based on all information of which I have knowledge.

Signature	Print or Type Your Name	G-28 ID Number	Date (mm/dd/yyyy)

Firm Name and Address	Daytime Telephone Number (with area code)
	E-Mail Address (if any)

Department of Homeland Security
U.S. Citizenship and Immigration Services

OMB #1615-0012; Expires 01/31/11

Instructions for I-130, Petition for Alien Relative

Instructions

Please read these instructions carefully to properly complete this form. If you need more space to complete an answer, use a separate sheet(s) of paper. Write your name and Alien Registration Number (A #), if any, at the top of each sheet of paper and indicate the part and number of the item to which the answer refers. If you do not follow the instructions, U.S. Citizenship and Immigration Services (USCIS) may have to return your petition, which may delay final action. The filing addresses provided on this form reflect the most current information as of the date this form was last printed. If you are filing Form I-130 more than 30 days after the latest edition date shown in the lower right-hand corner, please visit our website online at **www.uscis.gov** before you file, and check the Immigration Forms page to confirm the correct filing address and version currently in use. Check the edition date located in the lower right-hand corner of the form. If the edition date on your Form I-130 matches the edition date listed for Form I-130 on the online Immigration Forms page, your version is current and will be accepted by USCIS. If the edition date on the online version is later, download a copy and use the online version. If you do not have Internet access, call the National Customer Service Center at 1-800-375-5283 to verify the current filing address and edition date. **Improperly filed forms will be rejected, and the fee returned, with instructions to resubmit the entire filing using the current form instructions.**

What Is the Purpose of This Form?

A citizen or lawful permanent resident of the United States may file this form with U.S. Citizenship and Immigration Services (USCIS) to establish the existence of a relationship to certain alien relatives who wish to immigrate to the United States.

Who May File Form I-130?

1. If you are a U.S. citizen you must file a separate Form I-130 for each eligible relative. You may file a Form I-130 for:

   A. Your husband or wife;
   B. Your unmarried child under age 21;
   C. Your unmarried son or daughter age 21 or older;
   D. Your married son or daughter of any age;
   E. Your brother(s) or sister(s) (you must be age 21 or older);
   F. Your mother or father (you must be age 21 or older).

2. If you are a lawful permanent resident of United States, you may file this form for:

   A. Your husband or wife;
   B. Your unmarried child under age 21;
   C. Your unmarried son or daughter age 21 or older.

NOTE:

1. There is no visa category for married children of permanent residents. If an unmarried son or daughter of a permanent resident marries before the permanent resident becomes a U.S. citizen, any petition filed for that son or daughter will be automatically revoked.

2. If your relative qualifies under paragraph **1(C)**, **1(D)**, or **1(E)** above, separate petitions are not required for his or her husband or wife or unmarried children under 21 years of age.

3. If your relative qualifies under paragraph **2(B)** or **2(C)** above, separate petitions are not required for his or her unmarried children under 21 years of age.

4. The persons described in number 2 and 3 of the above **NOTE** will be able to apply for an immigrant visa along with your relative.

Who May Not File This Form I-130?

You may not file for a person in the following categories:

1. An adoptive parent or adopted child, if the adoption took place after the child's 16th birthday, or if the child has not been in the legal custody and living with the parent(s) for at least two years.

2. A natural parent, if the U.S. citizen son or daughter gained permanent residence through adoption.

3. A stepparent or stepchild, if the marriage that created the relationship took place after the child's 18th birthday.

4. A husband or wife, if you and your spouse were not both physically present at the marriage ceremony, and the marriage was not consummated.

5. A husband or wife, if you gained lawful permanent resident status by virtue of a prior marriage to a U. S. citizen or lawful permanent resident, unless:

   A. A period of five years has elapsed since you became a lawful permanent resident; or

   B. You can establish by clear and convincing evidence that the prior marriage through which you gained your immigrant status was not entered into for the purpose of evading any provision of the immigration laws; or

   C. Your prior marriage through which you gained your immigrant status was terminated by the death of your former spouse.

6. A husband or wife, if you married your husband or wife while your husband or wife was the subject of an exclusion, deportation, removal, or rescission proceeding regarding his or her right to be admitted into or to remain in the United States, or while a decision in any of these proceedings was before any court on judicial review, unless:

   You prove by clear and convincing evidence that the marriage is legally valid where it took place, **and** that you and your husband or wife married in good faith and not for the purpose of procuring the admission of your husband or wife as an immigrant, **and** that no fee or any other consideration (other than appropriate attorney fees) was given for your filing of this petition **OR**

   Your husband or wife has lived outside the United States, after the marriage, for a period of at least two years.

f www.facebook.com/become.citizen

7. A husband or wife, if it has been legally determined that such an alien has attempted or conspired to enter into a marriage for the purpose of evading the immigration laws.

8. A grandparent, grandchild, nephew, niece, uncle, aunt, cousin, or in-law.

General Instructions

Step 1. Fill Out Form I-130

1. Type or print legibly in black ink.

2. If extra space is needed to complete any item, attach a continuation sheet, indicate the item number, and date and sign each sheet.

3. Answer all questions fully and accurately. State that an item is not applicable with "N/A." If the answer is none, write "none."

Translations. Any foreign language document must be accompanied by a full English translation that the translator has certified as complete and correct, and by the translator's certification that he or she is competent to translate the foreign language into English.

Copies. If these instructions state that a copy of a document may be filed with this petition, submit a copy. If you choose to send the original, USCIS may keep that original for our records. If USCIS requires the original, it will be requested.

What Documents Do You Need to Show That You Are a U.S. Citizen?

1. If you were born in the United States, a copy of your birth certificate, issued by a civil registrar, vital statistics office, or other civil authority.

2. A copy of your naturalization certificate or certificate of citizenship issued by USCIS or the former INS.

3. A copy of Form FS-240, Report of Birth Abroad of a Citizen of the United States, issued by a U.S. Embassy or consulate.

4. A copy of your unexpired U.S. passport; or

5. An original statement from a U.S. consular officer verifying that you are a U.S. citizen with a valid passport.

6. If you do not have any of the above documents and you were born in the United States, see instructions under **Page 3**, **"What If a Document Is Not Available?"**

What Documents Do You Need to Show That You Are a Permanent Resident?

If you are a permanent resident, you must file your petition with a copy of the front and back of your permanent resident card. If you have not yet received your card, submit copies of your passport biographic page and the page showing admission as a permanent resident, or other evidence of permanent resident status issued by USCIS or the former INS.

What Documents Do You Need to Prove Family Relationship?

You have to prove that there is a family relationship between you and your relative. If you are filing for:

1. **A husband or wife,** submit the following documentation:

   A. A copy of your marriage certificate.

   B. If either you or your spouse were previously married, submit copies of documents showing that all prior marriages were legally terminated.

   C. A passport-style color photo of yourself and a passport-style color photo of your husband or wife, taken within 30 days of the date of this petition. The photos must have a white background and be glossy unretouched and not mounted. The dimensions of the full frontal facial image should be about 1 inch from the chin to top of the hair. Using pencil or felt pen, lightly print the name (and Alien Registration Number, if known) on the back of each photograph.

   D. A completed and signed Form G-325A, Biographic Information, for you and a Form G-325A for your husband or wife. Except for your name and signature you do not have to repeat on Form G-325A the information given on your Form I-130 petition.

NOTE: In addition to the required documentation listed above, you should submit one or more of the following types of documentation that may evidence that bona fides of your marriage:

   E. Documentation showing joint ownership or property; or

   F. A lease showing joint tenancy of a common residence; or

   G. Documentation showing co-mingling of financial resources; or

   H. Birth certificate(s) of child(ren) born to you, the petitioner, and your spouse together; or

   I. Affidavits sworn to or affirmed by third parties having personal knowledge of the bona fides of the marital relationship. (Each affidavit must contain the full name and address, date and place of birth of the person making the affidavit, his or her relationship to the petitioner of beneficiary, if any, and complete information and details explaining how the person acquired his or her knowledge of your marriage); or

   J. Any other relevant documentation to establish that there is an ongoing marital union.

NOTE: If you married your husband or wife while your husband or wife was the subject of an exclusion, deportation, removal, or rescission proceeding (including judicial review of the decision in one of these proceedings), this evidence must be sufficient to establish the bona fides or your marriage by clear and convincing evidence.

2. **A child and you are the mother:** Submit a copy of the child's birth certificate showing your name and the name of your child.

3. **A child and you are the father:** Submit a copy of the child's birth certificate showing both parents' names and your marriage certificate.

4. **A child born out of wedlock and you are the father**: If the child was not legitimated before reaching 18 years old, you must file your petition with copies of evidence that a bona fide parent-child relationship existed between the father and the child before the child reached 21 years. This may include evidence that the father lived with the child, supported him or her, or otherwise showed continuing parental interest in the child's welfare.

5. **A brother or sister:** Submit a copy of your birth certificate and a copy of your brother's or sister's birth certificate showing that you have at least one common parent. If you and your brother or sister have a common father but different mothers, submit copies of the marriage certificates of the father to each mother and copies of documents showing that any prior marriages of either your father or mothers were legally terminated. If you and your brother or sister are related through adoption or through a stepparent, or if you have a common father and either of you were not legitimated before your 18th birthday, see also **8** and **9** below.

6. **A mother:** Submit a copy of your birth certificate showing your name and your mother's name.

7. **A father:** Submit a copy of your birth certificate showing the names of both parents. Also give a copy of your parents' marriage certificate establishing that your father was married to your mother before you were born, and copies of documents showing that any prior marriages of either your father or mother were legally terminated. If you are filing for a stepparent or adoptive parent, or if you are filing for your father and were not legitimated before your 18th birthday, also see **4, 8,** and **9**.

8. **Stepparent/Stepchild:** If your petition is based on a stepparent-stepchild relationship, you must file your petition with a copy of the marriage certificate of the stepparent to the child's natural parent showing that the marriage occurred before the child's 18th birthday, copies of documents showing that any prior marriages were legally terminated and a copy of the stepchild's birth certificate.

9. **Adoptive parent or adopted child:** If you and the person you are filing for are related by adoption, you must submit a copy of the adoption decree(s) showing that the adoption took place before the child became 16 years old.

If you adopted the sibling of a child you already adopted, you must submit a copy of the adoption decree(s) showing that the adoption of the sibling occurred before that child's 18th birthday.

In either case, you must also submit copies of evidence that each child was in the legal custody of and resided with the parent(s) who adopted him or her for at least two years before or after adoption. Legal custody may only be granted by a court or recognized government entity and is usually granted at the time of the adoption is finalized. However, if legal custody is granted by a court or recognized government agency prior to the adoption, that time may count to fulfill the two-year legal custody requirement.

What If Your Name Has Changed?

If either you or the person you are filing for is using a name other than shown on the relevant documents, you must file your petition with copies of the legal documents that effected the change, such as a marriage certificate, adoption decree or court order.

What If a Document Is Not Available?

In such situation, submit a statement from the appropriate civil authority certifying that the document or documents are not available. You must also submit secondary evidence, including:

A. **Church record:** A copy of a document bearing the seal of the church, showing the baptism, dedication or comparable rite occurred within two months after birth, and showing the date and place of the child's birth, date of the religious ceremony, and the names of the child's parents.

B. **School record:** A letter from the authority (preferably the first school attended) showing the date of admission to the school, the child's date of birth or age at that time, place of birth, and names of the parents.

C. **Census record:** State or Federal census record showing the names, place of birth, date of birth, or the age of the person listed.

D. **Affidavits:** Written statements sworn to or affirmed by two persons who were living at the time and who have personal knowledge of the event you are trying to prove. For example, the date and place of birth, marriage or death. The person making the affidavit does not have to be a U.S. citizen. Each affidavit should contain the following information regarding the person making the affidavit: his or her full name, address, date and place of birth, and his or her relationship to you, if any, full information concerning the event, and complete details explaining how the person acquired knowledge of the event.

Where To File?

If you reside in the United States, file the I-130 form at the Lockbox according to following instructions:

If you are the petitioner and you reside in Alaska, Arizona, California, Colorado, Guam, Hawaii, Idaho, Illinois, Indiana, Iowa, Kansas, Michigan, Minnesota, Missouri, Montana, Nebraska, Nevada, North Dakota, Ohio, Oregon, South Dakota, Utah, Washington, Wisconsin, or Wyoming and you are filing only Form I-130, mail the petition to the USCIS Lockbox Facility. The address is as follows:

USCIS
P.O. Box 804625
Chicago, IL 60680-4107

If you are the petitioner and you reside in Alabama, Arkansas, Connecticut, Delaware, Florida, Georgia, Kentucky, Louisiana, Maine, Maryland, Massachusetts, Mississippi, New Hampshire, New Jersey, New Mexico, New York, North Carolina, Oklahoma, Pennsylvania, Puerto Rico, Rhode Island, South Carolina, Tennessee, Texas, Vermont, Virginia, U.S. Virgin Islands, West Virginia, or District of Columbia and you are filing only Form I-130, mail the petition to the USCIS Lockbox Facility. The address is as follows:

> **USCIS**
> **P.O. Box 804616**
> **Chicago, IL 60680-4107**

NOTE: If the Form I-130 petition is being filed concurrently with Form I-485, Application to Register Permanent Residence or Adjust Status, submit both forms concurrently to:

> **U.S. Citizenship and Immigration Services**
> **P.O. Box 805887**
> **Chicago, IL 60680-4107**

For couriers/express deliveries:

> **USCIS**
> **Attn: FBAS**
> **131 South Dearborn - 3rd Floor**
> **Chicago, IL 60603-5517**

Petitioners residing abroad: If you live in Canada, file your petition at the Vermont Service Center. **Exception:** If you are a U.S. citizen residing in Canada, and you are petitioning for your spouse, child, or parent, you may file the petition at the nearest U.S. Embassy or consulate, except for those in Quebec City. If you reside elsewhere outside the United States file, your relative petition at the USCIS office overseas or the U.S. Embassy or consulate having jurisdiction over the area where you live. For further information, contact the nearest U.S. Embassy or consulate.

What Is the Filing Fee?

The filing fee for a Form is **$355.**

Use the following guidelines when you prepare your check or money order for Form I-130:

1. The check or money order must be drawn on a bank or other financial institution located in the United States and must be payable in U.S. currency; and

2. Make the check or money order payable to **U.S. Department of Homeland Security**, unless:

   A. If you live in Guam and are filing your petition there, make it payable to **Treasurer, Guam**.

   B. If you live in the U.S. Virgin Islands and are filing your petition there, make it payable to **Commissioner of Finance of the Virgin Islands**.

   C. If you live outside the United States, Guam, or the U.S. Virgin Islands, contact the nearest U.S. Embassy or consulate for instructions on the method of payment.

NOTE: Please spell out U.S. Department of Homeland Security; do not use the initials "USDHS" or "DHS."

How to Check If the Fees Are Correct

The form fee on this form is current as of the edition date appearing in the lower right corner of this page. However, because USCIS fees change periodically, you can verify if the fees are correct by following one of the steps below:

1. Visit our website at **www.uscis.gov**, select "Immigration Forms," and check the appropriate fee;

2. Review the fee schedule included in your form package, if you called us to request the form, or

3. Telephone our National Customer Service Center at **1-800-375-5283** and ask for the fee information.

When Will a Visa Become Available?

When a petition is approved for the husband, wife, parent, or unmarried minor child of a United States citizen, these persons are classified as immmediate relatives. They do not have to wait for a visa number because immediate relatives are not subject to the immigrant visa limit.

For alien relatives in preference categories, a limited number of immigrant visas are issued each year. The visas are processed in the order in which the petitions are properly filed and accepted by USCIS. To be considered properly filed, a petition must be fully completed and signed, and the fee must be paid.

For a monthly report on the dates when immigrant visas are available, call the **U.S. Department of State** at **(202) 663-1541**, or visit: www.travel.state.gov.

Address Changes

If you change your address and you have an application or petition pending with USCIS, you may change your address online at **www.uscis.gov**, click on "Change your address with USCIS," and follow the prompts. Or you may complete and mail Form AR-11, Alien's Change of Address Card, to:

> **U.S. Citizenship and Immigration Services**
> **Change of Address**
> **P.O. Box 7134**
> **London, KY 40742-7134**

For commercial overnight or fast freight services only, mail to:

> **U.S. Citizenship and Immigration Services**
> **Change of Address**
> **1084-I South Laurel Road**
> **London, KY 40744**

Notice to Persons Filing for Spouses, If Married Less Than Two Years

Pursuant to section 216 of the Immigration and Nationality Act, your alien spouse may be granted conditional permanent resident status in the United States as of the date he or she is admitted or adjusted to conditional status by a USCIS officer. Both you and your conditional resident spouse are required to file Form I-751, Joint Petition to Remove Conditional Basis of Alien's Permanent Resident Status, during the 90-day period immediately before the second anniversary of the date your alien spouse was granted conditional permanent resident status.

Otherwise, the rights, privileges, responsibilites, and duties that apply to all other permanent residents apply equally to a conditional permanent resident. A conditional permanent resident is not limited to the right to apply for naturalization, file petitions on behalf of qualifying relatives, or reside permanently in the United States as an immigrant in accordance with our Nation's immigration laws.

NOTE: Failure to file the Form I-751 joint petition to remove the conditional basis of the alien spouse's permanent resident status will result in the termination of his or her permanent resident status and initiation of removal proceedings.

Processing Information

Acceptance. Any I-130 petition that is not properly signed or accompanied by the correct fee will be rejected with a notice that the petition is deficient. You may correct the deficiency and resubmit the petition. However, a rejected petition does not retain a filing date. A petition is not considered properly filed until accepted by USCIS.

Initial Processing. Once the petition has been accepted, it will be checked for completeness, including submission of the required initial evidence. If you do not completely fill out the form or file it without the required initial evidence, you will not establish a basis for eligibility, and USCIS may deny your petition.

Requests for More Information. We may request more information or evidence, or we may request that you appear at a USCIS office for an interview. We may also request that you submit the originals of any copy. We will return these originals when they are no longer needed.

Decision. The decision on Form I-130 involves a determination of whether you have established eligibility for the requested benefit. You will be notified of the decision in writing.

USCIS Forms and Information

To order USCIS forms, call our toll-free number at **1-800-870-3676**. You can also get USCIS forms and information on immigration laws, regulations, and procedures by telephoning our National Customer Service Center at **1-800-375-5283** or visiting our internet website at **www.uscis. gov**.

As an alternative to waiting in line for assistance at your local USCIS office, you can now schedule an appointment through our internet-based system, **InfoPass**. To access the system, visit our website. Use the **InfoPass** appointment scheduler and follow the screen prompts to set up your appointment. **InfoPass** generates an electronic appointment notice that appears on the screen.

Penalties

If you knowingly and willfully falsify or conceal a material fact or submit a false document with this request, we will deny the benefit you are filing for, and may deny any other immigration benefit.

In addition, you will face severe penalties provided by law, and may be subject to criminal prosecution.

Privacy Act Notice

We ask for the information on this form, and associated evidence, to determine if you have established eligibility for the immigration benefit for which you are filing. Our legal right to ask for this information is in 8 U.S.C. 1255. We may provide this information to other government agencies. Failure to provide this information, and any requested evidence, may delay a final decision or result in denial of your request.

Paperwork Reduction Act

An agency may not conduct or sponsor an information collection, and a person is not required to respond to a collection of information unless it displays a currently valid OMB control number. The public reporting burden for this collection of information is estimated at 90 minutes per response, including the time for reviewing instructions and completing and submitting the form. Send comments regarding this burden estimate or any other aspect of this collection of information, including suggestions for reducing this burden, to: U.S. Citizenship and Immigration Services, Regulatory Management Division, 111 Massachusetts Avenue, N.W., 3rd Floor, Suite 3008, Washington, DC 20529. OMB No. 1615-0012. **Do not mail your application to this address.**

Checklist

- Did you answer each question on the Form I-130 petition?
- Did you sign and date the petition?
- Did you enclose the correct filing fee for each petition?
- Did you submit proof of your U.S. citizenship or lawful permanent residence?
- Did you submit other required supporting evidence?

If you are filing for your husband or wife, did you include:

- His or her photograph?
- Your completed Form G-325A?
- His or her Form G-325A?

Department of Homeland Security
U.S. Citizenship and Immigration Services

OMB #1615-0012; Expires 01/31/11

I-130, Petition for Alien Relative

DO NOT WRITE IN THIS BLOCK - FOR USCIS OFFICE ONLY

A#	Action Stamp	Fee Stamp

Section of Law/Visa Category
- [ ] 201(b) Spouse - IR-1/CR-1
- [ ] 201(b) Child - IR-2/CR-2
- [ ] 201(b) Parent - IR-5
- [ ] 203(a)(1) Unm. S or D - F1-1
- [ ] 203(a)(2)(A)Spouse - F2-1
- [ ] 203(a)(2)(A) Child - F2-2
- [ ] 203(a)(2)(B) Unm. S or D - F2-4
- [ ] 203(a)(3) Married S or D - F3-1
- [ ] 203(a)(4) Brother/Sister - F4-1

Petition was filed on: _____ (priority date)
- [ ] Personal Interview   [ ] Previously Forwarded
- [ ] Pet. [ ] Ben. " A" File Reviewed   [ ] I-485 Filed Simultaneously
- [ ] Field Investigation   [ ] 204(g) Resolved
- [ ] 203(a)(2)(A) Resolved   [ ] 203(g) Resolved

Remarks:

A. Relationship   You are the petitioner.   Your relative is the beneficiary.

1. I am filing this petition for my:
- [ ] Husband/Wife [ ] Parent [ ] Brother/Sister [ ] Child

2. Are you related by adoption?
- [ ] Yes [ ] No

3. Did you gain permanent residence through adoption?
- [ ] Yes [ ] No

B. Information about you

1. Name (Family name in CAPS)   (First)   (Middle)

2. Address (Number and Street)   (Apt. No.)

(Town or City)   (State/Country)   (Zip/Postal Code)

3. Place of Birth (Town or City)   (State/Country)

4. Date of Birth

5. Gender
- [ ] Male
- [ ] Female

6. Marital Status
- [ ] Married [ ] Single
- [ ] Widowed [ ] Divorced

7. Other Names Used (including maiden name)

8. Date and Place of Present Marriage (if married)

9. U.S. Social Security Number (If any)   **10. Alien Registration Number**

11. Name(s) of Prior Husband(s)/Wive(s)   **12. Date(s) Marriage(s) Ended**

13. If you are a U.S. citizen, complete the following:

My citizenship was acquired through (check one):
- [ ] Birth in the U.S.
- [ ] Naturalization. Give certificate number and date and place of issuance.

- [ ] Parents. Have you obtained a certificate of citizenship in your own name?
  - [ ] Yes. Give certificate number, date and place of issuance.   [ ] No

14. If you are a lawful permanent resident alien, complete the following:

Date and place of admission for or adjustment to lawful permanent residence and class of admission.

14b. Did you gain permanent resident status through marriage to a U.S. citizen or lawful permanent resident?
- [ ] Yes [ ] No

C. Information about your relative

1. Name (Family name in CAPS)   (First)   (Middle)

2. Address (Number and Street)   (Apt. No.)

(Town or City)   (State/Country)   (Zip/Postal Code)

3. Place of Birth (Town or City)   (State/Country)

4. Date of Birth

5. Gender
- [ ] Male
- [ ] Female

6. Marital Status
- [ ] Married [ ] Single
- [ ] Widowed [ ] Divorced

7. Other Names Used (including maiden name)

8. Date and Place of Present Marriage (if married)

9. U.S. Social Security Number (If any)   **10. Alien Registration Number**

11. Name(s) of Prior Husband(s)/Wive(s)   **12. Date(s) Marriage(s) Ended**

13. Has your relative ever been in the U.S.? [ ] Yes [ ] No

14. If your relative is currently in the U.S., complete the following:
He or she arrived as a:
(visitor, student, stowaway, without inspection, etc.)

Arrival/Departure Record (I-94)   Date arrived

Date authorized stay expired, or will expire, as shown on Form I-94 or I-95

15. Name and address of present employer (if any)

Date this employment began

16. Has your relative ever been under immigration proceedings?
- [ ] No [ ] Yes Where _____ When _____
- [ ] Removal [ ] Exclusion/Deportation [ ] Rescission [ ] Judicial Proceedings

INITIAL RECEIPT _____ RESUBMITTED _____ RELOCATED: Rec'd _____ Sent _____ COMPLETED: Appv'd _____ Denied _____ Ret'd _____

Form I-130 (Rev. 05/27/08)Y

C. Information about your alien relative (continued)

17. List husband/wife and all children of your relative.

(Name)	(Relationship)	(Date of Birth)	(Country of Birth)

18. Address in the United States where your relative intends to live.

(Street Address)	(Town or City)	(State)

19. Your relative's address abroad. (Include street, city, province and country)   Phone Number (if any)

20. If your relative's native alphabet is other than Roman letters, write his or her name and foreign address in the native alphabet.

(Name)   Address (Include street, city, province and country):

21. If filing for your husband/wife, give last address at which you lived together. (Include street, city, province, if any, and country):

From: To:

22. Complete the information below if your relative is in the United States and will apply for adjustment of status.

Your relative is in the United States and will apply for adjustment of status to that of a lawful permanent resident at the USCIS office in:

If your relative is not eligible for adjustment of status, he or she will apply for a visa abroad at the American consular post in:

(City)	(State)	(City)	(Country)

NOTE: Designation of a U.S. embassy or consulate outside the country of your relative's last residence does not guarantee acceptance for processing by that post. Acceptance is at the discretion of the designated embassy or consulate.

D. Other information

1. If separate petitions are also being submitted for other relatives, give names of each and relationship.

2. Have you ever before filed a petition for this or any other alien? ☐ Yes ☐ No

If "Yes," give name, place and date of filing and result.

WARNING: USCIS investigates claimed relationships and verifies the validity of documents. USCIS seeks criminal prosecutions when family relationships are falsified to obtain visas.

PENALTIES: By law, you may be imprisoned for not more than five years or fined $250,000, or both, for entering into a marriage contract for the purpose of evading any provision of the immigration laws. In addition, you may be fined up to $10,000 and imprisoned for up to five years, or both, for knowingly and willfully falsifying or concealing a material fact or using any false document in submitting this petition.

YOUR CERTIFICATION: I certify, under penalty of perjury under the laws of the United States of America, that the foregoing is true and correct. Furthermore, I authorize the release of any information from my records that U.S. Citizenship and Immigration Services needs to determine eligiblity for the benefit that I am seeking.

E. Signature of petitioner.

Date   Phone Number (   )

F. Signature of person preparing this form, if other than the petitioner.

I declare that I prepared this document at the request of the person above and that it is based on all information of which I have any knowledge.

Print Name _____   Signature _____   Date _____

Address _____   **G-28 ID or VOLAG Number, if any.**

Form I-130 (Rev. 05/27/08)Y Page 2

Department of Homeland Security
U.S. Citizenship and Immigration Services

Instructions for I-134, Affidavit of Support

Instructions

Read these instructions carefully to properly complete this form. If you need more space to complete an answer, use a separate sheet of paper. Write your name and Alien Registration Number (A-Number), if any, at the top of each sheet of paper and indicate the part and number of the item to which the answer refers.

What Is the Purpose of This Form?

Section 212(a)(4) of the Immigration and Nationality Act (the Act) bars the admission into the United States any alien who, in the opinion of the U.S. Department of State officer adjudicating a visa application, a Department of Homeland Security officer, or an immigration judge adjudicating an application for admission, is likely at any time to become a public charge.

For aliens seeking admission or adjustment as permanent residents as immediate relatives, family-based immigrants, and certain employment based immigrants, as specified in sections 212(a)(4)(C) and 213A of the Act and 8 CFR Part 213a, the petitioning relative must file Form I-864.

Form I-134 may be used in any case in which you are inadmissible on public charge grounds, but in which you are not required to have Form I-864 filed on his or her behalf. Section 213 of the Act (*not* section 213A) permits the admission of an alien who is inadmissible on public charge grounds, in the discretion of the Secretary of Homeland Security (or, for immigration judge cases, the discretion of the Attorney General) upon the posting of a bond or other undertaking (method). Form I-134, is the "undertaking" prescribed in section 213 of the Act.

Do not use Form I-134 if the alien whom you are sponsoring is required to have Form I-864 instead.

Execution of Affidavit

If you are sponsoring more than one alien, you must submit a separate Form I-134 for each alien. You must sign Form I-134 in your full name. (Note: Signing Form I-134 is *under penalty of perjury under U.S. law).* For this reason, it is not necessary to sign Form I-134 before a notary, nor to have your signature notarized after you sign it.

General Instructions

Fill Out Form I-134

1. Type or print legibly in black ink.

2. If extra space is needed to complete any item, attach a continuation sheet, indicate the item number, and date and sign each sheet.

Supporting Evidence

As the sponsor, you must show you have sufficient income or financial resources to assure that the alien you are sponsoring will not become a public charge while in the United States.

Evidence should consist of copies of any of the documents listed below that applies to your situation.

Failure to provide evidence of sufficient income or financial resources may result in the denial of the alien's application for a visa or his or her removal from the United States.

You must submit in duplicate evidence of income and resources, as appropriate:

A. Statement from an officer of the bank or other financial institutions where you have deposits, identifying the following details regarding your account:

  1. Date account opened;

  2. Total amount deposited for the past year; and

  3. Present balance.

B. Statement of your employer on business stationery showing:

  1. Date and nature of employment;

  2. Salary paid; and

  3. Whether the position is temporary or permanent.

C. If self-employed:

  1. Copy of last income tax return filed; or

  2. Report of commercial rating concern.

D. List containing serial numbers and denominations of bonds and name of record owner(s).

Sponsor and Alien Liability

Under section 213 of the Act, if the person you are sponsoring becomes a public charge, the agency that provides assistance may be able to sue you to recover the cost of the assistance.

In addition to that provision, your income and assets may be combined with the income and assets of the person you are sponsoring in determining whether that person is eligible for Food Stamps, 7 U.S.C. 2014(i)(1), Supplemental Security Income (SSI), 42 U.S.C. 1382j, and Temporary Assistance for Needy Families (TANF), 42 U.S.C. 608.

Documentation of Income and Resources

An alien applying for SSI must make available to the Social Security Administration documentation concerning his or her income and resources and those of the sponsor, including information that was provided in the corresponding application.

An alien applying for TANF or Food Stamps must make similar information available to the State public assistance agency.

The U.S. Secretary of Health and Human Services and the U.S. Secretary of Agriculture are authorized to obtain copies of any such documentation submitted to USCIS or the U.S. Department of State and to release such documentation to a State public assistance agency.

Joint and Several Liability Issues

Sections 1621(e) of the Social Security Act and subsection 5(i) of the Food Stamp Act also provide that an alien and his or her sponsor shall be "jointly and severally liable" to repay any SSI, TANF, or Food Stamp benefits that are incorrectly paid because of misinformation provided by a sponsor or because of a sponsor's failure to provide information, except where the sponsor was without fault or where good cause existed. "Jointly and severally liable" means the alien and sponsors are each liable up to the full amount of any repayment due.

Incorrect payments that are not repaid will be withheld from any subsequent payments you or your sponsor are otherwise eligible under the Social Security Act or Food Stamp Act.

These provisions do not apply to SSI, TANF, or Food Stamp eligibility of aliens admitted as refugees, granted asylum or Cuban/Haitian entrants as defined in section 501(e) of P.L. 96-422, and to dependent children of the sponsor or sponsor's spouse.

Translations

Any document containing a foreign language submitted to USCIS shall be accompanied by a full English language translation which the translator has certified as complete and accurate, and by the translator's certification that he or she is competent to translate from the foreign language into English.

Copies

Unless specifically required that an original document be filed with an application or petition, an ordinary legible photocopy (standard 8 1/2 x 11 letter size) may be submitted. Original documents submitted when not required will remain a part of the record.

Where To File?

Where you submit the form depends on whether the alien you are sponsoring is in or outside the United States and what type of application is being submitted. See the instructions provided with the corresponding application for detailed information on where to submit this affidavit of support.

What Is the Filing Fee?

There is no filing fee for Form I-134.

Address Changes

If you change your address and you have an application or petition pending with USCIS, you may change your address online at **www.uscis.gov**, click on "Change your address with USCIS," and follow the prompts, or you may complete and mail Form AR-11, Alien's Change of Address Card, to:

U.S. Citizenship and Immigration Services
Change of Address
P.O. Box 7134
London, KY 40742-7134

For commercial overnight or fast freight services only, mail to:

U.S. Citizenship and Immigration Services
Change of Address
1084-I South Laurel Road
London, KY 40744

Processing Information

Any Form I-134 that is not signed will be rejected with a notice that your Form I-134 is deficient. You may correct the deficiency and resubmit Form I-134. Form I-134 is not considered properly filed until accepted by USCIS.

Initial processing

Upon your Form I-134 has been accepted, it will be checked for completeness, including submission of the required initial evidence. Failure to completely fill out the form, or file it without required initial evidence, may result in the denial of your application.

Requests for more information or interview

We may request more information or evidence, or we may request that you appear at a USCIS office for an interview. We may also request that you submit the originals of any copy. We will return these originals when they are no longer required.

USCIS Forms and Information

To order USCIS forms, call our toll-free number at **1-800-870-3676**. You can also get USCIS forms and information on immigration laws, regulations, and procedures by telephoning our National Customer Service Center at **1-800-375-5283** or visiting our Internet website at **www.uscis. gov**.

As an altenative to waiting in line for assistance at your local USCIS office, you can now schedule an appointment through our Internet-based system, **InfoPass**. To access the system, visit our website. Use the InfoPass appointment scheduler and follow the screen prompts to set up your appointment. InfoPass generates an electronic appointment notice that appears on the screen.

Penalties

If you knowingly and willfully make any false statement on Form I-134, or conceal any material fact, or submit a false document with Form I-134, we will deny the application for immigration benefits that the alien for whom you are submitting Form I-134 has filed, and may deny any other immigration benefits.

In addition, you will face severe penalties provided by law and may be subject to criminal prosecution.

Privacy Act Notice

We ask for the information on this form, and associated evidence, to determine if you have established eligibility for the immigration benefit for which you are seeking. Our legal right to ask for this information can be found in the Immigration and Nationality Act, as amended. We may provide this information to other government agencies. Failure to provide this information, and any requested evidence, may delay a final decision or result in denial of your request.

Authority for the collection of the information requested on this form is contained in 8 U.S.C. 1182(a)(4), 1183, 1184(a), and 1258.

The information will be used principally by USCIS, or by any consular officer to whom it may be furnished, to support an alien's application for benefits under the Immigration and Nationality Act and specifically the assertion that you have adequate means of financial support and will not become a public charge. Submission of the information is voluntary.

The information may also be disclosed to other Federal, State, local, and foreign law enforcement and regulatory agencies, including the U.S. Departments of Health and Human Services, Agriculture, State, Defense and any component (if the applicant has served or is serving in the U.S. Armed Forces), Central Intelligence Agency, and individuals and organizations during the course of any investigation to obtain further information required to carry out USCIS functions.

Paperwork Reduction Act

An agency may not conduct or sponsor an information collection, and a person is not required to respond to a collection of information unless it displays a currently valid OMB control number. The public reporting burden for this collection of information is estimated at 90 minutes per response, including the time for reviewing instructions and completing and submitting the form. Send comments regarding this burden estimate or any other aspect of this collection of information, including suggestions for reducing this burden, to: U.S. Citizenship and Immigration Services, Regulatory Management Division, 111 Massachusetts Avenue, N.W., 3rd Floor, Suite 3008, Washington, DC 20529. OMB No. 1615-0014. **Do not mail your application to this address.**

Department of Homeland Security
U.S. Citizenship and Immigration Services

Form I-134, Affidavit of Support

(Answer all items. Type or print in black ink.)

I, _____ residing at _____
       (Name)   (Street and Number)

_____
   (City)   (State)   (Zip Code if in U.S.)   (Country)

certify under penalty of perjury under U.S. law, that:

1. I was born on _____ in _____
                (Date-mm/dd/yyyy)   (City)   (Country)

If you are not a U.S. citizen based on your birth in the United States, or a non-citizen U.S. national based on your birth in American Samoa (including Swains Island), answer the following as appropriate:

    a. If a U.S.citizen through naturalization, give certificate of naturalization number _____

    b. If a U.S. citizen through parent(s) or marriage, give citizenship certificate number _____

    c. If U.S. citizenship was derived by some other method, attach a statement of explanation.

    d. If a lawfully admitted permanent resident of the United States, give A-Number _____

    e. If a lawfully admitted nonimmigrant, give Form I-94, Arrival-Departure Document, number _____

2. I am _____ years of age and have resided in the United States since (date) _____

3. This affidavit is executed on behalf of the following person:

Name (Family Name)	(First Name)	(Middle Name)	Gender	Age
Citizen of (Country)		Marital Status	Relationship to Sponsor	
Presently resides at (Street and Number)	(City)		(State)	(Country)

Name of spouse and children accompanying or following to join person:

Spouse	Gender	Age	Child		Gender	Age
Child	Gender	Age	Child		Gender	Age
Child	Gender	Age	Child		Gender	Age

4. This affidavit is made by me for the purpose of assuring the U.S. Government that the person(s) named in **item (3)** will not become a public charge in the United States.

5. I am willing and able to receive, maintain, and support the person(s) named in **item 3**. I am ready and willing to deposit a bond, if necessary, to guarantee that such person(s) will not become a public charge during his or her stay in the United States, or to guarantee that the above named person(s) will maintain his or her nonimmigrant status, if admitted temporarily, and will depart prior to the expiration of his or her authorized stay in the United States.

6. I understand that:
    a. Form I-134 is an "undertaking" under section 213 of the Immigration and Nationality Act, and I may be sued if the person named in **item 3** becomes a public charge after admission to the United States; and

    b. Form I-134 may be made available to any Federal, State, or local agency that may receive an application from the person named in **item 3** for Food Stamps, Supplemental Security Income, or Temporary Assistance to Needy Families;

    c. If the person named in **item 3** does apply for Food Stamps, Supplemental Security Income, or Temporary Assistance for Needy Families, my own income and assets may be considered in deciding the person's application. How long my income and assets may be attributed to the person named in **item 3** is determined under the statutes and rules governing each specific program.

7. I am employed as or engaged in the business of _____ with _____
                                                                    (Type of Business)   (Name of Concern)

at   _____
                    (Street and Number)   (City)   (State)   (Zip Code)

I derive an annual income of: *(If self-employed, I have attached a copy of my last income tax return or*
report of commercial rating concern which I certify to be true and correct to the best of my knowledge
and belief. See instructions for nature of evidence of net worth to be submitted.) $ _____

I have on deposit in savings banks in the United States: $ _____

I have other personal property, the reasonable value of which is: $ _____

I have stocks and bonds with the following market value, as indicated on the attached list, which I certify
to be true and correct to the best of my knowledge and belief: $ _____

I have life insurance in the sum of: $ _____

With a cash surrender value of: $ _____

I own real estate valued at: $ _____

    With mortgage(s) or other encumbrance(s) thereon amounting to: $ _____

    Which is located at: _____
                                            (Street and Number)   (City)   (State)   (Zip Code)

8. The following persons are dependent upon me for support: *(Check the box* in the appropriate column to indicate whether the person named is
wholly or **partially** dependent upon you for support.)

Name of Person	Wholly Dependent	Partially Dependent	Age	Relationship to Me
	☐	☐		
	☐	☐		
	☐	☐		

9. I have previously submitted affidavit(s) of support for the following person(s). If none, state "None".

Name of Person	Date submitted

10. I have submitted a visa petition(s) to U.S. Citizenship and Immigration Services on behalf of the following person(s). If none, state "None".

Name of Person	Relationship	Date submitted

11. I ☐ intend   ☐ do not intend to make specific contributions to the support of the person(s) named in **item 3**.

    (If you check "intend," indicate the exact nature and duration of the contributions. For example, if you intend to furnish room and board, state
    for how long and, if money, state the amount in U.S. dollars and whether it is to be given in a lump sum, weekly or monthly, and for how long.

    _____

    _____

    _____

Oath or Affirmation of Sponsor

I acknowledge that I have read "Sponsor and Alien Liability" on Page 2 of the instructions for this form, and am aware of my
responsibilities as a sponsor under the Social Security Act, as amended, and the Food Stamp Act, as amended.
I certify under penalty of perjury under United States law that I know the contents of this affidavit signed by me and that the statements are
true and correct.

Signature of sponsor _____   Date _____

Department of Homeland Security
U.S. Citizenship and Immigration Services

Instructions for I-140, Immigrant Petition for Alien Worker

Instructions

Read these instructions carefully to properly complete this form. If you need more space to complete an answer, use a separate sheet of paper. Write your name and Alien Registration Number (A-Number), if any, at the top of each sheet of paper and indicate the part and number of the item to which the answer refers.

What Is the Purpose of This Form?

This form is used to petition U.S. Citizenship and Immigration Services (USCIS) for an immigrant visa based on employment.

Who May File Form I-140?

A U.S. employer may file this petition for:

1. An outstanding professor or researcher with at least three years of experience in teaching or research in the academic area, who is recognized internationally as outstanding:

   A. In a tenured or tenure-track position at a university or institution of higher education to teach in the academic area; or

   B. In a comparable position at a university or institution of higher education to conduct research in the area; or

   C. In a comparable position to conduct research for a private employer that employs at least three persons in full-time research activities and which achieved documented accomplishments in an academic field.

2. An alien who, in the three years preceding the filing of this petition, has been employed for at least one year by a firm or corporation or other legal entity and who seeks to enter the United States to continue to render services to the same employer, or to a subsidiary or affiliate, in a capacity that is managerial or executive.

3. A member of the professions holding an advanced degree or an alien with exceptional ability in the sciences, arts, or business who will substantially benefit the national economy, cultural or educational interests, or welfare of the United States.

4. A skilled worker (requiring at least two years of specialized training or experience in the skill) to perform labor for which qualified workers are not available in the United States.

5. A member of the professions with a baccalaureate degree.

6. An unskilled worker (requiring less than two years of specialized training or experience) to perform labor for which qualified workers are not available in the United States.

In addition, a person may file this petition on his or her own behalf if he or she:

1. Has extraordinary ability in the sciences, arts, education, business, or athletics demonstrated by sustained national or international acclaim and whose achievements have been recognized in the field; or

2. Is a member of the profession holding an advanced degree or is claiming exceptional ability in the sciences, arts, or business, and is seeking an exemption of the requirement of a job offer in the national interest (NIW).

General Instructions

Step 1. Fill Out Form I-140

1. Type or print legibly in black ink.

2. If extra space is needed to complete any item, attach a continuation sheet, indicate the item number, and date and sign each sheet.

3. Answer all questions fully and accurately. State that an item is not applicable with "N/A." If the answer is none, write "None."

Step 2. General Requirements

Initial Evidence

1. **If you are filing for an alien of extraordinary ability in the sciences, arts, education, business, or athletics:**

   You must file your petition with evidence that the alien has sustained national or international acclaim and that the achievements have been recognized in the field of expertise.

   A. Evidence of a one-time achievement (i.e., a major internationally recognized award); or

B. At least three of the following:

1. Receipt of lesser nationally or internationally recognized prizes or awards for excellence in the field of endeavor;

2. Membership in associations in the field, which require outstanding achievements as judged by recognized national or international experts;

3. Published material about the alien in professional or major trade publications or other major media;

4. Participation on a panel or individually as a judge of the work of others in the field or an allied field;

5. Original scientific, scholarly, artistic, athletic, or business-related contributions of major significance in the field;

6. Authorship of scholarly articles in the field in professional or major trade publications or other major media;

7. Display of the alien's work at artistic exhibitions or showcases;

8. Evidence that the alien has performed in a leading or critical role for organizations or establishments that have distinguished reputations;

9. Evidence that the alien has commanded a high salary or other high remuneration for services;

10. Evidence of commercial successes in the performing arts, as shown by box office receipts or record, casette, compact disk, or video sales.

C. If the above standards do not readily apply to the alien's occupation, you may submit comparable evidence to establish the alien's eligibility; and

D. Evidence that the alien is coming to the United States to continue work in the area of expertise. Such evidence may include letter(s) from prospective employer(s), evidence of prearranged commitments such as contracts, or a statement from the alien detailing plans on how he or she intends to continue work in the United States.

2. **A U.S. employer filing for an outstanding professor or researcher must file the petition with:**

A. Evidence that the professor or researcher is recognized internationally as outstanding in the academic field

specified in the petition. Such evidence shall consist of at least two of the following:

1. Receipt of major prizes or awards for outstanding achievement in the academic field;

2. Membership in associations in the academic field that require outstanding achievements of their members;

3. Published material in professional publications written by others about the alien's work in the academic field;

4. Participation on a panel, or individually, as the judge of the work of others in the same or an allied academic field;

5. Original scientific or scholarly research contributions to the academic field; or

6. Authorship of scholarly books or articles in scholarly journals with international circulation in the academic field.

B. Evidence the beneficiary has at least three years of experience in teaching and/or research in the academic field; and

C. If you are a university or other institution of higher education, a letter indicating that you intend to employ the beneficiary in a tenured or tenure-track position as a teacher or in a permanent position as a researcher in the academic field; or

D. If you are a private employer, a letter indicating that you intend to employ the beneficiary in a permanent research position in the academic field, and evidence that you employ at least three full-time researchers and have achieved documented accomplishments in the field.

3. **A U.S. employer filing for a multinational executive or manager must file the petition with a statement which demonstrates that:**

A. If the worker is now employed outside the United States, he or she has been employed outside the United States for at least one year in the past three years in an executive or managerial capacity by the petitioner or by its parent, branch, subsidiary, or affiliate; or, if the worker is already employed in the United States, he or she was employed outside the United States for at least one year in the three years preceding admission as a nonimmigrant in an executive or managerial capacity by the petitioner or by its parent, branch, subsidiary, or affiliate;

B. The prospective employer in the United States is the same employer or a subsidiary or affiliate of the firm or corporation or other legal entity by which the alien was employed abroad;

C. The prospective U.S. employer has been doing business for at least one year; and

D. The alien is to be employed in the United States in a managerial or executive capacity. A description of the duties to be performed should be included.

4. **A U.S. employer filing for a member of the professions with an advanced degree or a person with exceptional ability in the sciences, arts, or business must file the petition with:**

A. A labor certification (see "**General Evidence**"), or a request for a waiver of a job offer because the employment is deemed to be in the national interest, with documentation provided to show that the beneficiary's presence in the United States would be in the national interest; and either:

1. An official academic record showing that the alien has a U.S. advanced degree or an equivalent foreign degree, or an official academic record showing that the alien has a U.S. baccalaureate degree or an equivalent foreign degree and letters from current or former employers showing that the alien has at least five years of progressive post baccalaureate experience in the specialty; or

2. At least three of the following:

a. An official academic record showing that the alien has a degree, diploma, certificate, or similar award from an institution of learning relating to the area of exceptional ability;

b. Letters from current or former employers showing that the alien has at least ten years of full-time experience in the occupation for which he or she is being sought;

c. A license to practice the profession or certification for a particular profession or occupation;

d. Evidence that the alien has commanded a salary, or other remuneration for services that demonstrates exceptional ability;

e. Evidence of membership in professional associations; or

f. Evidence of recognition for achievements and significant contributions to the industry or field by peers, governmental entities, or professional or business organizations.

3. If the above standards do not readily apply to the alien's occupation, you may submit comparable evidence to establish the alien's eligibility.

5. **A U.S. employer filing for a skilled worker must file the petition with:**

A. A labor certification (see "**General Evidence**"), and

B. Evidence that the alien meets the educational, training, or experience and any other requirements of the labor certification (the minimum requirement is two years of training or experience).

6. **A U.S. employer filing for a professional must file the petition with:**

A. A labor certification (see "**General Evidence**");

B. Evidence that the alien holds a U.S. baccalaureate degree or equivalent foreign degree; and

C. Evidence that a baccalaureate degree is required for entry into the occupation.

7. **A U.S. employer filing for an unskilled worker must file the petition with:**

A. A labor certification (see "**General Evidence**"); and

B. Evidence that the beneficiary meets any education, training, or experience requirements required in the labor certification.

General Evidence

1. Labor certification

Petitions for certain classifications must be filed with an **original** individual labor certification from the U.S. Department of Labor (DOL) or with documentation to establish that the alien qualifies for one of the shortage occupations designated in Group I or II of the DOL's Schedule A. If an individual labor certification is required, then the **original** individual labor certification must be submitted with the petition, unless the original labor certification has already been provided to USCIS in support of a different petition.

A labor certification establishes that there are insufficient U.S. workers who are able, willing, qualified, and available to fill the position being offered to the alien at the time and place where the alien is to be employed, and that the employment of the alien, if qualified, will not adversely affect the wages and working conditions of similarly employed U.S. workers. Application for labor certification is currently made on Form ETA-9089. Labor certification applications filed before March 28, 2005, were filed on Form ETA-750. If the alien is to be employed in a Schedule A, Group I or II shortage occupation, then you may file a fully completed, uncertified Form ETA-9089 in duplicate with your petition for determination by USCIS that the alien belongs to the shortage occupation.

See 20 CFR 656 or the DOL Web site, http://www.foreignlaborcert.doleta.gov, for further information about obtaining an individual labor certification or about Schedule A, Group I or II shortage occupations.

NOTE: Individual labor certifications issued by the DOL must be submitted in the **original**, unless the original labor certification has already been provided to USCIS in support of a different petition.

2. **Ability to pay wage**

Petitions which require job offers must be accompanied by evidence that the prospective U.S. employer has the ability to pay the proffered wage. Such evidence shall be in the form of copies of annual reports, Federal tax returns, or audited financial statements.

In a case where the prospective U.S. employer employs 100 or more workers, a statement from a financial officer of the organization that establishes ability to pay the wage may be submitted. In appropriate cases, additional evidence, such as profit/loss statements, bank account records, or personnel records, may be submitted.

Translations
Any document containing a foreign language submitted to USCIS must be accompanied by a full English language translation that the translator has certified as complete and accurate, and by the translator's certification that he or she is competent to translate from the foreign language into English.

Copies
Unless specifically required that an original document be filed with an application or petition, an ordinary legible photocopy may be submitted. Original documents submitted when not required will remain a part of the record, even if the submission was not required.

NOTE: Individual labor certifications issued by the DOL must be submitted in the **original**, unless the original labor certification has already been provided to USCIS in support of a different petition.

Where To File?

Updated Filing Address Information

The filing addresses provided on this form reflect the most current information as of the date this form was last printed. If you are filing Form I-140 more than 30 days after the latest edition date shown in the lower right-hand corner, visit us online at **www.uscis.gov** before you file, and check the "Immigration Forms" page to confirm the correct filing address and version currently in use. Check the edition date located in the lower right-hand corner of the form. If the edition date on your Form I-140 matches the edition date listed for Form I-140 on the online "Immigration Forms" page, your version is current and will be accepted by USCIS. If the edition date on the online version is later, download a copy and use the online version. If you do not have Internet access, call Customer Service at 1-800-375-5283 to verify the current filing address and edition date. **Improperly filed forms will be rejected and the fee returned with instructions to resubmit the entire filing using the current form instructions.**

E-Filing Form I-140

Certain Form I-140 filings may be electronically filed (e-filed) with USCIS. View our website at **www.uscis.gov** for a list of who is eligible to e-file this form and instructions.

Premium Processing

If you are requesting Premium Processing Services for Form I-140, you **must** also file Form I-907, Request for Premium Processing Service. Send Forms I-140 and I-907 together to the address listed in the **Form I-907 filing instructions.**
NOTE: Before you file the I-907/I-140 package, check the Premium Processing Service page, a link to which can be found on the "Services & Benefits" page on the USCIS Web site at **www.uscis.gov** to determine whether you may request Premium Processing for the requested classification.

Premium Processing Service for a Pending Form I-140

If you have already filed Form I-140 and you wish to request Premium Processing Service, file Form I-907 with the Service Center where your Form I-140 is pending. See Form I-907 for further instructions. Include a copy of Form I-797, Notice of Action, or a copy of the transfer notice, if applicable, showing the location of the relating petition. To ensure that Form I-907 is matched up with the pending Form I-140, you **must** fully answer questions 1 through 5 in Part 2 of Form I-907. If this information is not provided, Form I-907 will be rejected.

Processing Form I-140

All Form I-140s are filed either at the Nebraska Service Center or the Texas Service Center, depending on the location of the beneficiary's permanent employment. Before you file, note the different filing addresses. Failure to follow these instructions may result in your application or petition being rejected, delayed, or denied.

Nebraska Service Center Filings

File Form I-140 with the Nebraska Service Center if the beneficiary will be employed permanently in:

Alaska, Arizona, California, Colorado, Guam, Hawaii, Idaho, Illinois, Indiana, Iowa, Kansas, Michigan, Minnesota, Missouri, Montana, Nebraska, Nevada, North Dakota, Ohio, Oregon, South Dakota, Utah, Washington, Wisconsin, or Wyoming.

For Form I-140 filed alone, mail the form to:

USCIS Nebraska Service Center
P.O. Box 87140
Lincoln, NE 68501-7140

For Form I-140 filed concurrently with Form I-485, Application to Register Permanent Residence or Adjust Status, mail your forms package to:

USCIS Nebraska Service Center
P.O. Box 87485
Lincoln, NE 68501-7485

Texas Service Center Filings

File Form I-140 with the Texas Service Center if the beneficiary will be employed permanently in:

Alabama, Arkansas, Connecticut, Delaware, the District of Columbia, Florida, Georgia, Kentucky, Louisiana, Maine, Maryland, Massachusetts, Mississippi, New Hampshire,

New Jersey, New Mexico, New York, North Carolina, South Carolina, Oklahoma, Pennsylvania, Puerto Rico, Rhode Island, Tennessee, Texas, Vermont, Virginia, U.S. Virgin Islands, or West Virginia.

For Form I-140 filed alone, or concurrently with Form I-485, Application to Register Permanent Residence or Adjust Status, mail your forms package to:

USCIS Texas Service Center
P.O. Box 852135
Mesquite, TX 75185

Note on E-Filing

If you are e filing this application, it will automatically be routed to the appropriate Service Center, and you will receive a receipt indicating the location to which it was routed. This location may not necessarily be the same center shown in the filing addresses listed above. For e-filed applications, it is very important to review your filing receipt and make specific note of the receiving location. All further communication, including submission of supporting documents, must be directed to the receiving location indicated on your e-filing receipt.

What Is the Filing Fee?

The filing fee for Form I-140 is **$475.**

Use the following guidelines when you prepare your check or money order for the Form I-140 fee:

1. The check or money order must be drawn on a bank or other financial institution located in the United States and must be payable in U.S. currency; and

2. Make the check or money order payable to **U.S. Department of Homeland Security**, unless:

   A. If you live in Guam, make it payable to **Treasurer, Guam**.

B. If you live in the U.S. Virgin Islands, make it payable to **Commissioner of Finance of the Virgin Islands**.

NOTE: Spell out U.S. Department of Homeland Security; do not use the initials "USDHS" or "DHS."

Notice to Those Making Payment by Check

If you send us a check, it will be converted into an electronic funds transfer (EFT). This means we will copy your check and use the account information on it to electronically debit your account for the amount of the check. The debit from your account will usually take 24 hours and will be shown on your regular account statement.

You will not receive your original check back. We will destroy your original check, but we will keep a copy of it. If the EFT cannot be processed for technical reasons, you authorize us to process the copy in place of your original check. If the EFT cannot be completed because of insufficient funds, we may try to make the transfer up to two times.

How to Check If the Fees Are Correct

The form fee on this form is current as of the edition date appearing in the lower right corner of this page. However, because USCIS fees change periodically, you can verify if the fees are correct by following one of the steps below:

1. Visit our Web site at **www.uscis.gov**, select "Immigration Forms," and check the appropriate fee;

2. Review the Fee Schedule included in your form package, if you called us to request the form; or

3. Telephone our National Customer Service Center at **1-800-375-5283** and ask for the fee information.

Address Changes

If you change your address and you have an application or petition pending with USCIS, you may change your address online at **www.uscis.gov.** Click on "Change your address with USCIS" and follow the prompts, or you may complete and mail Form AR-11, Alien's Change of Address Card, to:

U.S. Citizenship and Immigration Services
Change of Address
P.O. Box 7134
London, KY 40742-7134

For commercial overnight or fast freight services only, mail to:

U.S. Citizenship and Immigration Services
Change of Address
1084-I South Laurel Road
London, KY 40744

Processing Information

Any Form I-140 that is not signed or accompanied by the correct fee will be rejected with a notice that Form I-140 is deficient. You may correct the deficiency and resubmit the Form I-140. An application or petition is not considered properly filed until accepted by USCIS.

Initial Processing

Once Form I-140 has been accepted, it will be checked for completeness, including submission of the required initial evidence. If you do not completely fill out the form, or file it without required initial evidence, you will not establish a basis for eligibility, and we may deny your Form I-140.

Requests for More Information or Interview

We may request more information or evidence, or we may request that you appear at a USCIS office for an interview. We may also request that you submit the originals of any copy. We will return these originals when they are no longer required.

Decision

The decision on a Form I-140 involves a determination of whether you have established eligibility for the requested benefit. You will be notified of the decision in writing.

Meaning of Petition Approval

Approval of a petition means you have established that the person you are filling for is eligible for the requested classification.

This is the first step towards permanent residence. However, this does not in itself grant permanent residence or employment authorization. You will be given information about the requirements for the person to receive an immigrant visa or to adjust status after your petition is approved.

Instructions for Industry and Occupation Codes

NAICS Code

The North American Industry Classification System (NAICS) code can be obtained from the U.S. Department of Commerce, U.S. Census Bureau at (www.census.gov/epcd/www/naics.html). Enter the code from left to right, one digit in each of the six boxes. If you use a code that is less than six digits, enter the code left to right and then add zeros in the remaining unoccupied boxes.

The code sequence 33466 would be entered as:

3	3	4	6	6	0

The code sequence 5133 would be entered as:

5	1	3	3	0	0

SOC Code

The Standard Occupational Classification (SOC) System codes can be obtained from the U.S. Department of Labor, Bureau of Labor Statistics (http://stats.bls.gov/soc/socguide.htm). Enter the code from left to right, one digit in each of the six boxes. If you use a code which is less than six digits, enter the code left to right and then add zeros in the remaining unoccupied boxes.

The code sequence 19-1021 would be entered as:

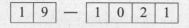

1	9	—	1	0	2	1

The code sequence 15-100 would be entered as:

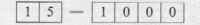

1	5	—	1	0	0	0

USCIS Forms and Information

To order USCIS forms, call our toll-free number at **1-800-870-3676**. You can also get USCIS forms and information on immigration laws, regulations, and procedures by telephoning our National Customer Service Center at **1-800-375-5283** or visiting our Internet Web site at **www.uscis.gov**.

As an alternative to waiting in line for assistance at your local USCIS office, you can now schedule an appointment through our Internet-based system, **InfoPass**. To access the system, visit our Web site. Use the **InfoPass** appointment scheduler and follow the screen prompts to set up your appointment. **InfoPass** generates an electronic appointment notice that appears on the screen.

Penalties

If you knowingly and willfully falsify or conceal a material fact or submit a false document with your Form I-140, we will deny your Form I-140 and may deny any other immigration benefit.

In addition, you will face severe penalties provided by law and may be subject to criminal prosecution.

Privacy Act Notice

We ask for the information on this form, and associated evidence, to determine if you have established eligibility for the immigration benefit for which you are filing. Our legal right to ask for this information can be found in the Immigration and Nationality Act, as amended. We may provide this information to other Government agencies. Failure to provide this information, and any requested evidence, may delay a final decision or result in denial of your Form I-140.

USCIS Compliance Review and Monitoring

By signing this form, you have stated under penalty of perjury (28 U.S.C.1746) that all information and documentation submitted with this form is true and correct. You also have authorized the release of any information from your records that USCIS may need to determine eligibility for the benefit you are seeking and consented to USCIS verification of such information.

The Department of Homeland Security has the right to verify any information you submit to establish eligibility for the immigration benefit you are seeking at any time. Our legal right to verify this information is in 8 U.S.C. 1103, 1155, 1184, and 8 CFR parts 103, 204, 205, and 214. To ensure compliance with applicable laws and authorities, USCIS may verify information before or after your case has been decided. Agency verification methods may include, but are not limited to: review of public records and information; contact via written correspondence, the Internet, facsimile or other electronic transmission, or telephone; unannounced physical site inspections of residences and places of employment; and interviews. Information obtained through verification will be used to assess your compliance with the laws and to determine your eligibility for the benefit sought.

Subject to the restrictions under 8 CFR part 103.2(b)(16), you will be provided an opportunity to address any adverse or derogatory information, that may result from a USCIS compliance review, verification, or site visit after a formal decision is made on your case or after the agency has initiated an adverse action which may result in revocation or termination of an approval.

Paperwork Reduction Act

An agency may not conduct or sponsor an information collection and a person is not required to respond to a collection of information unless it displays a currently valid OMB control number. The public reporting burden for this collection of information is estimated at 60 minutes per response, including the time for reviewing instructions and completing and submitting the form. Send comments regarding this burden estimate or any other aspect of this collection of information, including suggestions for reducing this burden, to: U.S. Citizenship and Immigration Services, Regulatory Management Division, 111 Massachusetts Avenue, N.W., 3rd Floor, Suite 3008, Washington, DC 20529-2210. OMB No. 1615-0015. **Do not mail your application to this address.**

Department of Homeland Security
U.S. Citizenship and Immigration Services

Form I-140, Immigrant Petition for Alien Worker

START HERE - Type or Print in Black Ink

Part 1. Information About the Person or Organization Filing this Petition. If an individual is filing, use the top name line. Organizations should use the *second* line.

Family Name (Last Name)　　Given Name (First Name)　　Full Middle Name

Company or Organization Name

Address: (Street Number and Name)　　Suite No.

Attn:

City　　State/Province

Country　　Zip/Postal Code

IRS Tax No.　　U.S. Social Security No. *(if any)*　　E-Mail Address *(if any)*

Part 2. Petition Type

This petition is being filed for: *(Check one)*

a. ☐ An alien of extraordinary ability
b. ☐ An outstanding professor or researcher
c. ☐ A multinational executive or manager
d. ☐ A member of the professions holding an advanced degree or an alien of exceptional ability (who is NOT seeking a National Interest Waiver)
e. ☐ A professional (at a minimum, possessing a bachelor's degree or a foreign degree equivalent to a U.S. bachelor's degree) or a skilled worker (requiring at least two years of specialized training or experience)
f. ☐ (Reserved)
g. ☐ Any other worker (requiring less than two years of training or experience)
h. ☐ Soviet Scientist
i. ☐ An alien applying for a National Interest Waiver (who IS a member of the professions holding an advanced degree or an alien of exceptional ability)

Part 3. Information About the Person For Whom You Are Filing

Family Name (Last Name)　　Given Name (First Name)　　Full Middle Name

Address: (Street Number and Name)　　Apt. No.

C/O: (In Care Of)

City　　State/Province

Country　　Zip/Postal Code　　E-Mail Address *(if any)*

Daytime Phone # *(with area/country codes)*　　Date of Birth *(mm/dd/yyyy)*

City/Town/Village of Birth　　State/Province of Birth　　Country of Birth

Country of Nationality/Citizenship　　A-Number *(if any)*　　U.S. Social Security # *(if any)*

If in the U.S.
Date of Arrival *(mm/dd/yyyy)*　　I-94 # *(Arrival/Departure Document)*
Current Nonimmigrant Status　　Date Status Expires *(mm/dd/yyyy)*

For USCIS Use Only

Returned	Receipt
Date	
Date	
Resubmitted	
Date	
Date	
Reloc Sent	
Date	
Date	
Reloc Rec'd	
Date	
Date	

Classification:
☐ 203(b)(1)(A) Alien of Extraordinary Ability
☐ 203(b)(1)(B) Outstanding Professor or Researcher
☐ 203(b)(1)(C) Multinational Executive or Manager
☐ 203(b)(2) Member of Professions w/Adv. Degree or Exceptional Ability
☐ 203(b)(3)(A)(i) Skilled Worker
☐ 203(b)(3)(A)(ii) Professional
☐ 203(b)(3)(A)(iii) Other Worker

Certification:
☐ National Interest Waiver (NIW)
☐ Schedule A, Group I
☐ Schedule A, Group II

Priority Date	Consulate

Concurrent Filing:
☐ I-485 filed concurrently

Remarks

Action Block

To Be Completed by *Attorney or Representative*, if any.
☐ Fill in box if G-28 is attached to represent the applicant.
ATTY State License #

Part 4. Processing Information

1. Complete the following for the person named in **Part 3**: *(Check one)*

☐ Alien will apply for a visa abroad at a U.S. Embassy or consulate at:

City   Foreign Country

[   ]   [   ]

☐ Alien is in the United States and will apply for adjustment of status to that of lawful permanent resident.

Alien's country of current residence or, if now in the U.S., last permanent residence abroad.

[   ]

2. If you provided a United States address in **Part 3**, print the person's foreign address:

[   ]

3. If the person's native alphabet is other than Roman letters, write the person's foreign name and address in the native alphabet:

[   ]

4. Are any other petition(s) or application(s) being filed with this Form I-140?

☐ No   ☐ Yes (check all that apply)   ☐ Form I-485   ☐ Form I-765
                                                     ☐ Form I-131   ☐ Other - Attach an explanation

5. Is the person for whom you are filing in removal proceedings?   ☐ No   ☐ Yes-Attach an explanation

6. Has any immigrant visa petition ever been filed by or on behalf of this person?   ☐ No   ☐ Yes-Attach an explanation

If you answered "Yes" to any of these questions, provide the case number, office location, date of decision, and disposition of the decision on a separate sheet of paper.

Part 5. Additional Information About the Petitioner

1. Type of petitioner *(Check one)*

☐ Employer   ☐ Self   ☐ Other (Explain, e.g., Permanent Resident, U.S. citizen or any other person filing on behalf of the alien)

[   ]

2. If a company, give the following:

Type of Business   Date Established *(mm/dd/yyyy)*   Current Number of Employees

[   ]   [   ]   [   ]

Gross Annual Income   Net Annual Income   NAICS Code

[   ]   [   ]   [   ][   ][   ][   ][   ][   ]

DOL/ETA Case Number   [   ]

3. If an individual, give the following:

Occupation   Annual Income

[   ]   [   ]

Part 6. Basic Information About the Proposed Employment

1. Job Title   2. SOC Code

[   ]   [   ][   ] — [   ][   ][   ][   ]

3. Nontechnical Description of Job

[   ]

4. Address where the person will work if different from address in **Part 1**.

[   ]

5. Is this a full-time position?   6. If the answer to **Number 5** is "No," how many hours per week for the position?

☐ Yes ☐ No   [   ]

7. Is this a permanent position?   8. Is this a new position?   9. Wages per week

☐ Yes ☐ No   ☐ Yes ☐ No $ [   ]

Part 7. Information on Spouse and All Children of the Person for Whom You Are Filing

List husband/wife and all children related to the individual for whom the petition is being filed. Provide an attachment of additional family members, if needed.

Name (First/Middle/Last)	Relationship	Date of Birth (mm/dd/yyyy)	Country of Birth

Part 8.   Signature.   *Read the information on penalties in the instructions before completing this section.   If someone helped you prepare this petition, he or she must complete Part 9.*

I certify, under penalty of perjury under the laws of the United States of America, that this petition and the evidence submitted with it are all true and correct. I authorize U.S. Citizenship and Immigration Services to release to other government agencies any information from my USCIS records, if USCIS determines that such action is necessary to determine eligibility for the benefit sought.

Petitioner's Signature   **Daytime Phone Number** *(Area/Country Codes)*   **E-Mail Address**

Print Name   **Date** *(mm/dd/yyyy)*

NOTE: *If you do not fully complete this form or fail to submit the required documents listed in the instructions, a final decision on your petition may be delayed or the petition may be denied.*

Part 9.   Signature of Person Preparing Form, If Other Than Above   *(Sign below)*

I declare that I prepared this petition at the request of the above person and it is based on all information of which I have knowledge.

Attorney or Representative: In the event of a Request for Evidence (RFE), may USCIS contact you by Fax or E-mail?   ☐ Yes   ☐ No

Signature   **Print Name**   **Date** *(mm/dd/yyyy)*

Firm Name and Address

Daytime Phone Number *(Area/Country Codes)*   **Fax Number** *(Area/Country Codes)*   **E-Mail Address**

www.facebook.com/become.citizen

OMB No. 1615-0023; Expires 11/30/2011

Department of Homeland Security
U.S. Citizenship and Immigration Services

I-485, Application to Register
Permanent Residence or Adjust Status

START HERE - Type or print in black ink.

Part 1.   Information About You

Family Name	Given Name	Middle Name

Address- C/O

Street Number and Name		Apt. #

City

State	Zip Code

Date of Birth *(mm/dd/yyyy)*	Country of Birth:
	Country of Citizenship/Nationality:

U.S. Social Security #	A # *(if any)*

Date of Last Arrival *(mm/dd/yyyy)*	I-94 #

Current USCIS Status	Expires on *(mm/dd/yyyy)*

For USCIS Use Only

Returned	Receipt
Resubmitted	
Reloc Sent	
Reloc Rec'd	
Applicant Interviewed	

Section of Law
- ☐ Sec. 209(b), INA
- ☐ Sec. 13, Act of 9/11/57
- ☐ Sec. 245, INA
- ☐ Sec. 249, INA
- ☐ Sec. 1 Act of 11/2/66
- ☐ Sec. 2 Act of 11/2/66
- ☐ Other

Country Chargeable

Eligibility Under Sec. 245
- ☐ Approved Visa Petition
- ☐ Dependent of Principal Alien
- ☐ Special Immigrant
- ☐ Other

Preference

Action Block

Part 2.   Application Type *(Check one)*

I am applying for an adjustment to permanent resident status because:

a. ☐ An immigrant petition giving me an immediately available immigrant visa number that has been approved. (Attach a copy of the approval notice, or a relative, special immigrant juvenile, or special immigrant military visa petition filed with this application that will give you an immediately available visa number, if approved.)

b. ☐ My spouse or parent applied for adjustment of status or was granted lawful permanent residence in an immigrant visa category that allows derivative status for spouses and children.

c. ☐ I entered as a K-1 fiancé(e) of a U.S. citizen whom I married within 90 days of entry, or I am the K-2 child of such a fiancé(e). (Attach a copy of the fiancé(e) petition approval notice and the marriage certificate).

d. ☐ I was granted asylum or derivative asylum status as the spouse or child of a person granted asylum and am eligible for adjustment.

e. ☐ I am a native or citizen of Cuba admitted or paroled into the United States after January 1, 1959, and thereafter have been physically present in the United States for at least one year.

f. ☐ I am the husband, wife, or minor unmarried child of a Cuban described above in **(e)**, and I am residing with that person, and was admitted or paroled into the United States after January 1, 1959, and thereafter have been physically present in the United States for at least one year.

g. ☐ I have continuously resided in the United States since before January 1, 1972.

h. ☐ Other basis of eligibility. Explain (for example, I was admitted as a refugee, my status has not been terminated, and I have been physically present in the United States for one year after admission). If additional space is needed, use a separate piece of paper.

I am already a permanent resident and am applying to have the date I was granted permanent residence adjusted to the date I originally arrived in the United States as a nonimmigrant or parolee, or as of May 2, 1964, whichever date is later, and: *(Check one)*

i. ☐ I am a native or citizen of Cuba and meet the description in **(e)** above.

j. ☐ I am the husband, wife, or minor unmarried child of a Cuban and meet the description in **(f)** above.

To be Completed by
Attorney or Representative, **if any**
☐ Fill in box if G-28 is attached to represent the applicant.

VOLAG #

ATTY State License #

Part 3. Processing Information

A. City/Town/Village of Birth	Current Occupation
Your Mother's First Name	Your Father's First Name

Give your name exactly as it appears on your Arrival-Departure Record (Form I-94)

Place of Last Entry Into the United States *(City/State)*	In what status did you last enter? *(Visitor, student, exchange alien, crewman, temporary worker, without inspection, etc.)*
Were you inspected by a U.S. Immigration Officer? ☐ Yes ☐ No	
Nonimmigrant Visa Number	Consulate Where Visa Was Issued

Date Visa Was Issued (mm/dd/yyyy)	Gender: ☐ Male ☐ Female	Marital Status: ☐ Married ☐ Single ☐ Divorced ☐ Widowed

Have you ever before applied for permanent resident status in the U.S.?   ☐ No   ☐ Yes. If you checked "Yes," give date and place of filing and final disposition.

B. List your present husband/wife, all of your sons and daughters (If you have none, write "None." If additional space is needed, use separate paper).

Family Name	Given Name	Middle Initial	Date of Birth *(mm/dd/yyyy)*
Country of Birth	Relationship	A #	Applying with you? ☐ Yes ☐ No
Family Name	Given Name	Middle Initial	Date of Birth *(mm/dd/yyyy)*
Country of Birth	Relationship	A #	Applying with you? ☐ Yes ☐ No
Family Name	Given Name	Middle Initial	Date of Birth *(mm/dd/yyyy)*
Country of Birth	Relationship	A #	Applying with you? ☐ Yes ☐ No
Family Name	Given Name	Middle Initial	Date of Birth *(mm/dd/yyyy)*
Country of Birth	Relationship	A #	Applying with you? ☐ Yes ☐ No
Family Name	Given Name	Middle Initial	Date of Birth *(mm/dd/yyyy)*
Country of Birth	Relationship	A #	Applying with you? ☐ Yes ☐ No

C. List your present and past membership in or affiliation with every organization, association, fund, foundation, party, club, society, or similar group in the United States or in other places since your 16th birthday. Include any foreign military service in this part. If none, write "None." Include the name(s) of organization(s), location(s), dates of membership from and to, and the nature of the organization(s). If additional space is needed, use a separate piece of paper.

Part 3. Processing Information *(Continued)*

Answer the following questions. (If your answer is **"Yes"** on any one of these questions, explain on a separate piece of paper and refer to "What Are the General Filing Instructions? Initial Evidence" to determine what documentation to include with your application. Answering **"Yes"** does not necessarily mean that you are not entitled to adjust status or register for permanent residence.)

1. Have you ever, in or outside the United States:

   a. Knowingly committed any crime of moral turpitude or a drug-related offense for which you have not been arrested? ☐ Yes ☐ No

   b. Been arrested, cited, charged, indicted, fined, or imprisoned for breaking or violating any law or ordinance, excluding traffic violations? ☐ Yes ☐ No

   c. Been the beneficiary of a pardon, amnesty, rehabilitation decree, other act of clemency, or similar action? ☐ Yes ☐ No

   d. Exercised diplomatic immunity to avoid prosecution for a criminal offense in the United States? ☐ Yes ☐ No

2. Have you received public assistance in the United States from any source, including the U.S.Government or any State, county, city, or municipality (other than emergency medical treatment), or are you likely to receive public assistance in the future? ☐ Yes ☐ No

3. Have you ever:

   a. Within the past ten years been a prostitute or procured anyone for prostitution, or intend to engage in such activities in the future? ☐ Yes ☐ No

   b. Engaged in any unlawful commercialized vice, including, but not limited to, illegal gambling? ☐ Yes ☐ No

   c. Knowingly encouraged, induced, assisted, abetted, or aided any alien to try to enter the United States illegally? ☐ Yes ☐ No

   d. Illicitly trafficked in any controlled substance, or knowingly assisted, abetted, or colluded in the illicit trafficking of any controlled substance? ☐ Yes ☐ No

4. Have you ever engaged in, conspired to engage in, or do you intend to engage in, or have you ever solicited membership or funds for, or have you through any means ever assisted or provided any type of material support to any person or organization that has ever engaged or conspired to engage in sabotage, kidnapping, political assassination, hijacking, or any other form of terrorist activity? ☐ Yes ☐ No

5. Do you intend to engage in the United States in:

   a. Espionage? ☐ Yes ☐ No

   b. Any activity a purpose of which is opposition to, or the control or overthrow of, the Government of the United States, by force, violence, or other unlawful means? ☐ Yes ☐ No

   c. Any activity to violate or evade any law prohibiting the export from the United States of goods, technology, or sensitive information? ☐ Yes ☐ No

6. Have you ever been a member of, or in any way affiliated with, the Communist Party or any other totalitarian party? ☐ Yes ☐ No

7. Did you, during the period from March 23, 1933, to May 8, 1945, in association with either the Nazi Government of Germany or any organization or government associated or allied with the Nazi Government of Germany, ever order, incite, assist, or otherwise participate in the persecution of any person because of race, religion, national origin, or political opinion? ☐ Yes ☐ No

8. Have you ever engaged in genocide, or otherwise ordered, incited, assisted, or otherwise participated in the killing of any person because of race, religion, nationality, ethnic origin, or political opinion? ☐ Yes ☐ No

9. Have you ever been deported from the United States, or removed from the United States at government expense, excluded within the past year, or are you now in exclusion, deportation, removal, or rescission proceedings? ☐ Yes ☐ No

10. Are you under a final order of civil penalty for violating section 274C of the Immigration and Nationality Act for use of fraudulent documents or have you, by fraud or willful misrepresentation of a material fact, ever sought to procure, or procured, a visa, other documentation, entry into the United States, or any immigration benefit? ☐ Yes ☐ No

11. Have you ever left the United States to avoid being drafted into the U.S. Armed Forces? ☐ Yes ☐ No

12. Have you ever been a J nonimmigrant exchange visitor who was subject to the two-year foreign residence requirement and have not yet complied with that requirement or obtained a waiver? ☐ Yes ☐ No

13. Are you now withholding custody of a U.S. citizen child outside the United States from a person granted custody of the child? ☐ Yes ☐ No

14. Do you plan to practice polygamy in the United States? ☐ Yes ☐ No

Part 4. Signature (Read the information on penalties in the instructions before completing this section. You must file this application while in the United States.)

Your Registration With U.S. Citizenship and Immigration Services

"I understand and acknowledge that, under section 262 of the Immigration and Nationality Act (Act), as an alien who has been or will be in the United States for more than 30 days, I am required to register with U.S. Citizenship and Immigration Services. I understand and acknowledge that, under section 265 of the Act, I am required to provide USCIS with my current address and written notice of any change of address within **ten** days of the change. I understand and acknowledge that USCIS will use the most recent address that I provide to USCIS, on any form containing these acknowledgements, for all purposes, including the service of a Notice to Appear should it be necessary for USCIS to initiate removal proceedings against me. I understand and acknowledge that if I change my address without providing written notice to USCIS, I will be held responsible for any communications sent to me at the most recent address that I provided to USCIS. I further understand and acknowledge that, if removal proceedings are initiated against me and I fail to attend any hearing, including an initial hearing based on service of the Notice to Appear at the most recent address that I provided to USCIS or as otherwise provided by law, I may be ordered removed in my absence, arrested, and removed from the United States."

Selective Service Registration

The following applies to you if you are a male at least 18 years of age, but not yet 26 years of age, who is required to register with the Selective Service System: "I understand that my filing Form I-485 with U.S. Citizenship and Immigration Services authorizes USCIS to provide certain registration information to the Selective Service System in accordance with the Military Selective Service Act. Upon USCIS acceptance of my application, I authorize USCIS to transmit to the Selective Service System my name, current address, Social Security Number, date of birth, and the date I filed the application for the purpose of recording my Selective Service registration as of the filing date. If, however, USCIS does not accept my application, I further understand that, if so required, I am responsible for registering with the Selective Service by other means, provided I have not yet reached age 26."

Applicant's Certification

I certify, under penalty of perjury under the laws of the United States of America, that this application and the evidence submitted with it is all true and correct. I authorize the release of any information from my records that U.S. Citizenship and Immigration Services (USCIS) needs to determine eligibility for the benefit I am seeking.

Signature	*Print Your Name*	*Date*	**Daytime Phone Number** *(Include Area Code)*

NOTE: *If you do not completely fill out this form or fail to submit required documents listed in the instructions, you may not be found eligible for the requested document and this application may be denied.*

Part 5. Signature of Person Preparing Form, If Other Than Above (Sign below)

I declare that I prepared this application at the request of the above person, and it is based on all information of which I have knowledge.

Signature	*Print Your Full Name*	*Date*	**Phone Number** *(Include Area Code)*

Firm Name and Address	*E-Mail Address (if any)*

OMB No. 1615-0003; Expires 02/29/12

Department of Homeland Security
U.S. Citizenship and Immigration Services

Instructions for Form I-539, Application to Extend/Change Nonimmigrant Status

Instructions

Read these instructions carefully to properly complete this form. If you need more space to complete an answer, use a separate sheet of paper. Write your name and Alien Registration Number (A-Number), if any, at the top of each sheet of paper and indicate the part and number of the item to which the answer refers.

NOTE: You have the option of submitting this paper version of Form I-539 according to the form's instructions, or you may file the application electronically. To file electronically, visit our Internet Web site at **www.uscis.gov** and follow the instructions on e-filing. Whether you submit this paper form or e-file, U.S. Citizenship and Immigration Services (USCIS) recommends that you retain a copy of your application and supporting documents for your records.

What Is the Purpose of This Form?

You should use this form if you are one of the nonimmigrants listed below and wish to apply to U.S. Citizenship and Immigration Services (USCIS) for an extension of stay or a change to another nonimmigrant status.

In certain situations, you may use this form to apply for an initial nonimmigrant status.

You may also use this form if you are a nonimmigrant F-1 or M-1 student applying for reinstatement.

When Should I Use Form I-539?

You must submit an application for extension of stay or change of status before your current authorized stay expires. We suggest you file at least 45 days before your stay expires, or as soon as you determine your need to change status. Failure to file before the expiration date may be excused if you demonstrate when you file the application that:

1. The delay was due to extraordinary circumstances beyond your control;

2. The length of the delay was reasonable;

3. You have not otherwise violated your status;

4. You are still a bona fide nonimmigrant; and

5. You are not in removal proceedings.

Who May File Form I-539?

Extension of Stay or Change of Status

Nonimmigrants in the United States may apply for an extension of stay or a change of status on this form, except as noted in these instructions under the heading, "Who May Not File Form I-539."

Multiple Applicants

You may include your spouse and your unmarried children under 21 years of age as co-applicants in your application for the same extension or change of status, but only if you are all now in the same status or they are all in derivative status.

Nonimmigrant Categories

This form may be used by the following nonimmigrants listed in alphabetical order:

1. **A, Ambassador, Public Minister, or Career Diplomatic or Consular Officer and Their Immediate Family Members**

   You must submit a copy, front and back, of Form I-94 of each person included in the application and Form I-566, Interagency Record of Request-A, G, or NATO Dependent Employment Authorization or Change/Adjustment to/from A,G, or NATO Status, certified by the U.S. Department of State to indicate your accredited status.

   NOTE: An A-1 or A-2 nonimmigrant is not required to pay a fee with Form I-539.

2. **A-3, Attendant or Servant of an A Nonimmigrant and the A-3's Immediate Family Members**

   You must submit a copy, front and back, of Form I-94 of each person included in the application.

   The application must be filed with:

   A. A copy of your employer's Form I-94 or approval notice demonstrating A status;

   B. An original letter from your employer describing your duties and stating that he or she intends to personally employ you, and arrangements you have made to depart from the United States; and

C. An original Form I-566, certified by the U.S. Department of State, indicating your employer's continuing accredited status.

3. B-1, Visitor for Business, or B-2, Visitor for Pleasure

If you are filing for an extension/change, you must file your application with the original Form I-94 of each person included in your application. In addition, you must submit a written statement explaining in detail:

A. The reasons for your request;

B. Why your extended stay would be temporary, including what arrangements you have made to depart from the United States; and

C. Any effect the extended stay may have on your foreign employment or residency.

If you are applying for an extension/change of B-1, visitor for business, you must designate your desired status using the following classification in **Part 2.1.b** of Form I-539:

A. B-1A, nonimmigrant who is the personal or domestic servant of a nonimmigrant employer;

B. B-1B, nonimmigrant domestic servant of a U.S. citizen;

C. B-1C, nonimmigrant who is employed by a foreign airline;

D. B-1D, nonimmigrant who is a missionary; and

E. B-1, all other visa classifications not designated above.

4. Dependents of an E, Treaty Trader or Investor, or Australian Specialty Occupation Worker

If you are filing for an extension/change of status as the dependent of an E worker, this application must be submitted with:

A. Form I-129, Petition for Alien Worker, filed for that E worker or a copy of the filing receipt noting that the petition is pending with USCIS;

B. A copy of the E's Form I-94 or approval notice showing that he or she has already been granted status to the period requested on your application; and

C. Evidence of relationship (example: birth or marriage certificate).

NOTE: An employer or investor must file Form I-129 to request an extension/change to E status for an employee, prospective employee, or the investor. Dependents of E employees must file for an extension/change of status on this form, not Form I-129.

5. F-1, Academic Student

To request a change to F-1 status or to apply for reinstatement as an F-1 student, you must submit your original Form I-94, as well as the original Form I-94 of each person included in the application.

Your application must include your original Form I-20, Certificate of Eligibility for Nonimmigrant Student, issued by the school where you will study. To request either a change or reinstatement, you must submit documentation that demonstrates your ability to pay for your studies, and support yourself while you are in the United States.

F-1 Extensions

Do not use this form to request an extension. For information concerning extensions, contact your designated school official at your institution.

F-1 Reinstatement

You will only be considered for reinstatement as an F-1 student if you establish:

A. That the violation of status was due solely to circumstances beyond your control or that failure to reinstate you would result in extreme hardship;

B. You are pursuing or will pursue a full course of study;

C. You have not been employed without authorization; and

D. You are not in removal proceedings.

6. G, Designated Principal Resident Representative of a Foreign Government and His or Her Immediate Family Members

You must submit a copy, front and back, of Form I-94 for each person included in the application, and Form I-566, certified by the U.S. Department of State to indicate your accredited status.

NOTE: A G-1 through G-4 nonimmigrant is not required to pay a fee with Form I-539.

The application must also be filed with:

A. A copy of your employer's Form I-94 or approval notice demonstrating G status; and

B. An original letter from your employer describing your duties and stating that he or she intends to personally employ you and arrangements you have made to depart from the United States.

7. Dependents of an H, Temporary Worker

If you are filing for an extension/change of status as the dependent of an employee who is an H temporary worker, this application must be submitted with:

A. Form I-129 filed for that employee or a copy of the filing receipt noting that the petition is pending with USCIS;

B. A copy of the employee's Form I-94 or approval notice showing that he or she has already been granted status to the period requested on your application; and

C. Evidence of relationship (example: birth or marriage certificate).

NOTE: An employer must file Form I-129 to request an extension/change to H status for an employee or prospective employee. Dependents of such employees must file for an extension/change of status on this form, not on Form I-129.

8. J-1, Exchange Visitor

If you are requesting a change of status to J-1 nonimmigrant classification, your application must be filed with an original DS-2019, Certificate of Eligibility for Exchange Visitor Status. You must also submit your original Form I-94, as well as the original Form I-94 for each person included in the application.

J-1 Extensions

If you are a J-1 exchange visitor seeking an extension of nonimmigrant status, contact the responsible officer of your program for information about this procedure.

J-1 Reinstatement

If you are a J-1 exchange visitor seeking reinstatement, you may need to apply to the U.S. Department of State's Office of Education and Cultural Affairs for such approval. Contact the responsible officer at your sponsoring program for information on the reinstatement filing procedure.

Notice to J Nonimmigrants

A J-1 exchange visitor whose status is to receive graduate medical education or training, and who has not received the appropriate waiver, is ineligible for change of status except to a nonimmigrant T or U visa. In addition, a J-1 exchange visitor who is subject to the foreign residence requirement, and who has not received a waiver of that requirement, is only eligible for a change of status to a nonimmigrant A, G, T, or U visa.

If a J-1 exchange visitor is subject to the foreign residence requirement, the J-2 dependant is also subject as a derivative to this requirement. If the J-1 exchange visitor obtains a waiver of the foreign residence requirement, the J-2 dependent is also exempt from the requirement. Under certain limited circumstances, a J-2 dependant may be independently eligible for a waiver of the foreign residence requirement.

A former J nonimmigrant (either a J-1 principal or a J-2 dependent) subject to the foreign residence requirement, who is currently maintaining another nonimmigrant visa status, continues to be subject to the foreign residence requirement. As noted above, the former J nonimmigrant is ineligible for a change of status until he or she fulfills the foreign residence requirement or obtains the appropriate waiver.

If you are a current or former J nonimmigrant, you must provide information about this status, including the dates you maintained status as a J-1 exchange visitor or a J-2 dependent. Willful failure to disclose this information (or other relevant information) can result in your application being denied. Provide proof of this status along with your application, such as a copy of Form DS-2019, Certificate of Eligibility for Exchange Visitor Status, or a copy of your passport that includes the J visa stamp.

9. Dependents of an L, Intracompany Transferee

If you are filing for an extension/change of status as the dependent of an employee who is an L intracompany transferee, this application must be submitted with:

A. Form I-129 filed for that employee, or a copy of the filing receipt noting that the petition is pending with USCIS;

B. A copy of the employee's Form I-94 or approval notice showing that he or she has already been granted status to the period requested on your application; and

C. Evidence of relationship (example: birth or marriage certificate).

NOTE: An employer should file Form I-129 to request an extension/change to L status for an employee or prospective employee. Dependents of such employees must file for an extension/change of status on this form, not on Form I-129.

10. M-1, Vocational or Non-Academic Student

To request a change to or extension of M-1 status, or apply for reinstatement as an M-1 student, you must submit your original Form I-94, as well as the original Form I-94 of each person included in the application.

M-1 Reinstatement

A. The violation of status was due solely to circumstances beyond your control or that failure to reinstate you would result in extreme hardship;

B. You are pursuing or will pursue a full course of study;

C. You have not been employed without authorization; and

D. You are not in removal proceedings.

NOTE: If you are an M-1 student, you are not eligible for a change to F-1 status, and you are not eligible for a change to any H status if the training you received as an M-1 helps you qualify for the H status. Also, you may not be granted a change to M-1 status for training to qualify for H status.

11. Dependents of a P, Artists, Athletes, and Entertainers

If you are filing for an extension/change of status as the dependent of an employee who is classified as a P nonimmigrant, this application must be submitted with:

A. Form I-129 filed for that employee or a copy of the filing receipt noting that the petition is pending with USCIS;

B. A copy of the employee's Form I-94 or approval notice showing that he or she has already been granted status to the period requested on your application; and

C. Evidence of relationship (example: birth or marriage certificate).

NOTE: An employer must file Form I-129 to request an extension/change to P status for an employee or prospective employee. Dependents of such employees must file for an extension/change of status on this form, not on Form I-129.

12. Dependents of an R, Religious Worker

If you are filing for an extension/change of status as the dependent of an employee who is classified as an R nonimmigrant, this application must be submitted with:

A. Form I-129 filed for that employee or a copy of the filing receipt noting that the petition is pending with USCIS;

B. A copy of the employee's Form I-94 or approval notice showing that he or she has already been granted status to the period requested on your application; and

C. Evidence of relationship (example: birth or marriage certificate).

13. TD Dependents of TN Nonimmigrants

TN nonimmigrants are citizens of Canada or Mexico who are coming to the United States to engage in business activities at a professional level under the North American Free Trade Agreement (NAFTA). The dependents (spouse or unmarried minor children) of a TN nonimmigrant are designated as TD nonimmigrants. A TD nonimmigrant may accompany or follow to join the TN professional. TD nonimmigrants may not work in the United States.

Form I-539 shall be used by a TD nonimmigrant to request an extension of stay or by an applicant to request a change of nonimmigrant status to TD classification.

If you are filing for an extension/change of status as the dependent of an employee who is classified as a TN nonimmigrant, this application must be submitted with:

A. Form I-129 filed for that employee or a copy of the filing receipt noting that the petition is pending with USCIS;

B. A copy of the employee's Form I-94 or approval notice showing that he or she has already been granted status to the period requested on your application; and

C. Evidence of relationship (example: birth or marriage certificate).

14. V, Spouse or Child of a Lawful Permanent Resident

Use Form I-539 if you are physically present in the United States and wish to request initial status or change status to a V nonimmigrant, or to request an extension of your current V nonimmigrant status.

Applicants must follow the instructions on this form and the attached instructions to Supplement A to Form I-539, Filing Instructions for V Nonimmigrants. The supplement contains additional information and the location where V applicants must file their applications.

NOTE: In addition to the **$300** application fee required to file Form I-539, V applicants are required to pay a **$80** biometric services fee for USCIS to take their fingerprints.

If necessary, USCIS may also take the V applicant's photograph and signature as part of the biometric services.

Notice to V Nonimmigrants

The Legal Immigration Family Equity Act (LIFE), signed into law on December 21, 2000, created a new V visa. This nonimmigrant status allows certain persons to reside legally in the United States and to travel to and from the United States while they wait to obtain lawful permanent residence.

In order to be eligible for a V visa, all of the following conditions must be met:

A. You must be the spouse or the unmarried child of a lawful permanent resident;

B. Form I-130, Petition for Alien Relative, must have been filed for you by your permanent resident spouse on or before December 21, 2000; and

C. You must have been waiting for at least 3 years after Form I-130 was filed for you; or

D. You must be the unmarried child (under 21 years of age) of a person who meets the three requirements listed above.

V visa holders will be eligible to adjust to lawful permanent resident status once an immigrant visa becomes available to them. While they are waiting, V visa holders may be authorized to work following their submission and USCIS approval of their Form I-765, Application for Employment Authorization.

> **WARNING:** Persons in V status who have been in the United States illegally for more than 180 days may trigger the grounds of inadmissibility regarding unlawful presence (for the applicable 3-year or 10-year bar to admission) if they leave the United States. Their departure may prevent them from adjusting status as a permanent resident.

Who May Not File Form I-539?

You may not be granted an extension or change of status if you were admitted under the Visa Waiver Program or if your current status is:

1. An alien in transit (C) or in transit without a visa (TWOV);

2. A crewman (D); or

3. A fiancé(e) or dependent of a fiancé(e)(K)(1) or (K)(2).

A spouse (K-3) of a U.S. citizen and his or her children (K-4), accorded such status under the LIFE Act, may not change to another nonimmigrant status.

EXCEPTION: A K-3 and K-4 are eligible to apply for an extension of status. They should file for an extension during the processing of Form I-130 filed on their behalf and up to completion of their adjustment-of-status application.

NOTE: Any nonimmigrant (A to V) may not change his or her status to K-3 or K-4.

General Instructions

Step 1. Fill Out Form I-539

1. Type or print legibly in black ink.

2. If extra space is needed to complete any item, attach a continuation sheet, indicate the item number, and date and sign each sheet.

3. Answer all questions fully and accurately. State that an item is not applicable with "N/A." If the answer is none, write "None."

Step 2. General Requirements

Required Documentation - Form I-94, Nonimmigrant Arrival-Departure Record. You are required to submit with your Form I-539 the original or copy, front and back, of Form I-94 of each person included in your application. If the original Form I-94 or required copy cannot be submitted with this application, include Form I-102, Application for Replacement/Initial Nonimmigrant Arrival/Departure Document, with the required fee.

Valid Passport

If you were required to have a passport to be admitted into the United States, you must maintain the validity of your passport during your nonimmigrant stay. If a required passport is not valid when you file Form I-539, submit an explanation with your form.

Additional Evidence

You may be required to submit additional evidence noted in these instructions.

Translations

Any document containing a foreign language submitted to USCIS must be accompanied by a full English language translation which the translator has certified as complete and accurate, and by the translator's certification that he or she is competent to translate from the foreign language into English.

Copies

Unless specifically required that an original document be filed with an application or petition, an ordinary legible photocopy may be submitted. Original documents submitted when not required will remain a part of the record, even if the submission was not required.

Where To File?

1. With some exceptions, Form I-539 is generally filed with the California Service Center or the Vermont Service Center.

   California Service Center fillings cover the following states: Alaska, Arizona, California, Colorado, Guam, Hawaii, Idaho, Illinois, Indiana, Iowa, Kansas, Michigan, Minnesota, Missouri, Montana, Nebraska, Nevada, North Dakota, Ohio, Oregon, South Dakota, Utah, Washington, Wisconsin, or Wyoming.

   The mailing address is:

   USCIS California Service Center
   P.O. Box 10539
   Laguna Niguel, CA 92607-1053

   Vermont Service Center filings cover the following states: Alabama, Arkansas, Connecticut, Delaware, Florida, Georgia, Kentucky, Louisiana, Maine, Maryland, Massachusetts, Mississippi, New Hampshire, New Jersey, New Mexico, New York, North Carolina, Oklahoma, Pennsylvania, Puerto Rico, Rhode Island, South Carolina, Tennessee, Texas, Vermont, Virginia, U.S. Virgin Islands, West Virginia, and the District of Columbia.

   The address for Vermont Service Center filings is:

   USCIS Vermont Service Center
   ATTN: I-539
   75 Lower Welden Street
   St. Albans, VT 05479

2. **Applicants for change of status to E-1, E-2, E-3, H-4, L-2, O-3, or P-4 as the dependent spouse or child or for an E-1, E-2, E-3, H-4, L-2, O-3, P-4, or TD extension, as the dependent spouse or child.**

A. **Filing Form I-539 at the same time as the principal:** If your Form I-539 for change of status or extension of stay is filed at the same time as the principal's Form I-129, Petition for Nonimmigrant Worker (which includes a request for change of status or extension of stay), send the entire Form I-129/I-539 package to the Vermont Service Center or the California Service Center, depending on the State where the principal is or will be employed temporarily.

B. **Filing Form I-539 separately from the principal and the principal's case is pending:** If the principal's Form I-129 (which includes a request for change of status or extension of stay) is pending, file Form I-539 with the same Service Center where the principal's Form I-129 is pending. Include a copy of Form I-129 filing receipt (or transfer notice) to show the pending Form I-129 location.

C. **Filing Form I-539 separately from the principal and the principal's case is approved:** If the principal's Form I-129 (which included a request for change of status or extension of stay) has already been approved, file Form I-539 with the Service Center that approved the principal's Form I-129. Include a copy of the Form I-129 approval notice to show the approved Form I-129 location.

D. **F-1 and M-1 students applying for F-1 and M-1 reinstatement:** File Form I-539 with the California Service Center or the Vermont Service Center, depending on the State in which the educational institution you attend or plan to attend is located.

E. **All other applicants for change of status or extension of stay (not listed above or in the exceptions):** File Form I-539 with the California Service Center or the Vermont Service Center, depending on the State where you live.

3. **Exceptions**

A. **R-2 Religious Worker Dependents:**

   File Form I-539 with the California Service Center, regardless of where the principal is/will be employed.

B. **H-1 C Nurses dependents:**

   File Form I-539 with the California Service Center, regardless of where the principal is/will be employed.

C. **TD dependents of TN principals (Free Trade-Canada and Mexico), H-4 dependents of H-1B1 principals (Free Trade-Singapore and Chile), and E-3 dependents of E-3 principals (Free Trade-Australia):**

www.facebook.com/become.citizen

File Form I-539 with the Vermont Service Center, regardless of where the principal is/will be employed.

D. Dependents of Major League Sports Athletes or Support Personnel:

File with the Vermont Service Center. This covers major league athletes, minor league sports, and any affiliates associated with the major leagues in baseball, hockey, soccer, basketball, and football. Support personnel include: coaches, trainers, broadcasters, referees, linesmen, umpires, and interpreters.

E. A, G, and NATO:

1. For change of status requests to A, G, or NATO classification for employment with an embassy, international organization, or NATO, mail Form I-539 through your embassy, international organization, or NATO to: U.S. Department of State, Office of Protocol, 3507 International Place, N.W., Suite 242, Washington, DC 20008.

2. For change of status requests to G classification for employment with a foreign government's mission to the United Nations or with the United Nations Secretariat, mail Form I-539 **through the foreign government's mission or the UN Secretariat** to: U.S. Mission to the United Nations, 799 United Nations Plaza, New York, NY 10017.

3. For a dependent spouse or child requesting a change of status to a NATO classification based on the principal's classification as a NATO nonimmigrant, mail Form I-539 to: NATO/HQ SACT Legal Affairs, 7857 Blandy Road, Suite 100, Norfolk, VA 23551. If you or the principal or the principal NATO nonimmigrant through whom you derive your status are posted at a national component or as an exchange officer, submit Form I-539 to your embassy for proper filing through official diplomatic channels.

4. For a change of status from A, G, or NATO classifications to another nonimmigrant classification, file Form I-539 with the USCIS Service Center designated to handle the new nonimmigrant classification sought. You must submit with Form I-539 an endorsement by the U.S. Department of State Visa Office, or a USUN official at **Part 7** on the Form I-566, Interagency Record of Request-A, G, or NATO Dependent Employment Authorization or Change/Adjustment to/from A,G, or NATO Status.

5. For extensions of stay for A-3, G-5, or NATO-7 nonimmigrants, submit your application through your embassy, international organization, or NATO command for proper filing through official diplomatic channels.

F. V Nonimmigrants

Follow the filing instructions on Form I-539, Supplement A, Filing Instructions for V Nonimmigrants.

G. Updated Filing Address Information

The filing addresses provided on this form reflect the most current information as of the date this form was last printed.

If you are filing Form I-539 more than 30 days after the latest edition date shown in the lower right corner, visit us online at **www.uscis.gov** before you file, and check the Immigration Forms page to confirm the correct filing address and version currently in use. Check the edition date located in the lower right corner of the form. If the edition date on your Form I-539 matches the edition date listed for Form I-539 on the online forms page, your version is current and will be accepted by USCIS. If the edition date on the online version is later, download a copy and use the online version. If you do not have Internet access, call Customer Service at **1-800-375-5283** to verify the current filing address and edition date.

H. Note on E-Filing

If you are e-filing this application, it will automatically be routed to the appropriate Service Center, and you will receive a receipt indicating the location to which it was routed. This location may not necessarily be the same center shown in the filing addresses listed above. For e-filed applications, it is very important to review your filing receipt and make specific note of the receiving location.

All further communication, including submission of supporting documents, should be directed to the receiving location indicated on your e-filing receipt.

What Is the Filing Fee?

The filing fee for Form I-539 is **$300** except for certain A and G nonimmigrants who are not required to pay a fee, as noted in these instructions.

An additional biometric fee of **$80** is required when filing this Form I-539 for V nonimmigrant status. After you submit Form I-539, USCIS will notify you about when and where to go for biometric services.

If biometric services are required, you may submit one check or money order for both the application and biometric fees, for a total of **$380**.

Use the following guidelines when you prepare your check or money order for the Form I-539 and the biometric service fee, if applicable:

1. The check or money order must be drawn on a bank or other financial institution located in the United States and must be payable in U.S. currency; and

2. Make the check or money order payable to **U.S. Department of Homeland Security**, unless:

   A. If you live in Guam, make it payable to **Treasurer, Guam**.

   B. If you live in the U.S. Virgin Islands, make it payable to **Commissioner of Finance of the Virgin Islands**.

NOTE: Spell out U.S. Department of Homeland Security; do not use the initials "USDHS" or "DHS."

Notice to Those Making Payment by Check

If you send us a check, it will be converted into an electronic funds transfer (EFT). This means we will copy your check and use the account information on it to electronically debit your account for the amount of the check. The debit from your account will usually take 24 hours and will be shown on your regular account statement.

You will not receive your original check back. We will destroy your original check, but we will keep a copy of it. If the EFT cannot be processed for technical reasons, you authorize us to process the copy in place of your original check. If the EFT cannot be completed because of insufficient funds, we may try to make the transfer up to two times.

How to Check If the Fees Are Correct

The form and biometric fees on this form are current as of the edition date appearing in the lower right corner of this page. However, because USCIS fees change periodically, you can verify if the fees are correct by following one of the steps below:

1. Visit our Web site at **www.uscis.gov**, select "Immigration Forms," and check the appropriate fee;

2. Review the Fee Schedule included in your form package, if you called us to request the form; or

3. Telephone our National Customer Service Center at **1-800-375-5283** and ask for the fee information.

NOTE: If your Form I-539 requires payment of a biometric service fee for USCIS to take your fingerprints, photograph, or signature, you can use the same procedure to obtain the correct biometric fee.

Address Changes

If you change your address and you have an application or petition pending with USCIS, you may change your address online at **www.uscis.gov**, click on "Change your address with USCIS," and follow the prompts. You may also complete and mail Form AR-11, Alien's Change of Address Card, to:

U.S. Citizenship and Immigration Services
Change of Address
P.O. Box 7134
London, KY 40742-7134

For commercial overnight or fast freight services only, mail to:

U.S. Citizenship and Immigration Services
Change of Address
1084-I South Laurel Road
London, KY 40744

Processing Information

Any Form I-539 that is not signed or accompanied by the correct fee will be rejected with a notice that Form I-539 is deficient. You may correct the deficiency and resubmit Form I-539. An application or petition is not considered properly filed until accepted by USCIS.

Initial processing

Once Form I-539 has been accepted, it will be checked for completeness, including submission of the required initial evidence. If you do not completely fill out the form, or file it without required initial evidence, you will not establish a basis for eligibility, and we may deny your Form I-539.

Requests for more information or interview

We may request more information or evidence, or we may request that you appear at a USCIS office for an interview. We may also request that you submit the originals of any copy. We will return these originals when they are no longer required.

Decision

The decision on Form I-539 involves a determination of whether you have established eligibility for the requested benefit. You will be notified of the decision in writing.

USCIS Forms and Information

To order USCIS forms, call our toll-free number at **1-800-870-3676.** You can also get USCIS forms and information on immigration laws, regulations, and procedures by telephoning our National Customer Service Center at **1-800-375-5283** or visiting our Internet Web site at **www.uscis.gov**.

As an alternative to waiting in line for assistance at your local USCIS office, you can now schedule an appointment through our Internet-based system, **InfoPass**. To access the system, visit our Web site. Use the **InfoPass** appointment scheduler and follow the screen prompts to set up your appointment. **InfoPass** generates an electronic appointment notice that appears on the screen.

Penalties

If you knowingly and willfully falsify or conceal a material fact or submit a false document with Form I-539, we will deny Form I-539 and may deny any other immigration benefit.

In addition, you will face severe penalties provided by law and may be subject to criminal prosecution.

Privacy Act Notice

We ask for the information on this form, and associated evidence, to determine if you have established eligibility for the immigration benefit for which you are filing. Our legal right to ask for this information can be found in the Immigration and Nationality Act, as amended. We may provide this information to other government agencies. Failure to provide this information, and any requested evidence, may delay a final decision or result in denial of your Form I-539.

USCIS Compliance Review and Monitoring

By signing this form, you have stated under penalty of perjury (28 U.S.C.1746) that all information and documentation submitted with this form is true and correct. You also have authorized the release of any information from your records that USCIS may need to determine eligibility for the benefit you are seeking and consented to USCIS verification of such information.

The Department of Homeland Security has the right to verify any information you submit to establish eligibility for the immigration benefit you are seeking at any time. Our legal right to verify this information is in 8 U.S.C. 1103, 1155, 1184, and 8 CFR parts 103, 204, 205, and 214. To ensure compliance with applicable laws and authorities, USCIS may verify information before or after your case has been decided. Agency verification methods may include, but are not limited to: review of public records and information; contact via written correspondence, the Internet, facsimile, or other electronic transmission, or telephone; unannounced physical site inspections of residences and places of employment; and interviews. Information obtained through verification will be used to assess your compliance with the laws and to determine your eligibility for the benefit sought.

Subject to the restrictions under 8 CFR part 103.2(b)(16), you will be provided an opportunity to address any adverse or derogatory information that may result from a USCIS compliance review, verification, or site visit after a formal decision is made on your case or after the agency has initiated an adverse action which may result in revocation or termination of an approval.

Paperwork Reduction Act

An agency may not conduct or sponsor an information collection and a person is not required to respond to a collection of information unless it displays a currently valid OMB control number. The public reporting burden for this collection of information is estimated at 45 minutes per response, including the time for reviewing instructions and completing and submitting the form. Send comments regarding this burden estimate or any other aspect of this collection of information, including suggestions for reducing this burden, to: U.S. Citizenship and Immigration Services, Regulatory Products Division, 111 Massachusetts Avenue, N. W., 3rd Floor, Suite 3008, Washington, DC 20529-2210. OMB No. 1615-0003. **Do not mail your application to this address.**

OMB No. 1615-0003; Expires 02/29/12

Department of Homeland Security
U.S. Citizenship and Immigration Services

I-539, Application to Extend/ Change Nonimmigrant Status

START HERE - Please type or print in black ink

For USCIS Use Only

Part 1.   Information About You

Family Name	Given Name	Middle Name

Address -
In care of -

Street Number and Name		Apt. Number

City	State	Zip Code	Daytime Phone Number

Country of Birth	Country of Citizenship

Date of Birth (mm/dd/yyyy)	U. S. Social Security # (if any)	A- Number (if any)

Date of Last Arrival Into the U.S.	I-94 Number

Current Nonimmigrant Status	Expires on (mm/dd/yyyy)

For USCIS Use Only

Returned

Date

Resubmitted

Date

Reloc Sent

Date

Reloc Rec'd

Date

☐ Applicant Interviewed on

Date

Part 2. Application Type *(See instructions for fee)*

1. I am applying for: *(Check one)*
   a. ☐ An extension of stay in my current status.
   b. ☐ A change of status. The new status I am requesting is: _____
   c. ☐ Reinstatement to student status.

2. Number of people included in this application: *(Check one)*
   a. ☐ I am the only applicant.
   b. ☐ Members of my family are filing this application with me.
      The total number of people (including me) in the application is: _____
      (Complete the supplement for each co-applicant.)

Part 3. Processing Information

1. I/We request that my/our current or requested status be extended until (mm/dd/yyyy):

2. Is this application based on an extension or change of status already granted to your spouse, child, or parent?
   ☐ No ☐ Yes. USCIS Receipt # _____

3. Is this application based on a separate petition or application to give your spouse, child, or parent an extension or change of status? ☐ No ☐ Yes, filed with this I-539.
   ☐ Yes, filed previously and pending with USCIS. Receipt #: _____

4. If you answered "Yes" to Question 3, give the name of the petitioner or applicant:

   If the petition or application is pending with USCIS, also give the following data:

Office filed at _____	Filed on (mm/dd/yyyy) _____

Part 4. Additional Information

1. For applicant #1, provide passport information: Valid to: (mm/dd/yyyy)
   Country of Issuance:

2. Foreign Address: Street Number and Name | Apt. Number

City or Town	State or Province

Country	Zip/Postal Code

☐ *Extension Granted to (Date):*
_____

Change of Status/Extension Granted
New Class: From *(Date)*: _____
_____   To *(Date)*: _____

If Denied:
☐ Still within period of stay
☐ S/D to: _____
☐ Place under docket control

Remarks:

Action Block

To Be Completed by
Attorney or Representative, **if any**

☐ Fill in box if G-28 is attached to represent the applicant.

ATTY State License #

Form I-539 (Rev. 06/12/09)Y

3. Answer the following questions. If you answer "Yes" to any question, describe the circumstances in detail and explain on a separate sheet of paper.

	Yes	No
a. Are you, or any other person included on the application, an applicant for an immigrant visa?	☐	☐
b. Has an immigrant petition ever been filed for you or for any other person included in this application?	☐	☐
c. Has Form I-485, Application to Register Permanent Residence or Adjust Status, ever been filed by you or by any other person included in this application?	☐	☐
d. 1. Have you, or any other person included in this application, ever been arrested or convicted of any criminal offense since last entering the United States?	☐	☐

d. 2. Have you EVER ordered, incited, called for, commited, assisted, helped with, or otherwise participated in any of the following:

(a) Acts involving torture or genocide?

(b) Killing any person?

(c) Intentionally and severely injuring any person?

(d) Engaging in any kind of sexual contact or relations with any person who was being forced or threatened?

(e) Limiting or denying any person's ability to exercise religious beliefs?

	Yes	No
	☐	☐

d. 3. Have you EVER:

(a) Served in, been a member of, assisted in, or participated in any military unit, paramilitary unit, police unit, self-defense unit, vigilante unit, rebel group, guerrilla group, militia, or insurgent organization?

(b) Served in any prison, jail, prison camp, detention facility, labor camp, or any other situation that involved detaining persons?

	Yes	No
	☐	☐
d. 4. Have you EVER been a member of, assisted in, or participated in any group, unit, or organization of any kind in which you or other persons used any type of weapon against any person or threatened to do so?	☐	☐
d. 5. Have you EVER assisted or participated in selling or providing weapons to any person who to your knowledge used them against another person, or in transporting weapons to any person who to your knowledge used them against another person?	☐	☐
d. 6. Have you EVER received any type of military, paramilitary, or weapons training?	☐	☐
e. Have you, or any other person included in this application, done anything that violated the terms of the nonimmigrant status you now hold?	☐	☐
f. Are you, or any other person included in this application, now in removal proceedings?	☐	☐
g. Have you, or any other person included in this application, been employed in the United States since last admitted or granted an extension or change of status?	☐	☐

1. If you answered "Yes" to Question 3f, give the following information concerning the removal proceedings on the attached page entitled "Part 4. Additional information. Page for answers to 3f and 3g." Include the name of the person in removal proceedings and information on jurisdiction, date proceedings began, and status of proceedings.

2. If you answered "No" to Question 3g, fully describe how you are supporting yourself on the attached page entitled "Part 4. Additional information. Page for answers to 3f and 3g." Include the source, amount, and basis for any income.

3. If you answered "Yes" to Question 3g, fully describe the employment on the attached page entitled "Part 4. Additional information. Page for answers to 3f and 3g." Include the name of the person employed, name and address of the employer, weekly income, and whether the employment was specifically authorized by USCIS.

	Yes	No
h. Are you currently or have you ever been a J-1 exchange visitor or a J-2 dependent of a J-1 exchange visitor?	☐	☐

If "Yes," you must provide the dates you maintained status as a J-1 exchange visitor or J-2 dependent. Willful failure to disclose this information (or other relevant information) can result in your application being denied. Also, provide proof of your J-1 or J-2 status, such as a copy of Form DS-2019, Certificate of Eligibility for Exchange Visitor Status, or a copy of your passport that includes the J visa stamp.

Part 5. Applicant's Statement and Signature *(Read the information on penalties in the instructions before completing this section. You must file this application while in the United States.)*

Applicant's Statement (Check One):

☐ I can read and understand English, and have read and understand each and every question and instruction on this form, as well as my answer to each question.

☐ Each and every question and instruction on this form, as well as my answer to each question, has been read to me by the person named below in _____, a language in which I am fluent. I understand each and every question and instruction on this form, as well as my answer to each question.

Applicant's Signature

I certify, under penalty of perjury under the laws of the United States of America, that this application and the evidence submitted with it is all true and correct. I authorize the release of any information from my records that U.S. Citizenship and Immigration Services needs to determine eligibility for the benefit I am seeking.

Signature	Print your Name	Date
Daytime Telephone Number	E-Mail Address	

NOTE: *If you do not completely fill out this form or fail to submit required documents listed in the instructions, you may not be found eligible for the requested benefit and this application may be denied.*

Part 6. Interpreter's Statement

Language used: _____

I certify that I am fluent in English and the above-mentioned language. I further certify that I have read each and every question and instruction on this form, as well as the answer to each question, to this applicant in the above-mentioned language, and the applicant has understood each and every instruction and question on the form, as well as the answer to each question.

Signature	Print Your Name	Date
Firm Name (if applicable)	Daytime Telephone Number *(Area Code and Number)*	
Address	Fax Number *(Area Code and Number)*	E-Mail Address

Part 7. Signature of Person Preparing Form, if Other Than Above *(Sign Below)*

Signature	Print Your Name	Date
Firm Name (if applicable)	Daytime Telephone Number *(Area Code and Number)*	
Address	Fax Number *(Area Code and Number)*	E-Mail Address

I declare that I prepared this application at the request of the above person and it is based on all information of which I have knowledge.

Part 4. (Continued) Additional Information. (Page 2 for answers to 3f and 3g.)

If you answered "Yes" to Question 3f in Part 4 on Page 3 of this form, give the following information concerning the removal proceedings. Include the name of the person in removal proceedings and information on jurisdiction, date proceedings began, and status of proceedings.

If you answered "No" to Question 3g in Part 4 on Page 3 of this form, fully describe how you are supporting yourself. Include the source, amount and basis for any income.

If you answered "Yes" to Question 3g in Part 4 on Page 3 of this form, fully describe the employment. Include the name of the person employed, name and address of the employer, weekly income, and whether the employment was specifically authorized by USCIS.

Form I-539 (Rev. 06/12/09)Y Page 4

Supplement -1
Attach to Form I-539 when more than one person is included in the petition or application.
(List each person separately. Do not include the person named in Form I-539.)

Family Name	Given Name	Middle Name	Date of Birth (mm/dd/yyyy)	
Country of Birth	Country of Citizenship	U.S. Social Security # (if any)	A-Number (if any)	
Date of Arrival (mm/dd/yyyy)		I-94 Number		
Current Nonimmigrant Status:		Expires on (mm/dd/yyyy)		
Country Where Passport Issued		Expiration Date (mm/dd/yyyy)		

Family Name	Given Name	Middle Name	Date of Birth (mm/dd/yyyy)	
Country of Birth	Country of Citizenship	U.S. Social Security # (if any)	A-Number (if any)	
Date of Arrival (mm/dd/yyyy)		I-94 Number		
Current Nonimmigrant Status:		Expires on (mm/dd/yyyy)		
Country Where Passport Issued		Expiration Date (mm/dd/yyyy)		

Family Name	Given Name	Middle Name	Date of Birth (mm/dd/yyyy)	
Country of Birth	Country of Citizenship	U.S. Social Security # (if any)	A-Number (if any)	
Date of Arrival (mm/dd/yyyy)		I-94 Number		
Current Nonimmigrant Status:		Expires on (mm/dd/yyyy)		
Country Where Passport Issued		Expiration Date (mm/dd/yyyy)		

Family Name	Given Name	Middle Name	Date of Birth (mm/dd/yyyy)	
Country of Birth	Country of Citizenship	U.S. Social Security # (if any)	A-Number (if any)	
Date of Arrival (mm/dd/yyyy)		I-94 Number		
Current Nonimmigrant Status:		Expires on (mm/dd/yyyy)		
Country Where Passport Issued		Expiration Date (mm/dd/yyyy)		

Family Name	Given Name	Middle Name	Date of Birth (mm/dd/yyyy)	
Country of Birth	Country of Citizenship	U.S. Social Security # (if any)	A-Number (if any)	
Date of Arrival (mm/dd/yyyy)		I-94 Number		
Current Nonimmigrant Status:		Expires on (mm/dd/yyyy)		
Country Where Passport Issued		Expiration Date (mm/dd/yyyy)		

If you need additional space, attach a separate sheet of paper.
Place your name, A-Number, if any, date of birth, form number, and application date at the top of the sheet of paper.

Form I-539 (Rev. 06/12/09)Y Page 5

Department of Homeland Security
U.S. Citizenship and Immigration Services

I-693, Report of Medical Examination and Vaccination Record

Instructions

Please read these instructions carefully to properly complete this form. If you need more space to complete an answer, use a separate sheet(s) of paper. Write your name and Alien Registration Number (A #), if you have one, at the top of each sheet and indicate the number of the item that refers to your answer.

Section I. Applicant's Instructions

What Is the Purpose of Form I-693?

Generally, all applicants filing for adjustment of status to that of a permanent resident must submit a Form I-693 completed by a designated civil surgeon. Form I-693 is used to report results of a medical examination to U.S. Citizenship and Immigration Services (USCIS). The examination is required to establish that you are not inadmissible to the United States on public health grounds. A list of those health grounds can be found in section 212(a)(1) of the Immigration and Nationality Act. The list is also available in **Question 7** of Section III, Frequently Asked Questions.

The results of your medical examination are confidential and are used for immigration purposes only. When required to do so by law, the civil surgeon may share your results with public health authorities.

NOTE: If you are applying for adjustment of status at least one year after your first admission to the United States as a refugee or as a "K" or "V" nonimmigrant visa holder, see Questions 1-3 in Section III, Frequently Asked Questions, before proceeding any further.

How Do I File Form I-693?

A separate Form I-693 is required for **each** applicant. **There is no filing fee for this form.** Follow these steps:

Step 1 - Carefully read all these instructions, including Section III, Frequently Asked Questions.

Step 2 - Call a designated physician (also known as a civil surgeon) to make an appointment.

Step 3 - Fill out **Part 1** of the form. **Do not sign the form.**

Step 4 - Attend your medical exam appointment and all follow-up exams, as may be required. Sign Form I-693 in front of the civil surgeon.

Step 5 - Submit Form I-693 in the sealed envelope to USCIS according to the instructions on Form I-485, Application to Register Permanent Residence or Adjust Status. USCIS will return the form to you and/or request another Form I-693 if it is not in an envelope or if the envelope has been opened or altered.

NOTE: The civil surgeon will ask you to verify your identity. Take a government-issued photo identification to your appointment. (Example: your valid unexpired passport or driver's license.) For applicants under 14 years, USCIS will accept other proof of identity that shows name, date and place of birth, parents' full names, and any other identifying information about the applicant. Acceptable documents include birth certificates (with translations, if necessary) or affidavits. Also take any vaccination records you may have to the appointment.

How Do I Find a Designated Civil Surgeon in the Area Where I Live?

To find a designated civil surgeon in your area, you can call the USCIS National Customer Service Center (NCSC) at **1-800-375-5283** and follow the instructions in the automated menu. Service is available in English and Spanish. A list of the designated civil surgeons in your area can also be generated by going to the civil surgeon page from the USCIS website at **www.uscis.gov** and clicking on the Civil Surgeon Locator link.

How Do I Fill Out My Portion of Form I-693?

1. **Use black ink only.** Type or print clearly. If an item does not apply to you, write "N/A" unless the specific instruction states otherwise.

2. **You should fill out only Part 1.** The civil surgeon and any other doctors, clinics, or health departments receiving a referral are required to complete **Parts 2** through **6**.

    A. **Part 1 -** Information about you - Fill this part out **before** your medical exam appointment.

    B. **Family name** (Last Name) - Use your legal name. If you have two last names, include both and use a hyphen (-) between the names, if appropriate.

C. **Home address** - Give your physical street address. This must include a street number and name or a rural route number. Do not put a post office box (P.O. Box) number here.

D. **Date of birth** - Use eight numbers to show your date of birth (example: May 1, 1979, should be written 05/01/1979).

E. **Place of birth** - Give the name of the city/town/village where you were born.

F. **Country of birth** - Give the name of the country where you were born.

G. **A-number** - This is your alien registration file number. If you are not sure if you have one, look at any letters or notices you have received from the Department of Homeland Security (DHS). Look for a **number** that begins with a letter "A" and is followed by 8 or 9 numbers (example: A 000 000 000). If you do not have one or if you cannot remember what it is, leave this space blank.

H. **U.S. Social Security #** - If you do not have a U.S. Social Security Number, leave this blank.

I. **Certification** - Do not sign here until the civil surgeon tells you to do so.

How Do I Submit Form I-693 to USCIS?

1. **The civil surgeon is required to give you the completed Form I-693 in a sealed envelope**. Do not accept the form from the civil surgeon if it is not in a sealed envelope. USCIS will return the form to you if it is not in an envelope or if the envelope has been opened or altered.

2. **Adjustment of status applicants:** If you are applying for adjustment of status, submit Form I-693 according to the instructions on Form I-485, Application to Register for Permanent Residence or Adjust Status.

3. **Other applicants:** Follow the instructions on or included with the application form or the instructions given to you by the office requesting the medical exam.

Section II. Civil Surgeon's Instructions

What Are My Responsibilities as a Designated Civil Surgeon?

1. **Truthfully and Accurately Report the Results.** You are responsible for reporting the results of the medical exam and all laboratory reports on Form I-693 where indicated, and for signing the civil surgeon's certification provided on the form.

In this regard, you must take reasonable steps to ensure that the person appearing for the medical exam is the same person applying for the requested immigration benefit. All applicants must present a valid government-issued photo identification. The law imposes severe penalties for knowingly and willfully falsifying or concealing a material fact or using any false documents in connection with this medical exam.

2. **Follow HHS Guidelines.** USCIS has designated you as a civil surgeon with the understanding that you will perform the medical exam according to U.S. Department of Health and Human Services' regulations. These regulations include the specific guidelines found in the *Technical Instructions for the Medical Examination of Aliens in the United States (Technical Instructions),* published by the Centers for Disease Control and Prevention (CDC) in Atlanta, Georgia. The *Technical Instructions* are available on the CDC's website at **http://www.cdc.gov/ncidod/dq/civil.htm**. CDC also posts periodic updates to the *Technical Instructions* at **http://www.cdc.gov/ncidod/dq/updates.htm**.

3. **Give Pre-Test and Post-Test Counseling for HIV/AIDS.** All civil surgeons must give pre-test counseling to any applicant who is tested for HIV. The pre-test counseling must include an explanation of the purpose of the test and basic information about HIV. Civil surgeons must also provide post-test counseling to all applicants who test HIV positive. You must provide information to the applicant about the test results, the prognosis, the ways the applicant can protect himself or herself from opportunistic infections, the ways the applicant can protect others from HIV transmission, and referrals for counseling and early medical intervention. You will find specific instructions about these pre-test and post-test requirements in CDC's *Technical Instructions*.

4. **Make Referrals and File Case Reports, as Required.** According to CDC's *Technical Instructions*, you are required to:

A. **Refer** the applicant to the local health department if the chest X-ray suggests TB or other circumstances are present as described in CDC's *Technical Instructions*. **NOTE:** CDC also recommends referral to the local health department when the chest X-ray is normal or not suggestive of TB, but the applicant has a tuberculin skin test reaction of ≥ 10 mm, in order to evaluate the possible need for preventive therapy.

B. Ensure that any applicant diagnosed with syphilis is treated with the standard treatment regimen described in CDC's *Technical Instructions*.

C. Ensure that testing and therapy are given for diagnoses of chancroid, gonorrhea, granuloma inguinale, or lymphogranuloma venereum.

D. Refer the applicant to a Hansen's disease specialist for evaluation to confirm a suspected diagnosis of Hansen's disease (leprosy).

E. File a case report with the appropriate public health authorities if: **(1)** the applicant tests positive for HIV infection; and **(2)** a case report is required by local laws or regulations. You must also advise the applicant that a case report is being filed.

How Do I Fill Out My Portion of This Form?

The applicant fills out **Part 1** of Form I-693 before the medical exam appointment. You, the civil surgeon, are responsible for ensuring the remaining parts are completed and signed, as follows.

1. **Part 2 - Medical examination -** You must fill out this part and provide the results of each component of the medical exam relating to: communicable disease of public health significance, vaccinations, physical or mental disorder with associated harmful behavior, and substance or drug abuse/substance or drug addiction. In **Part 2**, you must also include the results of any lab work or other studies required to determine whether the applicant is inadmissible on health grounds. You must instruct applicants who have had a tuberculin skin test (TST) to return to your office within 48-72 hours to have the TST read.

2. **Part 3 - Referral to Health Department or Other Doctor/Facility.** If you refer the applicant to a local health department or to another physician or clinic, you must also fill out **Part 3**. **Also see Part 5.**

3. **Part 4 - Physician or Health Department Receiving the Referral.** If you refer the applicant for further tests or evaluation, the health care professional receiving the referral must fill out and sign **Part 4**.

4. **Part 5 - Civil Surgeon's Certification.** You must sign the certification after the initial medical exam and all referrals/follow-up examinations (if required) have been completed. Complete the identifying information in this part before referring an applicant for further tests or evaluation. **Do not sign and date** this part until the referral/follow-up evaluation (if required) has been completed and the applicant has been medically cleared.

5. **Part 6 - Health Department Identifying Information.** If you are a State or local health department that is completing the vaccination record on behalf of a refugee, you must complete this part.

How Do I Complete Form I-693 If I Need to Make a Referral?

Advise the applicant that the appropriate follow-up must be obtained before medical clearance can be granted. In **Part 3**, include the name, address, and telephone number of the onward physician or public health service facility that will conduct further evaluation or provide treatment. Specify the type of examination and additional tests or treatment the applicant should receive. Complete the identifying information in **Part 5**, but **do not sign or date**. Make a copy of the Form I-693 for your records and give the original form to the applicant in a sealed envelope.

What Do I Do After the Medical Exam and Follow-Up (If Required) Are Completed?

You and the applicant should sign your respective certifications. After the medical exam (and any follow-up if required) is complete, write the results in **Part 2** of the Form I-693 as they relate to the specific component of the medical exam. The applicant should sign the certification in **Part 1** and you should sign the civil surgeon's certification in **Part 5**. All signatures on the form must be originals (no stamps or facsimiles). **Do not sign the form or have the applicant sign the form** until the applicant has met all health follow-up requirements.

Give the results to the applicant. Give the completed Form I-693 to the applicant in a sealed envelope. On the front of the envelope write in capital letters: "**DO NOT OPEN. FOR USCIS USE ONLY.**" On the back of the envelope, write your initials across the line where the flap of the envelope and the envelope meet. Then, with clear cellophane tape, place the tape with half on the flap of the envelope and half on the envelope across the envelope's entire width (and across your initials). USCIS will not accept Form I-693 if it is not in a sealed envelope or if the envelope is altered in any way. Also, you should keep a copy of the I-693 for your records.

Return all supporting medical documents to the applicant and give them a copy of the vaccination record. Return all supporting medical documents, including chest X-rays (if obtained), directly to the applicant. In addition, give the applicant a copy of the completed vaccination record in **Part 2**. This will serve as the applicant's official vaccination record and may be retained by the applicant for future use in establishing compliance with vaccination requirements. (Example: school, day care, employment, etc.)

Section III. Frequently Asked Questions

1. What if I am a refugee and already had a medical exam overseas?

If you were admitted to the United States as a refugee and are now applying for adjustment of status one year following your first admission, you do not need to repeat the entire medical exam you had overseas, unless a Class A medical condition was found during that exam.

If a complete medical exam is not required, you only need to comply with the vaccination requirements. This means you only need to complete **Part 1**, Information about you, and the vaccination section of **Part 2**, not Form I-693. Contact your State or local refugee health coordinator to find out whether it may be possible for you to have the vaccination portion of Form I-693 completed by a State or local health department. The State or local health department must also complete **Part 6** of the Form.

2. What if I am a K nonimmigrant visa holder and already had a medical exam overseas?

If you were admitted as a:

A. K-1 fiancé(e) or a K-2 child of a K-1 fiancé(e), or as a

B. K-3 spouse of a U.S. citizen or a K-4 child of a K-3 spouse of a U.S. citizen, and

C. You received a medical examination prior to admission, then-

    a. You are not required to have another medical examination as long as your Form I-485, Application to Register Permanent Residence or Adjust Status, is filed within one year of your overseas medical examination.

    b. You will, however, be required to complete **Part 1**, Information about you, and submit the vaccination section of **Part 2** with your adjustment of status application. A designated civil surgeon must complete the vaccination section and **Part 5**, the Civil Surgeon's Certification.

3. What if I am a V nonimmigrant visa holder and already had a medical exam overseas?

If you were admitted to the United States or obtained status while in the United States as a:

A. V-1 spouse of a permanent resident or awaiting a V-1 visa, or as a

B. V-2 child of a V-1 spouse of a permanent resident, or as a

C. V-3 child of a V-2 unmarried son or daughter of a V-1 spouse of a permanent resident, and

D. You received a medical examination prior to admission or obtaining V status, then-

    a. You are not required to have another medical examination as long as your Form I-485, Application to Register Permanent Residence or Adjust Status, is filed within one year of your overseas medical examination.

    b. You will, however, be required to **Part 1**, Information about you, and submit the vaccination section of **Part 2** with your adjustment of status application. A designated civil surgeon must complete the vaccination section and **Part 5**, the Civil Surgeon's Certification.

4. May any doctor perform the required medical exam?

Only a doctor who has been specially designated by USCIS as a civil surgeon may perform the medical exam. USCIS will not accept a Form I-693 completed by a doctor who is not a **currently** designated civil surgeon.

5. How do I know whether a doctor is a designated civil surgeon?

You can obtain a list of the designated civil surgeons by calling the USCIS National Customer Service Center at **1-800-375-5283**, visiting the civil surgeon page from the USCIS website at **www.uscis.gov** and clicking on the Civil Surgeon Locator link, or by visiting your local USCIS office.

NOTE: If you choose to visit your local USCIS office, you must first get an InfoPass appointment. For information on **InfoPass**, visit the USCIS website at **www. uscis.gov**.

6. Who pays for the medical exam?

The applicant is responsible for paying all costs of the medical exam, including the cost of any follow-up tests or treatment that may be required. Payments are made directly to the civil surgeon or other health care facility.

7. What are the medical grounds of inadmissibility?

The medical grounds of inadmissibility under U.S. immigration laws are divided into four categories communicable diseases of public health significance, lack of required vaccinations, physical or mental disorders with harmful behavior, and drug abuse/drug addiction. The civil surgeon is required to perform a general physical exam and specific evaluations, as described below.

Communicable Diseases of Public Health Significance

The civil surgeon is required to perform specific tests for TB, syphilis, and human immunodeficiency virus (HIV) infection. The medical exam also indicates an evaluation for other sexually transmitted diseases and Hansen's Disease (leprosy).

To test for:	Then:
Tuberculosis (TB)	All applicants two years of age and older are required to have a tuberculin skin test (TST) given by the Mantoux technique. **(Civil surgeons may require an applicant younger than two years to undergo a TST if there is evidence of contact with a person known to have tuberculosis or other reason to suspect tuberculosis.)** After the skin test, the applicant will need to return to the civil surgeon within 48 to 72 hours to have the results read. If you have a reaction of four millimeters or less, generally you will not need any further tests for TB. A chest X-ray is required when the reaction to the TST is five millimeters or more. The civil surgeon will explain the medical requirements to you in more detail.
Syphilis	All applicants age 15 and older must have a blood test for syphilis. Civil surgeons may require applicants under age 15 to be tested if there is reason to suspect the possibility of infection.
HIV	All applicants age 15 or older must have a blood test for HIV. Civil surgeons can require applicants under age 15 to be tested for HIV if there is reason to suspect the possibility of infection. Civil surgeons are required to provide pre-test counseling to all applicants who take the HIV test. Civil surgeons are also required to provide post-test counseling to any applicant who tests positive for HIV.

If you are found to have a communicable disease of public health significance, the civil surgeon will advise you how to obtain any necessary treatment. It also may be necessary for you to apply for a waiver of inadmissibility. USCIS will advise you if this is necessary. To obtain more information about this waiver, visit the USCIS website at **www.uscis.gov**.

Vaccination Requirements

All applicants for adjustment of status must present documents showing they have been vaccinated against a broad range of vaccine-preventable diseases. The civil surgeon will review your vaccination history with you to determine whether you have all the required vaccinations. Make sure you take your vaccination records with you to your appointment with the civil surgeon.

NOTE: Please do not attempt to meet the requirements before you are evaluated by the civil surgeon, in case it is not medically appropriate for you to have one or more of the required vaccines.

By law, the required vaccines include: mumps, measles, rubella, polio, tetanus and diphtheria toxoids, pertussis, influenza, hepatitis B, haemophilus influenzae type B, varicella, pneumococcal, rotavirus, hepatitis A, meningococcal, human papillomavirus, zoster, and any other vaccinations recommended by the Advisory Committee for Immunization Practices (ACIP).

If you never received or are unable to prove you received certain vaccines, the civil surgeon can administer them to you. After evaluation by the civil surgeon, you also have the option of asking your family doctor to administer those vaccines to you and showing the records to the civil surgeon to note on Form I-693.

If you initially did not have documents proving you received all the required vaccines but later submit those documents, or if the civil surgeon certifies that it is not medically appropriate for you to have one or more of the missing vaccine(s), USCIS may grant you a waiver based on the civil surgeon's certification on the vaccination supplement.

HHS has determined that a vaccine is "not medically appropriate" if : **(a)** the vaccine is not recommended for your specific age group; **(b)** there is a medical reason why it would not be safe to have the vaccine (for example, allergies to eggs and yeast, pregnancy, hypersensitivity to prior vaccines, or other medical reasons); or **(c)** you are unable to complete the entire series of a required vaccine within a reasonable amount of time.

If you object to receiving the recommended vaccinations because of your sincerely held religious beliefs or moral convictions, you may apply for a waiver of these requirements. If you hold these objections, inform the civil surgeon that you will apply for a waiver. If the waiver application is denied, you may be ineligible for the immigration benefit that you are seeking. To obtain more information about these waivers, visit the USCIS website at **www.uscis.gov**.

Physical or Mental Disorders

Are all physical or mental disorders considered health-related grounds of inadmissibility?

No. The emphasis is more on the behavior associated with the physical or mental disorder, instead of the physical or mental disorder itself. This means that the civil surgeon must determine that there is behavior associated with the disorder that is harmful either to you, to others, or to property. If you have had a history of a physical or a mental disorder, there must be associated harmful behavior that is likely to recur in order for you to be considered inadmissible.

The civil surgeon will ask you general questions during the medical exam to determine whether you have such a condition. Depending on the outcome of the initial exam, the civil surgeon may find it necessary to refer you to a specialist for further testing.

If the civil surgeon finds that you have a physical or mental disorder with associated harmful behavior, you may apply for a waiver according to the terms, conditions, and controls determined necessary by USCIS in consultation with HHS. To obtain more information about these waivers, visit the USCIS website at **www.uscis.gov**.

Drug Addiction/Drug Abuse

What are the guidelines for determining whether someone is a drug abuser/drug addict?

The civil surgeon will review your medical history during the medical exam and ask you questions necessary to determine whether you are currently using or have used in the past any drugs or other psychoactive substances. The medical guidelines for determining drug abuse and drug addiction are determined by HHS.

If the civil surgeon determines you have a medical condition of drug addiction/abuse, you are **not** eligible to apply for a waiver **unless** you are applying for adjustment of status one year after you were admitted as a refugee, or you are applying for adjustment of status one year after you were granted asylum. If you are ineligible to apply for a waiver, but are later found by the civil surgeon to be in remission from the drug abuse or drug addiction (as determined by HHS), you may proceed with your adjustment of status application, if eligible.

Section IV. USCIS Information

How Do I Get USCIS Forms and Related Information?

To request USCIS forms, call our toll-free forms line at **1-800-870-3676**. You may also obtain USCIS forms and information about immigration laws and regulations, policy, and procedures by calling our National Customer Service Center at **1-800-375-5283** or visiting the USCIS Internet website at **www.uscis.gov**.

Address Changes. If you change your address, you must fill out and give us a Form AR-11, Alien's Change of Address Card. Mail the completed form to:

> **U.S. Citizenship and Immigration Services**
> **Change of Address**
> **P.O. Box 7134**
> **London, KY 40742-7134**

For commercial overnight or fast freight services only, mail to:

> **U.S. Citizenship and Immigration Services**
> **Change of Address**
> **1084-I South Laurel Road**
> **London, KY 40744**

You may also complete Form AR-11, Alien's Change of Address Card, on the USCIS Internet website at **www.uscis.gov**.

Visiting a USCIS Office in Person - InfoPass. To visit a USCIS office in person, you must first have an appointment. **InfoPass** is an Internet-based system that allows you to make an appointment to talk to an Immigration Information Officer in person. To access **InfoPass**, log onto the Internet website at **www.uscis.gov**.

Processing Information

Initial Processing. Once the application has been accepted, it will be checked for completeness, including submission of the required initial evidence. If you do not completely fill out the form or file it without the required initial evidence, you will not establish a basis for eligibility and we may deny your application.

Requests for More Information. We may request more information or evidence, or we may request that you appear at a USCIS office for an interview. Unless specifically required that an original document be filed with an application or petition, an ordinary legible photocopy (standard 8 1/2 x 11 letter size) may be submitted. Original documents submitted when not required will remain a part of the record.

Decision. The decision on the Form I-693 involves a determination of whether you have established eligibility for the requested benefit. You will be notified of the decision in writing.

Privacy Act Notice

We ask for the information on this form, and associated evidence, to determine if you have established eligibility for the immigration benefit for which you are filing. Our legal right to ask for this information can be found in the Immigration and Nationality Act, as amended. We may provide this information to other government agencies. Failure to provide this information, and any requested evidence, may delay a final decision or result in denial of your Form I-693.

Penalties

If you knowingly and willfully falsify or conceal a material fact or submit a false document with this Form I-693, we will deny the Form I-693 and may deny any other immigration benefit.

In addition, you will face severe penalties provided by law and may be subject to criminal prosecution.

Paperwork Reduction Act

An agency may not conduct or sponsor an information collection and a person is not required to respond to a collection of information unless it displays a currently valid OMB control number. The public reporting burden for this collection of information is estimated at 2 hours, 30 minutes per response, including the time for reviewing instructions, completing and submitting the form. Send comments regarding this burden estimate or any other aspect of this collection of information, including suggestions for reducing this burden, to: U.S. Citizenship and Immigration Services, Regulatory Management Division, 111 Massachusetts Avenue, N.W., 3rd Floor, Suite 3008, Washington, DC 20529, OMB No. 1615-0033. **Do not mail your application to this address.**

Department of Homeland Security
U.S. Citizenship and Immigration Services

I-693, Report of Medical
Examination and Vaccination Record

START HERE - Please type or print in CAPITAL letters *(Use black ink)*

Part 1. Information about you *(The person requesting a medical examination or vaccinations must complete this part)*

Family Name (Last Name)

Given Name (First Name)

Full Middle Name

Home Address: Street Number and Name

Apt. Number

Gender:
☐ Male   ☐ Female

City

State

Zip Code

Phone # *(Include Area Code) no dashes or ()*

Date of Birth *(mm/dd/yyyy)*   Place of Birth *(City/Town/Village)*   Country of Birth   A-number *(if any)*   U.S. Social Security # *(if any)*

Applicant's Certification

I certify under penalty of perjury under United States law that I am the person who is identified in **Part 1** of this Form I-693, Report of Medical Examination and Vaccination Record, and that the information in **Part 1** of this form is true to the best of my knowledge. I understand the purpose of this medical exam, and I authorize the required tests and procedures to be completed. If it is determined that I willfully misrepresented a material fact or provided false/altered information or documents with regard to my medical exam, I understand that any immigration benefit I derived from this medical exam may be revoked, that I may be removed from the United States, and that I may be subject to civil or criminal penalties.

Signature - Do not sign or date this form until instructed to do so by the civil surgeon

Date *(mm/dd/yyyy)*

Part 2. Medical examination *(The civil surgeon completes this part)*

1. Examination

Date of First
Examination

Date(s) of Follow-up Examination(s) if Required:

Date of Exam

Date of Exam

Date of Exam

Summary of Overall Findings:

☐ No Class A or Class B Condition   ☐ Class A Conditions (see **2** through **5** below)   ☐ Class B Conditions (see **2** through **6** below)

2. Communicable Diseases of Public Health Significance

A. Tuberculosis (TB)

☐ Tuberculin Skin Test (TST) (Required for applicants 2 years of age and older; for children under 2 years of age, see pp. 11-12 of Technical Instructions at **http://www.cdc.gov/ncidod/dq/civil.htm.**)

Date TST Applied

Date TST Read

Size of Reaction *(mm)*

☐ Chest X-Ray - Required **ONLY** for TST reactions of ≥ 5mm or if specific TST exception criteria met, or for an applicant with TB symptoms or immunosuppression (e.g., HIV). **Attach copy of X-Ray Report.**

Date Chest X-Ray
Taken

Date Chest X-Ray
Read

Results
☐ Normal
☐ Abnormal (Describe results in remarks.)

Findings:

☐ No Class A or Class B TB   ☐ Class B1 Pulmonary TB   ☐ Class B2 Pulmonary TB   ☐ Class B, Other Chest Condition (non-TB)
☐ Class A Pulmonary TB Disease   ☐ Class B1 Extra Pulmonary TB   ☐ Class B, Latent TB Infection

Remarks: (Include any signs or symptoms of TB, additional tests, and therapy given, with stop and start dates and any changes.)

Part 2. Medical Examination *(Continued)*

B. Syphilis

☐ Serologic Test for Syphilis (Required for applicants 15 years and older)

Date Screening Run

[   ]

☐ Screening Nonreactive

☐ Screening Reactive, Titer 1: [   ]

If Reactive, Date Confirmation Run

[   ]

☐ Confirmation Nonreactive

☐ Confirmation Reactive

Findings:

☐ No Class A or Class B Syphilis   ☐ Syphilis, Class A (untreated)   ☐ Syphilis, Class B (with residual deficit, treated in the past year)

Remarks: (Include any therapy given with doses and dates.)

[   ]

C. HIV/AIDS

☐ Serologic Test for HIV Antibody (Required for applicants 15 years and older)

Date Screening Run

[   ]

☐ Screening Negative

☐ Screening Positive

☐ Screening Indeterminate

If Positive or Indeterminate, Date Confirmation Run

[   ]

☐ Confirmation Negative

☐ Confirmation Positive

Findings:

☐ No Class A HIV   ☐ HIV, Class A

Remarks: (Include any signs or symptoms of HIV infection, therapy given, and any counseling, or referrals.)

[   ]

D. Other Class A/Class B Conditions for Communicable Diseases of Public Health Significance

Findings:

☐ Chancroid, Class A   ☐ Gonorrhea, Class A   ☐ Hansen's Disease (Leprosy, Infectious), Class A

☐ Granuloma Inguinale, Class A   ☐ Lymphogranuloma Venereum, Class A   ☐ Hansen's Disease (Leprosy, Noninfectious), Class B

Remarks: (Include any therapy given and any counseling, or referrals.)

[   ]

---

3. Physical or Mental Disorders With Associated Harmful Behavior

☐ Physical/Mental Disorder, With Associated Harmful Behavior, Class A

☐ Physical/Mental Disorder, Without Associated Harmful Behavior, Class B

Remarks: (Include diagnosis, with likelihood of harmful behavior to recur, therapy given, and any counseling, or referrals.)

[   ]

---

4. Drug Abuse/Drug Addiction

☐ Substance (Drug) Use, Listed in Section 202 of Controlled Substance Act, Class A

☐ Substance (Drug) Use, Not Listed in Section 202 of Controlled Substance Act, But With Associated Harmful Behavior, Class A

☐ Prior Substance (Drug) Use in Remission, Class B

Remarks: (Include any therapy given, rehabilitation, counseling, or referrals.)

[   ]

Part 2. Medical examination   *(Continued)*

5. Vaccinations (See Technical Instructions at **http://www.cdc.gov/ncidod/dq/civil.htm** for list of required vaccines.)

Vaccine History Transferred From a Written Record				Vaccine Given	Completed Series	Waiver(s) to Be Requested From USCIS			
						Blanket			
						Not Medically Appropriate			
Vaccine	Date Received mm/dd/yyyy	Date Received mm/dd/yyyy	Date Received mm/dd/yyyy	Date Given by Civil Surgeon mm/dd/yyyy	Mark an X if completed; write date of lab test if immune or "VH" if varicella history	Not Age Appropriate	Contra-indication	Insufficient Time Interval	Not Flu Season
Specify Vaccine: DT ☐ DTP ☐ DTaP ☐									██
Specify Vaccine: Td ☐ Tdap ☐									██
Specify Vaccine: OPV ☐ IPV ☐									██
MMR (Measles Mumps-Rubella) or if monovalent or other combination of the vaccines are given, specify vaccine(s):									██
Hib									██
Hepatitis B									██
Varicella									██
Pneumococcal									██
Influenza									
Rotavirus									██
Hepatitis A									██
Meningococcal									██
Human Papillomavirus									██
Zoster									██

Give Copy to Applicant

Results:
☐ Applicant may be eligible for blanket waiver(s) as indicated above.
☐ Applicant will request an individual waiver based on religious or moral convictions.
☐ Vaccine history complete for each vaccine, all requirements met.
☐ Applicant does not meet immunization requirements.

A-number *(if any)*

Name *(Type or print your name)*

Part 2. Medical examination   *(Continued)*

6. List other medical conditions, Class B other (e.g. hypertension, diabetes)

Part 3. Referral to health department or other doctor/facility   *(To be completed by Civil Surgeon, if referral was made)*

Type or Print Name of Doctor or Health Department

Date of Referral *(mm/dd/yyyy)*

Address: (Street Number and Name, City, State and Zip Code)

Daytime Phone # *(Include Area Code) no dashes or ( )*

Remarks: (Include name of medical condition and reasons for referral.)

Part 4. To Be Completed by Physician or Health Department Performing Referral Evaluation

The applicant identified on this form was referred to me by the civil surgeon named in **Part 5** of this form. I have provided appropriate evaluation/treatment.

Type or Print Full Name of Evaluating Physician or Health Department

Signature

Address: (Street Number and Name, City, State and Zip Code)

Date *(mm/dd/yyyy)*

Name of Medical Practice or Health Department

Daytime Phone # *(Include Area Code) no dashes or ( )*

Remarks: (Attach a separate sheet of paper, if needed.)

Part 5.   Civil Surgeon's Certification *(Do not sign form or have the applicant sign in Part 1 until all health follow-up requirements have been met.)*

I certify under penalty of perjury under United States law that: I am a civil surgeon in current status designated to examine applicants seeking certain immigration benefits in the United States; I have a currently valid and unrestricted license to practice medicine in the state where I am performing medical examinations; I performed this examination of the person identified in **Part 1** of this Form I-693, after having made every reasonable effort to verify that person whom I examined is the person identified in **Part 1**; that I performed the examination in accordance with the Centers for Disease Control and Prevention's *Technical Instructions*, and all supplemental information or updates provided to me; and that all information provided by me on this form is true and correct to the best of my information, knowledge, and belief.

Type or Print Full Name   *(First, Middle, Last)*

Signature

Address (Street Number and Name, City, State and Zip Code)

Date *(mm/dd/yyyy)*

Name of Medical Practice or Health Department

Daytime Phone # *(Include Area Code) no dashes or ( )*

E-Mail Address

Part 6. Health department identifying information. *(If completed by State or local health department on behalf of a refugee, place a stamp or seal where indicated.)*

Type or Print Name

(Place State or local health department stamp/seal below.)

Signature

Date *(mm/dd/yyyy)*

Daytime Phone #   *(Include Area Code) no dashes or ( )*

Department of Homeland Security
U.S. Citizenship and Immigration Services

Instructions for I-751, Petition to Remove Conditions on Residence

Instructions

Please read these instructions carefully to properly complete this form. If you need more space to complete an answer, use a separate sheet(s) of paper. Write your name and Alien Registration Number (A #), if any, at the top of each sheet of paper and indicate the section and number of the item to which the answer refers.

What Is the Purpose of This Form?

This form is for a conditional resident who obtained such status through marriage to petition to U.S. Citizenship and Immigration Services (USCIS) to remove the conditions on his or her residence.

Who May File Form I-751?

If you were granted conditional resident status through marriage to a U.S. citizen or permanent resident, use this form to petition for the removal of those conditions.

If you are still married, the petition should be filed jointly by you and the spouse through whom you obtained conditional status. However, you may apply for a waiver of this joint filing requirement if:

1. You entered the marriage in good faith, but your spouse subsequently died;

2. You entered the marriage in good faith, but the marriage was later terminated due to divorce or annulment;

3. You entered the marriage in good faith and have remained married, but have been battered or subjected to extreme cruelty by your U.S. citizen or permanent resident spouse; or

4. The termination of your status and removal would result in extreme hardship.

Conditional Resident Children

In Part 5 of the form, please make sure to include any conditional resident children applying with you in order to have their conditional basis removed, or they may file separately. Please remember to provide their A-number.

When Should I File Form I-751?

1. **Filing jointly.** If you are filing this petition jointly with your spouse, you must file it during the **90 days** immediately before the second anniversary of the date you were accorded conditional resident status. This is the date your conditional residence expires.

2. **Filing with a request that the joint filing requirement be waived.** You may file this petition at any time after you are granted conditional resident status and before you are removed.

3. **Effect of not filing.** If this petition is not filed, you will automatically lose your permanent resident status as of the second anniversary of the date on which you were granted conditional status.

You will then become removable from the United States. If your failure to file was through no fault of your own, you may file your petition late with a written explanation and request that USCIS excuse the late filing. Failure to file before the expiration date may be excused if you demonstrate when you submit the application that the delay was due to extraordinary circumstances beyond your control and that the length of the delay was reasonable.

General Instructions

Step 1. Fill Out Form I-751

1. Type or print legibly in black ink.

2. If extra space is needed to complete any item, attach a continuation sheet, indicate the item number, and date and sign each sheet.

3. Answer all questions fully and accurately. State that an item is not applicable with "N/A." If the answer is none, write "NONE."

Translations. Any document containing a foreign language submitted to the Service shall be accompanied by a full English language translation which the translator has certified as complete and accurate, and by the translator's certification that he or she is competent to translate from the foreign language into English.

Copies. Unless specifically required that an original document be filed with an application or petition, an ordinary legible photocopy may be submitted. Original documents submitted when not required will remain a part of the record, even if the submission was not required.

What Initial Evidence Is Required?

Permanent Resident Card
You must file your petition with a copy of your Permanent Resident Card or Alien Registration Card, and a copy of the Permanent Resident or Alien Registration cards of any of your conditional resident children you are including in your petition. Submit copies of both front and back sides of the card.

Exception
Those who reside overseas pursuant to military or government orders, including conditional resident dependents residing overseas and listed under Part 5 of the form, must submit the following items with Form I-751:

1. Two passport-style photos for applicants and dependents, regardless of age.

2. Two completed fingerprint cards (Form FD-258) for applicants and dependents between the ages of 14 and 79. You must indicate your Alien Registration Number (A#) on the fingerprint card and ensure that the completed cards are not bent, folded, or creased. The fingerprint cards must be prepared by a U.S. Embassy or U.S. consulate, USCIS Office, or U.S. Military installation.

In order for USCIS to identify filings based on military or government orders, applicants are required to indicate on top of Form I-751, **"ACTIVE MILITARY"** or **"GOVERNMENT ORDERS"** and submit a copy of their current military or government orders.

Evidence of the Relationship
Submit copies of documents indicating that the marriage upon which you were granted conditional status was entered in "good faith" and was not for the purpose of circumventing immigration laws. Submit copies of as many documents as you wish to establish this fact and to demonstrate the circumstances of the relationship from the date of the marriage to the present date, and to demonstrate any circumstances surrounding the end of the relationship, if it has ended. The documents should cover, but not limited to, the following examples:

1. Birth certificate(s) of child(ren) born to the marriage.

2. Lease or mortgage contracts showing joint occupancy and/or ownership of your communal residence.

3. Financial records showing joint ownership of assets and joint responsibility for liabilities, such as joint savings and checking accounts, joint federal and state tax returns, insurance policies that show the other spouse as the beneficiary, joint utility bills, joint installments or other loans.

4. Other documents you consider relevant to establish that your marriage was not entered into in order to evade the U.S. immigration laws.

5. Affidavits sworn to or affirmed by at least two people who have known both of you since your conditional residence was granted and have personal knowledge of your marriage and relationship. (Such persons may be required to testify before an immigration officer as to the information contained in the affidavit.) The original affidavit must be submitted and also contain the following information regarding the person making the affidavit: his or her full name and address; date and place of birth; relationship to you or your spouse, if any; and full information and complete details explaining how the person acquired his or her knowledge. Affidavits must be supported by other types of evidence listed above.

If you are filing to waive the joint filing requirement due to the death of your spouse, also submit a copy of the death certificate with your petition.

If you are filing to waive the joint filing requirement because your marriage has been terminated, also submit a copy of the divorce decree or other document terminating or annulling the marriage with your petition.

If you are filing to waive the joint filing requirement because you and/or your conditional resident child were battered or subjected to extreme cruelty, also file your petition with the following:

A. Evidence of the physical abuse, such as copies of reports or official records issued by police, judges, medical personnel, school officials and representatives of social service agencies, and original affidavits as described under *Evidence of the Relationship*; or

B. Evidence of the abuse, such as copies of reports or official records issued by police, courts, medical personnel, school officials, clergy, social workers and other social service agency personnel. You may also submit any legal documents relating to an order of protection against the abuser or relating to any legal steps you may have taken to end the abuse. You may also submit evidence that you sought safe haven in a battered women's shelter or similar refuge, as well as photographs evidencing your injuries.

C. A copy of your divorce decree, if your marriage was terminated by divorce on grounds of physical abuse or extreme cruelty.

If you are filing for a waiver of the joint filing requirement because the termination of your status and removal would result in "extreme hardship," you must submit with your petition evidence that your removal would result in hardship significantly greater than the hardship encountered by other aliens who are removed from this country after extended stays. The evidence must relate only to those factors that arose since you became a conditional resident.

If you are a child filing separately from your parent, also submit your petition with a full explanation as to why you are filing separately, along with copies of any supporting documentation.

Criminal History
If you have ever been arrested or detained by any law enforcement officer for any reason, and no charges were filed, submit:

1. An original official statement by the arresting agency or applicable court order confirming that no charges were filed.

If you have ever been arrested or detained by any law enforcement officer for any reason, and charges were filed, or if charges were filed against you without an arrest, submit:

2. An original or court-certified copy of the complete arrest record and/or disposition for each incident, (e. g. dismissal order, conviction record, or acquittal order).

If you have ever been convicted or placed in an alternative sentencing program or rehabilitative program (such as a drug treatment or community service program), submit:

1. An original or court-certified copy of your sentencing record for each incident, and evidence that you completed your sentence, specifically;

    A. An original or certified copy of your probation or parole record, or

    B. Evidence that you completed an alternative sentencing program, or rehabilitative program set aside, sealed, expunged, or otherwise removed from your record, submit:

2. An original or court-certified copy of the court order vacating, setting aside, sealing, expunging, or otherwise removing the arrest or conviction, or

3. An original statement from the court that no record exists of your arrest or conviction.

NOTE: Unless a traffic incident was alcohol or drug related, you do not need to submit documentation for traffic fines and incidents that did not involve an actual arrest if the only penalty was a fine of less than $500.00 and or points on your driver's license.

Where to File?

If you live in Alaska, American Samoa, Arizona, California, Colorado, Guam, Hawaii, Idaho, Illinois, Indiana, Iowa, Kansas, Michigan, Minnesota, Missouri, Montana, Nebraska, Nevada, North Dakota, Ohio, Oregon, South Dakota, Utah, Washington, Wisconsin, or Wyoming, mail your petition to the California Service Center:

USCIS California Service Center
P.O. Box 10751
Laguna Niguel, CA 92607-1075

If you live in Alabama, Arkansas, Connecticut, Delaware, Washington, D.C., Florida, Georgia, Kentucky, Louisiana, Maine, Maryland, Massachusetts, Mississippi, New Hampshire, New Jersey, New Mexico, New York, North Carolina, Oklahoma, Pennsylvania, Puerto Rico, Rhode Island, South Carolina, Tennessee, Texas, Vermont, Virginia, U.S. Virgin Islands, or West Virginia, mail your petition to the Vermont Service Center:

USCIS Vermont Service Center
75 Lower Welden St.
P.O. Box 200
St. Albans, VT 05479-0001

NOTE: If you or your spouse are currently serving with or employed by the U.S. Government, either in a civilian or military capacity and assigned outside the United States, mail your petition to the USCIS Service Center having jurisdiction over your residence of record in the United States. Include a copy of the U.S. Government orders assigning you and your spouse abroad.

What Is the Filing Fee?

The filing fee for a Form is **$465.**

An additional biometric fee of **$80** is required when filing Form I-751. **After you submit Form I-751, USCIS will notify you about when and where to go for biometric services.**

You may submit one check or money order for both the application and biometric fees, for a total of **$545.00**.

NOTE: Each conditional resident dependent, eligible to be included on the principal applicant's Form I-751 and listed under Part 5 of Form I-751, is required to submit an additional biometric services fee of **$80.00**, including dependents residing overseas pursuant to military or government orders, regardless of age.

Use the following guidelines when you prepare your check or money order for the Form I-751 and the biometric service fee:

1. The check or money order must be drawn on a bank or other financial institution located in the United States and must be payable in U.S. currency; and

2. Make the check or money order payable to **U.S. Department of Homeland Security**, unless:

    A. If you live in Guam, make it payable to **Treasurer, Guam**.

    B. If you live in the U.S. Virgin Islands, make it payable to **Commissioner of Finance of the Virgin Islands**.

    C. If you live outside the United States, Guam, or the U.S. Virgin Islands, contact the nearest U.S. Embassy or consulate for instructions on the method of payment.

NOTE: Please spell out U.S. Department of Homeland Security; do not use the initials "USDHS" or "DHS."

How to Check If the Fees Are Correct?

The form and biometric fees on this form are current as of the edition date appearing in the lower right corner of this page. However, because USCIS fees change periodically, you can verify if the fees are correct by following one of the steps below:

1. Visit our website at **www.uscis.gov**, select "Immigration Forms" and check the appropriate fee;

2. Review the Fee Schedule included in your form package, if you called us to request the form; or

3. Telephone our National Customer Service Center at **1-800-375-5283** and ask for the fee information.

NOTE: If your Form I-751 requires payment of a biometric service fee for USCIS to take your fingerprints, photograph or signature, you can use the same procedure to obtain the correct biometric fee.

Address Changes

If you change your address and you have an application or petition pending with USCIS, you may change your address on-line at www.uscis.gov, click on "Change your address with USCIS" and follow the prompts or by completing and mailing Form AR-11, Alien's Change of Address Card, to:

> **U.S. Citizenship and Immigration Services**
> **Change of Address**
> **P.O. Box 7134**
> **London, KY 40742-7134**

For commercial overnight or fast freight services only, mail to:

> **U.S. Citizenship and Immigration Services**
> **Change of Address**
> **1084-I South Laurel Road**
> **London, KY 40744**

Processing Information

Acceptance. Any application that is not signed or accompanied by the correct fee will be rejected with a notice that the application is deficient. You may correct the deficiency and resubmit the application. However, an application is not considered properly filed until accepted by USCIS.

Initial Processing. Once the application has been accepted, it will be checked for completeness, including submission of the required initial evidence. If you do not completely fill out the form or file it without the required initial evidence, you will not establish a basis for eligibility and we may deny your application.

Requests for More Information. We may request more information or evidence, or we may request that you appear at a USCIS office for an interview. We may also request that you submit the originals of any copy. We will return these originals when they are no longer needed.

Decision. The decision on Form I-751 involves a determination of whether you have established eligibility for the requested benefit. You will be notified of the decision in writing.

USCIS Forms and Information

To order USCIS forms, call our toll-free number at **1-800-870-3676**. You can also get USCIS forms and information on immigration laws, regulations, and procedures by telephoning our National Customer Service Center at **1-800-375-5283** or visiting our internet website at **www.uscis. gov**.

As an alternative to waiting in line for assistance at your local USCIS office, you can now schedule an appointment through our internet-based system, **InfoPass**. To access the system, visit our website. Use the **InfoPass** appointment scheduler and follow the screen prompts to set up your appointment. **InfoPass** generates an electronic appointment notice that appears on the screen.

Penalties

If you knowingly and willfully falsify or conceal a material fact or submit a false document with your Form I-751, we will deny your Form I-751 and may deny any other immigration benefit.

In addition, you will face severe penalties provided by law and may be subject to criminal prosecution.

Privacy Act Notice

We ask for the information on this form, and associated evidence, to determine if you have established eligibility for the immigration benefit for which you are filing. Our legal right to ask for this information can be found in the Immigration and Nationality Act, as amended. We may provide this information to other government agencies. Failure to provide this information, and any requested evidence, may delay a final decision or result in denial of your Form I-751.

Paperwork Reduction Act

An agency may not conduct or sponsor an information collection and a person is not required to respond to a collection of information unless it displays a currently valid OMB control number. The public reporting burden for this collection of information is estimated at 3 hours and 20 minutes per response, including the time for reviewing instructions, and completing and submitting the form. Send comments regarding this burden estimate or any other aspect of this collection of information, including suggestions for reducing this burden, to: U.S. Citizenship and Immigration Services, Regulatory Management Division, 111 Massachusetts Avenue, N.W., 3rd Floor, Suite 3008, Washington, DC 20529. OMB No. 1615-0038. **Do not mail your application to this address.**

Department of Homeland Security
U.S. Citizenship and Immigration Services

I-751, Petition to Remove Conditions on Residence

START HERE - Please type or print in black ink.

Part 1. Information About You

Family Name (Last Name)	Given Name (First Name)	Full Middle Name

Address: (Street number and name) | Apt. #

C/O: (In care of)

City	State/Province

Country	Zip/Postal Code

Mailing Address, if different than above (Street number and name): | Apt. #

C/O: (In care of)

City	State/Province

Country	Zip/Postal Code

Date of Birth (mm/dd/yyyy)	Country of Birth	Country of Citizenship

Alien Registration Number (#A)	Social Security # (If any)

Conditional Residence Expires on (mm/dd/yyyy)	Daytime Phone # (Area/Country codes)

Part 2. Basis for Petition   *(Check one)*

a. ☐ My conditional residence is based on my marriage to a U.S. citizen or permanent resident, and we are filing this petition together.

b. ☐ I am a child who entered as a conditional permanent resident and I am unable to be included in a joint Petition to Remove the Conditions on Residence (Form 1-751) filed by my parent(s)

OR

My conditional residence is based on my marriage to a U.S. citizen or permanent resident, but I am unable to file a joint petition and I request a waiver because: **(Check one)**

c. ☐ My spouse is deceased.

d. ☐ I entered into the marriage in good faith but the marriage was terminated through divorce or annulment.

e. ☐ I am a conditional resident spouse who entered a marriage in good faith, and during the marriage I was battered by or was the subject of extreme cruelty by my U.S. citizen or permanent resident spouse or parent.

f. ☐ I am a conditional resident child who was battered by or subjected to extreme cruelty by my U.S. citizen or conditional resident parent(s).

g. ☐ The termination of my status and removal from the United States would result in an extreme hardship.

For USCIS Use Only

Returned	Receipt
Date	
Date	
Resubmitted	
Date	
Date	
Reloc Sent	
Date	
Date	
Reloc Rec'd	
Date	
Date	
☐ Petitioner Interviewed on _____	

Remarks

Action Block

To Be Completed by
Attorney or Representative, if any.

☐ Fill in box if G-28 is attached to represent the applicant.

ATTY State License #

Part 3. Additional Information About You

1. Other Names Used *(including maiden name):*

2. Date of Marriage *(mm/dd/yyyy)*   **3.** Place of Marriage   **4.** If your spouse is deceased, give the date of death *(mm/dd/yyyy)*

5. Are you in removal, deportation, or rescission proceedings? ☐ Yes ☐ No

6. Was a fee paid to anyone other than an attorney in connection with this petition? ☐ Yes ☐ No

7. Have you ever been arrested, detained, charged, indicted, fined, or imprisoned for breaking or violating any law or ordianance (excluding traffic regulations), or committed any crime which you were not arrested in the United States or abroad? ☐ Yes ☐ No

8. If you are married, is this a different marriage than the one through which conditional residence status was obtained? ☐ Yes ☐ No

9. Have you resided at any other address since you became a permanent resident? *(If yes, attach a list of all addresses and dates.)* ☐ Yes ☐ No

10. Is your spouse currently serving with or employed by the U.S. government and serving outside the United States? ☐ Yes ☐ No

If you answered "Yes" to any of the above, provide a detailed explanation on a separate sheet(s) of paper and refer to "What Initial Evidence Is Required?" to determine what criminal history documentation to include with your petition. Place your name and Alien Registration Number (A#) at the top of each sheet and give the number of the item that refers to your response.

Part 4. Information About the Spouse or Parent Through Whom You Gained Your Conditional Residence

Family Name   First Name   Middle Name

Address

Date of Birth *(mm/dd/yyyy)*   Social Security # *(if any)*   A# *(if any)*

Part 5. Information About Your Children-List all your children *(Attach other sheet(s) if necessary)*

Name *(First/Middle/Last)*	Date of Birth *(mm/dd/yyyy)*	A # *(If any)*	If in U.S., give address/immigration status	Living with you?
				☐ Yes ☐ No
				☐ Yes ☐ No
				☐ Yes ☐ No
				☐ Yes ☐ No
				☐ Yes ☐ No

Part 6. Signature.

Read the information on penalties in the instructions before completing this section. If you checked block "a" in Part 2, your spouse must also sign below.

I certify, under penalty of perjury of the laws of the United States of America, that this petition and the evidence submitted with it is all true and correct. If conditional residence was based on a marriage, I further certify that the marriage was entered in accordance with the laws of the place where the marriage took place and was not for the purpose of procuring an immigration benefit. I also authorize the release of any information from my records that the U.S. Citizenship and Immigration Services needs to determine eligibility for the benefit sought.

Signature   Print Name   Date *(mm/dd/yyyy)*

Signature of Spouse   Print Name   Date *(mm/dd/yyyy)*

NOTE: If you do not completely fill out this form or fail to submit any required documents listed in the instructions, you may not be found eligible for the requested benefit and this petition may be denied.

Part 7. Signature of Person Preparing Form, If Other than Above

I declare that I prepared this petition at the request of the above person and it is based on all information of which I have knowledge.

Signature   Print Name   Date *(mm/dd/yyyy)*

Firm Name and Address   Daytime Phone Number *(Area/Country codes)*

E-Mail Address *(If any)*

Department of Homeland Security
U.S. Citizenship and Immigration Services

Instructions for I-765, Application for Employment Authorization

Instructions

Read these instructions carefully to properly complete this form. If you need more space to complete an answer, use a separate sheet of paper. Write your name and Alien Registration Number (A-Number), if any, at the top of each sheet of paper and indicate the part and number of the item to which the answer refers.

The filing addresses provided on this form reflect the most current information as of the date this form was last printed. If you are filing Form I-765 more than 30 days after the latest edition date shown in the lower right-hand corner, please visit our website at www.uscis.gov **before you file**, and check the Forms and Fees page to confirm the correct filing address and version currently in use. Check the edition date located in the lower right-hand corner of the form. If the edition date on your Form I-765 matches the edition date listed for Form I-765 on the online Forms and Fees page, your version is current and will be accepted by USCIS. If the edition date on the online version is later, download a copy and use the online version. If you do not have Internet access, call the National Customer Service Center at 1-800-375-5283 to verify the current filing address and edition date. **Improperly filed forms will be rejected and the fee returned, with instructions to resubmit the entire filing using the current form instructions.**

Index

What Is the Purpose of This Form?

Certain aliens who are temporarily in the United States may file Form I-765, Application for Employment Authorization, to request an Employment Authorization Document (EAD). Other aliens who are authorized to work in the United States without restrictions should also use this form to apply to USCIS for a document evidencing such authorization. Please review **Eligibility Categories** to determine whether you should use this form.

If you are a lawful permanent resident, a conditional resident, or a nonimmigrant authorized to be employed with a specific employer under 8 CFR 274a.12(b), please do **not** use this form.

Definitions

Employment Authorization Document (EAD): Form I-688, Form I-688A, Form I-688B, Form I-766, or any successor document issued by USCIS as evidence that the holder is authorized to work in the United States.

Renewal EAD: An EAD issued to an eligible applicant at or after the expiration of a previous EAD issued under the same category.

Replacement EAD: An EAD issued to an eligible applicant when the previously issued EAD has been lost, stolen, mutilated, or contains erroneous information, such as a misspelled name.

Interim EAD: An EAD issued to an eligible applicant when USCIS has failed to adjudicate an application within 90 days of receipt of a properly filed EAD application, or within 30 days of a properly filed initial EAD application based on an asylum application filed on or after January 4, 1995. The interim EAD will be granted for a period not to exceed 240 days and is subject to the conditions noted on the document.

Who May File This Form I-765?

USCIS adjudicates a request for employment authorization by determining whether an applicant has submitted the required information and documentation, and whether the applicant is eligible. In order to determine your eligibility, you must identify the category in which you are eligible and fill in that category in **Question 16** on Form I-765. Enter only **one** of the following category numbers on the application form. For example, if you are a refugee applying for an EAD, you should write **"(a)(3)"** at **Question 16**.

For easier reference, the categories are subdivided as follows:

1. Asylee/Refugee Categories

A. Refugee--(a)(3). File your EAD application with either a copy of your Form I-590, Registration for Classification as Refugee, approval letter, or a copy of a Form I-730, Refugee/Asylee Relative Petition, approval notice.

B. Paroled as a Refugee--(a)(4). File your EAD application with a copy of your Form I-94, Arrival-Departure Record.

C. Asylee (Granted Asylum)--(a)(5). File your EAD application with a copy of the USCIS letter, or judge's decision, granting you asylum. It is not necessary to apply for an EAD as an asylee until 90 days before the expiration of your current EAD.

D. Asylum Applicant (With a Pending Asylum Application)Who Filed for Asylum on or After January 4, 1995--(c)(8). (For specific instructions for applicants with pending asylum claims, see Page 6).

2. Nationality Categories

A. Citizen of Micronesia, the Marshall Islands, or Palau--(a)(8). File your EAD application if you were admitted to the United States as a citizen of the Federated States of Micronesia (CFA/FSM), the Marshall Islands (CFA/MIS), or Palau, under agreements between the United States and the former trust territories.

B. Deferred Enforced Departure (DED) / Extended Voluntary Departure--(a)(11). File your EAD application with evidence of your identity and nationality.

C. Temporary Protected Status (TPS)--(a)(12). File your EAD application with Form I-821, Application for Temporary Protected Status. If you are filing for an initial EAD based on your TPS status, include evidence of identity and nationality as required by the Form I-821 instructions.

D. Temporary Treatment Benefits--(c)(19). For an EAD based on 8 CFR 244.5. Include evidence of nationality and identity as required by the Form I-821 instructions.

1. Extension of TPS status: Include a copy (front and back) of your last available TPS document: EAD, Form I-94, or approval notice.

2. Registration for TPS only without employment authorization: File Form I-765, Form I-821, and a letter indicating that this form is for registration purposes only. No fee is required for Form I-765 filed as part of TPS registration. (Form I-821 has separate fee requirements.)

E. NACARA Section 203 Applicants Who Are Eligible to Apply for NACARA Relief With USCIS--(c)(10). See the instructions to Form I-881, Application for Suspension of Deportation or Special Rule Cancellation of Removal, to determine if you are eligible to apply to USCIS for NACARA 203 relief.

If you are eligible, follow the instructions below and submit your Form I-765 at the same time you file your Form I-881 with USCIS:

1. If you are filing a Form I-881 with USCIS, file your EAD application at the same time and at the same filing location. Your response to Question 16 on the Form I-765 should be "(c)(10)."

2. If you have already filed your Form I-881 at the Service Center specified on Form I-881, and now wish to apply for employment authorization, your response to **Question 16** on Form I-765 should be **"(c)(10)."** You should file your EAD application at the Service Center designated in "Where to File?" of these instructions.

3. If you are a NACARA Section 203 applicant who previously filed Form I-881 with USCIS, and the application is still pending, you may renew your EAD. Your response to **Question 16** on Form I-765 should be **"(c)(10)."** Submit the required fee and the EAD application to the Service Center designated in "Where to File?" of these instructions.

F. Dependent of TECRO E-1 Nonimmigrant--(c) (2). File your EAD application with the required certification from the American Institute in Taiwan if you are the spouse or unmarried dependent son or daughter of an E-1 employee of the Taipei Economic and Cultural Representative Office.

3. Foreign Students

A. F-1 Student Seeking Optional Practical Training in an Occupation Directly Related to Studies: (c)(3)(A) - Pre-completion Optional Practical Training; (c)(3)(B) - Post-completion Optional Practical Training; (c)(3)(C) - 17-month extension for STEM Students (Students with a degree in Science, Technology, Engineering, or Mathematics). File your EAD application with a Certificate of Eligibility of Nonimmigrant (F-1) Student Status (Form I-20 A-B /I-20 ID) endorsed by a Designated School Official within the past 30 days. If you are a STEM student requesting a 17-month extension under the eligibility code (c)(3)(C), you must also submit a copy of your degree and the employer name as listed in E-Verify, along with the E-Verify Company Identification Number, or a valid E-Verify Client Company Identification Number, for the employer with whom you are seeking the 17-month OPT extension. This information must be provided in Item #17 of the form.

B. F-1 Student Offered Off-Campus Employment Under the Sponsorship of a Qualifying International Organization--(c)(3)(ii). File your EAD application with the international organization's letter of certification that the proposed employment is within the scope of its sponsorship, and a Certificate of Eligibility of Nonimmigrant (F-1) Student Status -- For Academic and Language Students (Form I-20 A-B/ -20 ID) endorsed by the Designated School Official within the past 30 days.

C. F-1 Student Seeking Off-Campus Employment Due to Severe Economic Hardship--(c)(3)(iii). File your EAD application with Form I-20 A-B/I-20 ID, Certificate of Eligibility of Nonimmigrant (F-1) Student Status -- For Academic and Language Students, and any evidence you wish to submit, such as affidavits, that detail the unforeseen economic circumstances that cause your request, and evidence that you have tried to find off-campus employment with an employer who has filed a labor and wage attestation.

D. J-2 Spouse or Minor Child of an Exchange Visitor--(c)(5). File your EAD application with a copy of your J-1's (principal alien's) Certificate of Eligibility for Exchange Visitor (J-1) Status (Form IAP-66). You must submit a written statement with any supporting evidence showing that your employment is not necessary to support the J-1 but is for other purposes.

E. M-1 Student Seeking Practical Training After Completing Studies--(c)(6). File your EAD application with a completed Form I-539, Application to Change/Extend Nonimmigrant Status. Form I-20 M-N, Certificate of Eligibility for Nonimmigrant (M-1) Student Status -- For Vocational Students endorsed by the Designated School Official within the past 30 days.

4. Eligible Dependents of Employees of Diplomatic Missions, International Organizations, or NATO

A. Dependent of A-1 or A-2 Foreign Government Officials--(c)(1). Submit your EAD application with Form I-566, Interagency Record of Request-A, G, or NATO Dependent Employment Authorization or Change/Adjustment to/from A, G, or NATO Status, Dependent Employment Authorization, through your diplomatic mission to the Department of State (DOS). The DOS will forward all favorably endorsed applications directly to the Nebraska Service Center for adjudication.

B. Dependent of G-1, G-3 or G-4 Nonimmigrant--(c)(4). Submit your EAD application with a Form I-566, Interagency Record of Request-A, G, or NATO Dependent Employment Authorization or Change/Adjustment to/from A, G, or NATO Status, Dependent Employment Authorization, through your international organization to the Department of State (DOS). [In New York City, the United Nations (UN) and UN missions should submit such applications to the United States Mission to the UN (USUN).] The DOS or USUN will forward all favorably endorsed applications directly to the Nebraska Service Center for adjudication.

C. Dependent of NATO-1 Through NATO-6--(c)(7). Submit your EAD application with Form I-566, Interagency Record of Request-A, G, or NATO Dependent Employment Authorization or Change/Adjustment to/from A, G, or NATO Status, Dependent Employment Authorization, to NATO SACLANT, 7857 Blandy Road, C-027, Suite 100, Norfolk, VA 23551-2490. NATO/SACLANT will forward all favorably endorsed applications directly to the Nebraska Service Center for adjudication.

5. Employment-Based Nonimmigrant Categories

A. B-1 Nonimmigrant Who Is the Personal or Domestic Servant of a Nonimmigrant Employer--(c)(17)(i). File the EAD application with:

1. Evidence from your employer that he or she is a B, E, F, H, I, J, L, M, O, P, R, or TN nonimmigrant and you were employed for at least one year by the employer before the employer entered the United States or your employer regularly employs personal and domestic servants and has done so for a period of years before coming to the United States; and

2. Evidence that you have either worked for this employer as a personal or domestic servant for at least one year, or evidence that you have at least one year's experience as a personal or domestic servant; and

3. Evidence establishing that you have a residence abroad which you have no intention of abandoning.

B. B-1 Nonimmigrant Domestic Servant of a U.S. Citizen--(c)(17)(ii). File your EAD application with:

1. Evidence from your employer that he or she is a U.S. citizen; and

2. Evidence that your employer has a permanent home abroad or is stationed outside the United States and is temporarily visiting the United States or the citizen's current assignment in the United States will not be longer than four years; and

3. Evidence that he or she has employed you as a domestic servant abroad for at least six months prior to your admission to the United States.

C. B-1 Nonimmigrant Employed by a Foreign Airline--(c)(17)(iii). File your EAD application with a letter from the airline fully describing your duties and indicating that your position would entitle you to E nonimmigrant status except for the fact that you are not a national of the same country as the airline or because there is no treaty of commerce and navigation in effect between the United States and that country.

D. Spouse of an E-1/E-2 Treaty Trader or Investor--(a)(17). File your EAD application with evidence of your lawful status and evidence you are a **spouse** of a principal E-1/E-2, such as your Form I-94. (Other relatives or dependents of E-1/E-2 aliens who are in E status are not eligible for employment authorization and may not file under this category.)

E. Spouse of an L-1 Intracompany Transferee--(a)(18). File your EAD application with evidence of your lawful status and evidence you are a **spouse** of a principal L-1, such as your Form I-94. (Other relatives or dependents of L-1 aliens who are in L status are not eligible for employment authorization and may not file under this category.)

6. Family-Based Nonimmigrant Categories

A. K-1 Nonimmigrant Fiance(e) of U.S. Citizen or K-2 Dependent--(a)(6). File your EAD application if you are filing within 90 days from the date of entry. This EAD cannot be renewed. Any EAD application other than for a replacement must be based on your pending application for adjustment under (c)(9).

B. K-3 Nonimmigrant Spouse of U.S. Citizen or K-4 Dependent--(a)(9). File your EAD application along with evidence of your admission such as copies of your Form I-94, passport, and K visa.

C. Family Unity Program--(a)(13). If you are filing for initial or extension Family Unity benefits complete and submit Form I-817, Application for Voluntary Departure Under the Family Unity Program. An EAD will be issued if your Form I-817 is approved; no I-765 application is necessary.

If your non-expired Family Unity EAD is lost or stolen, file Form I-765 with proper fee(s), along with a copy of your approval notice for Family Unity benefits, to request a replacement.

D. LIFE Family Unity (a)(14). If you are applying for initial employment authorization under Family Unity provisions of section 1504 of the LIFE Act Amendments, or an extension of such authorization, you should not be using this form. Please obtain and complete Form I-817, Application for Family Unity Benefits. If you are applying for a replacement EAD that was issued under LIFE Act Amendments Family Unity provisions, file your EAD application with the required evidence listed in the "Required Document" section of these instructions.

E. V-1, V-2, or V-3 Nonimmigrant--(a)(15). If you have been inspected and admitted to the United States with a valid V visa, file this application along with evidence of your admission, such as copies of your Form I-94, passport, and K visa. If you have been granted V status while in the United States, file this application along with evidence of your V status, such as an approval notice. If you are in the United States but you have not yet filed an application for V status, you may file this application at the same time as you file your application for V status. USCIS will adjudicate this application after adjudicating your application for V status.

7. EAD Applicants Who Have Filed for Adjustment of Status

A. Adjustment Applicant--(c)(9). File your EAD application with a copy of the receipt notice or other evidence that your Form I-485, Application for Permanent Residence or Adjust Status, is pending. You may file Form I-765 together with your Form I-485.

B. Adjustment Applicant Based on Continuous Residence Since January 1, 1972--(c)(16). File your EAD application with your Form I-485, Application for Permanent Residence; a copy of your receipt notice; or other evidence that the Form I-485 is pending.

C. Renewal EAD for National Interest Waiver Physicians: If you are filing for a renewal EAD based on your pending adjustment status and an approved National Interest Waiver Physician petition, you must also include evidence of your meaningful progress toward completing the national interest waiver obligation. Such evidence includes documentation of employment in any period during the previous 12 months (e.g., copies of W-2 forms). If you did not work as a national interest waiver physician during any period of the previous 12 months, you must explain and provide a statement of future intent to work in the national interest waiver employment.

8. Other Categories

A. N-8 or N-9 Nonimmigrant--(a)(7). File your EAD application with the required evidence listed in the "Required Document" section of these instructions.

B. Granted Withholding of Deportation or Removal (a)(10). File your EAD application with a copy of the Immigration Judge's order. It is not necessary to apply for a new EAD until 90 days before the expiration of your current EAD.

C. Applicant for Suspension of Deportation--(c)(10). File your EAD application with evidence that your Form I-881, Application for Suspension of Deportation, or EOIR-40, is pending.

D. Paroled in the Public Interest--(c)(11). File your EAD application if you were paroled into the United States for emergent reasons or reasons strictly in the public interest.

E. Deferred Action--(c)(14). File your EAD application with a copy of the order, notice, or document placing you in deferred action and evidence establishing economic necessity for an EAD.

F. Final Order of Deportation--(c)(18). File your EAD application with a copy of the order of supervision and a request for employment authorization which may be based on but not limited to the following:

1. Existence of a dependent spouse and/or children in the United States who rely on you for support;

2. Existence of economic necessity to be employed; and

3. Anticipated length of time before you can be removed from the United States.

G. LIFE Legalization Applicant--(c)(24). We encourage you to file your EAD application together with your Form I-485, Application to Register Permanent Residence or Adjust Status, to facilitate processing. However, you may file Form I-765 at a later date with evidence that you were a CSS, LULAC, or Zambrano class member applicant before October 1, 2000, and with a copy of the receipt notice or other evidence that your Form I-485 is pending.

H. T-1 Nonimmigrant--(a)(16). If you are applying for initial employment authorization as a T-1 nonimmigrant, file this form only if you did not request an employment authorization document when you applied for T nonimmigrant status. If you have been granted T nonimmigrant status and this is a request for a renewal or replacement of an employment authorization document, file this application along with evidence of your T nonimmigrant status, such as an approval notice.

I. T-2, T-3, or T-4 Nonimmigrant--(c)(25). File the form with a copy of your T-1's (principal alien's) approval notice and proof of your relationship to the T-1 principal.

J. U-1 Nonimmigrant--(a)(19). If you are applying for initial employment authorization as a U-1 nonimmigrant, file this form only if you did not request an employment authorization document when you applied for U nonimmigrant status. If you have been granted U nonimmigrant status and this is a request for a renewal or replacement of an employment authorization document, file this application along with evidence of your U nonimmigrant status, such as an approval notice.

K. U-2, U-3, U-4, or U-5--(a)(20). If you obtained U nonimmigrant status while in the United States, then you must submit a copy of the approval notice for your U nonimmigrant status. If you were admitted to the United States as a U nonimmigrant, then you must submit a copy of your passport with your U nonimmigrant visa.

Required Documentation

All applications must be filed with the documents required below, in addition to the particular evidence required for the category listed in "Who May File This Form I-765?" with fee, if required.

If you are required to show economic necessity for your category, submit a list of your assets, income, and expenses.

Please assemble the documents in the following order:

1. Your application with the filing fee. See **"What Is the Filing Fee?"** for details.

2. If you are mailing your application to USCIS, you must also submit:

   A. A copy of Form I-94, Arrival-Departure Record (front and back), if available. If you are filing Form I-765 under the(c) (9) category, Form I-94 is not required.

   B. A copy of your last EAD (front and back). If no prior EAD has been issued, you must submit a copy of a Federal Government-issued identity document, such as a passport showing your picture, name, and date of birth; a birth certificate with photo ID; a visa issued by a foreign consulate; or a national ID document with photo and/or fingerprint. The identity document photocopy must clearly show the facial features of the applicant and the biographical information.

   C. You **must** submit two identical color photographs of yourself taken within 30 days of filing your application. The photos must have a white to off-white background, be printed on thin paper with a glossy finish, and be unmounted and unretouched.

   The passport-style photos must be 2" by 2". The photos must be in color with full face, frontal view on a white to off-white background. Head height should measure 1" to 1 3/8" from top to bottom of chin, and eye height is between 1 1/8" to 1 3/8" from bottom of photo. Your head must be bare unless you are wearing a headdress as required by a religious order of which you are a member. Using pencil or felt pen, lightly print your name and Alien Receipt Number on the back of the photo.

Special Filing Instructions for Those With Pending Asylum Applications ((c)(8))

Asylum Applicant (with a pending asylum application) who filed for asylum on or after January 4, 1995. *You must wait at least 150 days following the filling of your asylum claim before you are eligible to apply for an EAD.*

Any delay in processing the asylum application that is caused by you, including unexcused failure to appear for fingerprinting and other biometric capture, will not be counted as part of that 150 days. If you fail to appear for your asylum interview or for a hearing before an immigration judge, you will be ineligible for an EAD. If you have received a recommended approval for a grant of asylum, you do not need to wait the 150 days and may apply for an EAD immediately upon receipt of your recommended approval. If you file your EAD application early, it will be denied. File your EAD application with:

1. A copy of the USCIS acknowledgement mailer which was mailed to you; or

2. Other evidence that your Form I-589 was filed with USCIS; or

3. Evidence that your Form I-589 was filed with an Immigration Judge at the Executive Office for Immigration Review (EOIR); or

4. Evidence that your asylum application remains under administrative or judicial review

Asylum applicant (with a pending asylum application) who filed for asylum and for withholding of deportation prior to January 4, 1995, and is *NOT* in exclusion or deportation proceedings.

You may file your EAD application at any time; however, it will only be granted if USCIS finds that your asylum application is not frivolous. File your EAD application with:

1. A complete copy of your previously filed Form I-589; AND

2. A copy of your USCIS receipt notice; or

3. A copy of the USCIS acknowledgement mailer; or

4. Evidence that your Form I-589 was filed with EOIR; or

5. Evidence that your asylum application remains under administrative or judicial review; or

6. A copy of the USCIS acknowledgement mailer.

Asylum applicant (with a pending asylum application) who filed an initial request for asylum prior to January 4, 1995, and *IS IN* exclusion or deportation proceedings. If you filed your Request for Asylum and Withholding of Deportation (Form I-589) prior to January 4, 1995, and you ARE IN exclusion or deportation proceedings, file your EAD application with:

1. A date-stamped copy of your previously filed Form I-589; or

2. A copy of Form I-221, Order to Show Cause and Notice of Hearing, or Form I-122, Notice to Applicant for Admission Detained for Hearing Before Immigration Judge; or

3. A copy of EOIR-26, Notice of Appeal, date stamped by the Office of the Immigration Judge; or

4. A date-stamped copy of a petition for judicial review or for *habeas corpus* issued to the asylum applicant; or

5. Other evidence that you filed an asylum application with EOIR.

Asylum application under the ABC Settlement Agreement--(c)(8). If you are a Salvadoran or Guatemalan national eligible for benefits under the ABC settlement agreement, American Baptist Churches v. Thornburgh , 760 F. Supp. 976 (N.D. Cal. 1991), please follow the instructions contained in this section when filing your Form I-765.

You must have an asylum application (Form I-589) on file either with USCIS or with an Immigration Judge in order to receive work authorization. Therefore, please submit evidence that you have previously filed an asylum application when you submit your EAD application. You are not required to submit this evidence when you apply, but it will help USCIS process your request efficiently.

If you are renewing or replacing your EAD, you must pay the filing fee.

Mark your application as follows:

1. Write "ABC" in the top right corner of your EAD application. You must identify yourself as an ABC class member if you are applying for an EAD under the ABC settlement agreement.

2. Write "(c)(8)" in **Section 16** of the application.

You are entitled to an EAD without regard to the merits of your asylum claim. Your application for an EAD will be decided within 60 days if: (1) you pay the filing fee, (2) you have a complete pending asylum application on file, and (3) write "ABC" in the top right corner of your EAD application. If you do not pay the filing fee for an initial EAD request, your request may be denied if USCIS finds that your asylum application is frivolous. However, if you cannot pay the filing fee for an EAD, you may qualify for a fee waiver under 8 CFR 103.7(c).

What Is the Filing Fee?

The filing fee for Form I-765 is $340.

Exceptions:

Initial EAD: If this is your initial application and you are applying under one of the following categories, a filing fee is **not** required:

1. (a)(3) Refugee;

2. (a)(4) Paroled as Refugee;

3. (a)(5) Asylee;

4. (a)(7) N-8 or N-9 nonimmigrant;

5. (a)(8) Citizen of Micronesia, Marshall Islands, or Palau;

6. (a)(10) Granted Withholding of Deportation;

7. (a)(11) Deferred Enforced Departure;

8. (a)(16) Victim of Severe Form of Trafficking (T-1);

9. (a)(19) U-1 Nonimmigrant;

10. (c)(1), (c)(4), or (c)(7) Dependent of certain foreign government, international organization, or NATO personnel; or

11. (c)(8) Applicant for asylum (an applicant filing under the special ABC procedures must pay the fee).

Renewal EAD: If this is a renewal application and you are applying under one of the following categories, a filing fee is **not** required:

1. (a)(8) Citizen of Micronesia, Marshall Islands, or Palau;

2. (a)(10) Granted Withholding of Deportation;

3. (a)(11) Deferred Enforced Departure; or

4. (c)(l), (c)(4), or (c)(7) Dependent of certain foreign government, international organization, or NATO personnel;

5. (c)(9) or (c)(16) Adjustment applicant who filed for adjustment under the fee structure implemented July 30, 2007.

Replacement EAD: If this is your replacement application, and you are applying under one of the following categories, a filing fee is **not** required:

1. (c)(l), (c)(4), or (c)(7) Dependent of certain foreign government, international organization, or NATO personnel.

NOTE: If you are requesting a replacement EAD under the (c)(9) or (c)(16) Adjustment applicant filed under the fee structure implemented July 30, 2007, then the full filing fee will be required; however, no biometrics fee is required.

Incorrect Card: No fee is required if you are filing only because the card issued to you was incorrect due to a USCIS administrative error. However, if the error was not caused by USCIS, both application and biometrics fees are required.

You may be eligible for a fee waiver under 8 CFR 103.7(c).

USCIS will use the Poverty Guidelines published annually by the U.S. Department of Health and Human Services as the basic criteria in determining the applicant's eligibility when economic necessity is identified as a factor.

The Poverty Guidelines will be used as a guide, but not as a conclusive standard, in adjudicating fee waiver requests for employment authorization applications requiring a fee.

Use the following guidelines when you prepare your check or money order for the Form I-765 fee:

1. The check or money order must be drawn on a bank or other financial institution located in the United States and must be payable in U.S. currency; and

2. Make the check or money order payable to **U.S. Department of Homeland Security**, unless:

    A. If you live in Guam, make it payable to **Treasurer, Guam**.

    B. If you live in the U.S. Virgin Islands, make it payable to **Commissioner of Finance of the Virgin Islands**.

NOTE: If you filed Form I-485, Application to Register Permanent Residence or Adjust Status, as of July 30, 2007, no fee is required to also file a request for employment authorization on Form I-765. You may file the I-765 concurrently with your I-485, or you may submit the I-765 at a later date. If you file Form I-765 separately, you must also submit a copy of your Form I-797C, Notice of Action, receipt as evidence of the filing of Form I-485 as of July 30, 2007.

NOTE: Please spell out U.S. Department of Homeland Security; do not use the initials "USDHS" or "DHS."

Notice to Those Making Payment by Check. If you send us a check, it will be converted into an electronic funds transfer (EFT). This means we will copy your check and use the account information on it to electronically debit your account for the amount of the check. The debit from your account will usually take 24 hours and will be shown on your regular account statement.

You will not receive your original check back. We will destroy your original check, but we will keep a copy of it. If the EFT cannot be processed for technical reasons, you authorize us to process the copy in place of your original check. If the EFT cannot be completed because of insufficient funds, we may try to make the transfer up to two times.

How to Check If the Fees Are Correct

The form fee on this form is current as of the edition date appearing in the lower right corner of this page. However, because USCIS fees change periodically, you can verify if the fees are correct by following one of the steps below:

1. Visit our website at **www.uscis.gov**, select "Immigration Forms," and check the appropriate fee;

2. Review the Fee Schedule included in your form package, if you called us to request the form; or

3. Telephone our National Customer Service Center at **1-800-375-5283** and ask for the fee information.

Where to File?

E-Filing Form I-765: Certain Form I-765 filings may be electronically filed (e-filed) with USCIS. Please view our website at www.uscis.gov for a list of who is eligible to e-file this form and instructions.

If your response to **Question 16** is **(a)(3)**, admitted as a refugee, **(a)(4)**, paroled as a refugee, **(a)(5)**, asylum granted, **(a)(7)**, N-8 or N-9 nonimmigrant, or **(a)(8)**, admitted as citizen of the Federated States of Micronesia or of the Marshall Islands, mail your application to:

> **USCIS**
> Nebraska Service Center
> P.O. Box 87765
> Lincoln, NE 68501-7765

For courier/express deliveries:

> **USCIS**
> Nebraska Service Center
> 850 S. Street
> Lincoln, NE 68508-1225

If your response to **Question 16** is:

1. **(a)(10)**, an alien granted withholding of deportation or removal;

2. **(c)(11)**, an alien paroled into the United States temporarily for emergency reasons, or reasons deemed strictly in the public interest;

3. **(c)(14)**, an alien who has been granted deferred action, (Exception: If the grant of deferred action was based on an approved Form I-360 filed for a battered or abused spouse or child, file your Form I-765 with the Vermont Service Center at the address below.);

4. **(c)(16)**, an alien who has filed an application for creation of record of lawful admission for permanent residence; or

5. **(c)(18)**, an alien against whom a final order of deportation or removal exists and who is released on an order of supervision, mail your application to the following address:

USCIS
P.O. Box 805887
Chicago, IL 60680-4120

If your response to **Question 16** is **(c)(14)**, an alien who has been granted deferred action based on an approved Form I-360 filed for a battered or abused spouse or child, **(a)(16)**, victim of trafficking, or **(c)(25)**, immediate family member of a T-1 victim of severe form of trafficking in persons, **(a)(19)** U-1 nonimmigrant, or **(a)(20)**, immediate family member of a U-1 victim of criminal activity, send your application to:

USCIS
Vermont Service Center
Attn: I-765
75 Lower Welden St.
St. Albans, VT 05479-0001

Note: This address may be used for both U.S. Postal Service and private courier deliveries.

If your response to **Question 16** is **(a)(14)**, an alien granted family unity benefits under Section 1504 of the LIFE Act, or **(c)(24)**, an alien who has filed for adjustment under section 1104 of the LIFE Act, mail your application to:

USCIS
P.O. Box 7219
Chicago, IL 60680-7219

If your response to **Question 16** is **(a)(15)**, any alien in V nonimmigrant status, mail your application to:

USCIS
P.O. Box 7216
Chicago, IL 60680-7216

If your response to **Question 16** is **(a)(12)**, alien granted Temporary Protected Status (TPS), or **(c)(19)**, alien who has a pending application for TPS, mail your application according to the instructions in the Federal Register notice for your particular country's TPS designation.

If you need to replace a valid lost, stolen, or mutilated Temporary Protected Status EAD, send your application to:

USCIS
Vermont Service Center
Attn: TPS
75 Lower Welden St.
St. Albans, VT 05479-0001

Note: This address may be used for both U.S. Postal Service and private courier deliveries.

If your response to **Question 16** is **(c)(1)**, alien spouse or unmarried dependent child, son, or daughter of a foreign government official, or **(c)(4)**, eligible dependent of a G-1, G-3, or G-4 non-immigrant, or **(c)(7)**, dependent of a NATO 1 through NATO 7, submit your application through your principal's sponsoring organization. Your application will be reviewed and forwarded by DOS, USUN, or NATO/SACLANT to the Nebraska Service Center following certification of your eligibility for an EAD.

If your response to **Question 16** is **(c)(8)** under the special ABC filing instructions, and you are filing your Form I-589, Application for Asylum, and this application together, mail your applications to the office where you will file your asylum application. Otherwise, for all other (c)(8) filings, see additional instructions below.

If your response to **Question 16** is **(c)(9)** and you filed your Form I-485 with the USCIS Chicago Lockbox Facility, file your Form I-765 with the following address (if you filed your Form I-485 with a USCIS Service Center, see instructions below):

USCIS Lockbox Addresses:

For U. S. Postal Service (USPS) deliveries:

USCIS
P.O. Box 805887
Chicago, IL 60680-4120

For courier/express deliveries:

USCIS
Attn: FBAS
131 South Dearborn - 3rd Floor
Chicago, IL 60603-5517

Otherwise, if you filed your Form I-485 with a USCIS Service Center, you must file Form I-765 at the Nebraska Service Center or the Texas Service Center, depending on where you live (see the following addresses).

Nebraska Service Center Filings

File Form I-765 alone or concurrently with Form I-485 with the Nebraska Service Center if you live in:

Alaska, Arizona, California, Colorado, Guam, Hawaii, Idaho, Illinois, Indiana, Iowa, Kansas, Michigan, Minnesota, Missouri, Montana, Nebraska, Nevada, North Dakota, Ohio, Oregon, South Dakota, Utah, Washington, Wisconsin, or Wyoming.

If you are filing Form I-765 alone, mail your Form I-765 package to:

> **USCIS**
> Nebraska Service Center
> P.O. Box 87765
> Lincoln, NE 68501-7765

If you are filing Form I-765 concurrently with Form I-485, mail to:

> **USCIS**
> Nebraska Service Center
> P.O. Box 87485
> Lincoln, NE 68501-7485

For private courier (non-USPS) deliveries:

> **USCIS**
> Nebraska Service Center
> 850 S. Street
> Lincoln, NE 68508-1225

Texas Service Center Filings

File Form I-765 with the Texas Service Center if you live in:

Alabama, Arkansas, Connecticut, Florida, Georgia, Kentucky, Louisiana, Maine, Maryland, Massachusetts, Mississippi, New Hampshire, New Jersey, New Mexico, New York, North Carolina, South Carolina, Oklahoma, Pennsylvania, Puerto Rico, Rhode Island, Tennessee, Texas, Vermont, Virginia, U.S. Virgin Islands, West Virginia, or Washington, DC.

If you are filing Form I-765 concurrently with Form I-485, mail your Form I-765 to the address you will use to file Form I-485.

If you are filing Form I-765 alone, mail your Form I-765 package to:

> **USCIS**
> Texas Service Center
> P.O. Box 851041
> Mesquite, TX 75185-1041

For private courier (non-USPS) deliveries:

> **USCIS**
> Texas Service Center
> 4141 North St. Augustine Road
> Dallas, TX 75227

If your response to **Question 16** is:

1. **(a)(6)**, alien admitted as a nonimmigrant fiancé(e) pursuant to section 101(a)(15) (K)(i);

2. **(a)(11)**, alien granted extended voluntary departure by the Secretary as a member of a nationality group pursuant to a request by the Secretary of State;

3. **(a)(13)**, alien granted voluntary departure under the Family Unity Program;

4. **(a)(17)**, spouse of a treaty trader, investor;

5. **(a)(18)**, spouse of an intracompany transferee;

6. **(c)(2)**, alien spouse or unmarried dependent son or daughter of an employee of the Coordination Council for North American Affairs;

7. **(c)(3)(A), (c)(3)(B), or (c)(3)(C)**, F-1 student seeking optional practical training;

8. **(c)(3)(ii)**, F-1 student offered employment under the sponsorship of an international organization;

9. **(c)(3)(iii)**, F-1 student seeking employment because of severe economic hardship;

10. **(c)(5)**, spouse or minor child of an exchange visitor (J-2);

11. **(c)(6)**, M-1 student seeking employment for practical training;

12. **(c)(8)**, an alien who has filed an application for asylum or withholding of deportation or removal;

13. **(c)(17)(i)**, a visitor for business (B-1) who is the personal or domestic servant who is accompanying or following to join an employer;

14. **(c)(17)(ii)**, a domestic servant of a U.S. citizen accompanying or following to join his or her U.S. citizen employer who has a permanent home or is stationed in a foreign country; or

15. **(c)(17)(iii)**, an employee of a foreign airline engaged in international transportation of passengers freight:

Mail your application to the appropriate Service Center depending on where you live (see chart on the following page).

If you live in:		Mail your application to:
Connecticut D.C. Maryland New Hampshire New York Puerto Rico Vermont West Virginia	Delaware Maine Massachusetts New Jersey Pennsylvania Rhode Island Virginia U.S.V.I.	For both U.S. Postal Service and private courier deliveries: **USCIS** Vermont Service Center ATTN: I-765 75 Lower Welden Street St. Albans, VT 05479-0001
Arizona Guam Nevada	California Hawaii	U.S. Postal Service deliveries: **USCIS** California Service Center P.O. Box 10765 Laguna Niguel, CA 92607-1076 For courier/express deliveries: **USCIS** California Service Center 24000 Avila Road 2nd Floor, Room 2312 Laguna Niguel, CA 92677
Alabama Florida Kentucky Mississippi North Carolina South Carolina Texas	Arkansas Georgia Louisiana New Mexico Oklahoma Tennessee	U.S. Postal Service deliveries: **USCIS Service Center** Texas Service Center P.O. Box 851041 Mesquite, TX 75185-1041 For courier/express deliveries: **USCIS** Texas Service Center 4141 N St. Augustine Rd Dallas, TX 75227
Alaska Idaho Indiana Kansas Minnesota Montana North Dakota Oregon Utah Wisconsin	Colorado Illinois Iowa Michigan Missouri Nebraska Ohio South Dakota Washington Wyoming	US Postal Service deliveries: **USCIS Service Center** Nebraska Service Center P.O. Box 87765 Lincoln, NE 68501-7765 For courier/express deliveries: **USCIS** Nebraska Service Center 850 S. Street Lincoln, NE 68508-1225

If your response to **Question 16** is:

1. **(a)(9)**, admitted as a K-3 spouse or K-4 dependant; or

2. **(c)(10)**, and you are a NACARA 203 applicant eligible to apply for relief with USCIS, or if your I-881 application is still pending with USCIS and you wish to renew your EAD:

Mail your EAD application with the required fee to the appropriate USCIS Service Center below:

If you live in Alabama, Arkansas, Colorado, Connecticut, Delaware, the District of Columbia, Florida, Georgia, Louisiana, Maine, Maryland, Massachusetts, Mississippi, New Hampshire, New Jersey, New Mexico, New York, North Carolina, Oklahoma, Pennsylvania, Puerto Rico, Rhode Island, South Carolina, Tennessee, Texas, Utah, the U.S. Virgin Islands, Vermont, Virginia, West Virginia, or Wyoming, send your application to:

> **USCIS**
> Vermont Service Center
> Attn: I-765
> 75 Lower Welden St.
> St. Albans, VT 05479-0001

Note: This address may be used for both U.S. Postal Service and private courier deliveries.

If you live in Alaska, Arizona, California, the Commonwealth of Guam, Hawaii, Idaho, Illinois, Indiana, Iowa, Kansas, Kentucky, Michigan, Minnesota, Missouri, Montana, Nebraska, Nevada, North Dakota, Oregon, Ohio, South Dakota, Washington, or Wisconsin, mail your application to:

> **USCIS**
> California Service Center
> P.O. Box 10765
> Laguna Niguel, CA 92607-1076

For courier/express deliveries:

> **USCIS**
> California Service Center
> 24000 Avila Road
> 2nd Floor, Room 2312
> Laguna Niguel, CA 92677

NOTE: You should submit the fee for the EAD application on a separate check or money order. Do not combine your check or money order with the fee for Form I-881.

If your response to **Question 16** is **(c)(10)** and you are not eligible to apply for NACARA 203 relief with USCIS, but you are eligible for other deportation or removal relief, mail your application to the following address:

USCIS
P.O. Box 805887
Chicago, IL 60680-4120

Questions Regarding Form I-765

For additional information about Form I-765, including how to file your application or filing locations not mentioned, call the USCIS National Customer Service Center at **1-800-375-5283** or visit our website at **www.uscis.gov.**

Processing Information

Any Form I-765 that is not signed or accompanied by the correct fee will be rejected with a notice that Form I-765 is deficient. You may correct the deficiency and resubmit Form I-765. An application or petition is not considered properly filed until accepted by USCIS.

Initial processing

Once Form I-765 has been accepted, it will be checked for completeness, including submission of the required initial evidence. If you do not completely fill out the form, or file it without required initial evidence, you will not establish a basis for eligibility, and we may deny your Form I-765.

Requests for more information or interview

We may request more information or evidence, or we may request that you appear at a USCIS office for an interview. We may also request that you submit the originals of any copy. We will return these originals when they are no longer required.

Interim EAD

If you have not received a decision within 90 days of receipt by USCIS of a properly filed EAD application or within 30 days of a properly filed initial EAD application based on an asylum application filed on or after January 4, 1995, you may obtain interim work authorization by appearing in person at your local USCIS District Office. You must bring proof of identity and any notices that you have received from USCIS in connection with your application for employment authorization.

Approval

If approved, your EAD will either be mailed to you or you may be required to appear at your local USCIS office to pick it up.

Denial

If your application cannot be granted, you will receive a written notice explaining the basis of your denial.

Penalties

If you knowingly and willfully falsify or conceal a material fact or submit a false document with your Form I-765, we will deny your Form I-765 and may deny any other immigration benefit.

In addition, you will face severe penalties provided by law and may be subject to criminal prosecution.

USCIS Forms and Information

To order USCIS forms, call our toll-free number at **1-800-870-3676**. You can also get USCIS forms and information on immigration laws, regulations, and procedures by telephoning our National Customer Service Center at **1-800-375-5283** or visiting our Internet website at **www.uscis.gov**.

As an alternative to waiting in line for assistance at your local USCIS office, you can now schedule an appointment through our Internet-based system, **InfoPass**. To access the system, visit our website. Use the **InfoPass** appointment scheduler and follow the screen prompts to set up your appointment. **InfoPass** generates an electronic appointment notice that appears on the screen.

Paperwork Reduction Act

An agency may not conduct or sponsor an information collection and a person is not required to respond to a collection of information unless it displays a currently valid OMB control number. The public reporting burden for this collection of information is estimated at 3 hours and 25 minutes per response, including the time for reviewing instructions and completing and submitting the form. Send comments regarding this burden estimate or any other aspect of this collection of information, including suggestions for reducing this burden, to: U.S. Citizenship and Immigration Services, Regulatory Management Division, 111 Massachusetts Avenue, N.W., 3rd Floor, Suite 3008, Washington, DC 20529-2210. OMB No. 1615-0040. **Do not mail your application to this address.**

Department of Homeland Security
U.S. Citizenship and Immigration Services

I-765, Application For
Employment Authorization

Do not write in this block.

Remarks	Action Block	Fee Stamp
A#		

Applicant is filing under §274a.12 _____

☐ Application Approved. Employment Authorized / Extended *(Circle One)*   until _____ (Date).
_____ (Date).

Subject to the following conditions: _____
Application Denied.
☐ Failed to establish eligibility under 8 CFR 274a.12 (a) or (c).
☐ Failed to establish economic necessity as required in 8 CFR 274a.12(c)(14), (18) and 8 CFR 214.2(f)

I am applying for:
☐ Permission to accept employment.
☐ Replacement *(of lost employment authorization document)*
☐ Renewal of my permission to accept employment *(attach previous employment authorization document).*

1. Name (Family Name in CAPS)   (First)   (Middle)

Which USCIS Office?   Date(s)

2. Other Names Used (Include Maiden Name).

Results (Granted or Denied - attach all documentation)

3. Address in the United States (Number and Street)   (Apt. Number)

12. Date of Last Entry into the U.S.   (mm/dd/yyyy)

(Town or City)   (State/Country)   (ZIP Code)

13. Place of Last Entry into the U.S.

4. Country of Citizenship/Nationality

14. Manner of Last Entry (Visitor, Student, etc.)

5. Place of Birth (Town or City)   (State/Province)   (Country)

15. Current Immigration Status (Visitor, Student, etc.)

6. Date of Birth   (mm/dd/yyyy)   7. Gender
☐ Male   ☐ Female

8. Marital Status   ☐ Married   ☐ Single
☐ Widowed   ☐ Divorced

16. Go to **Part 2** of the Instructions, Eligibility Categories. In the space below, place the letter and number of the category you selected from the instructions (For example, (a)(8), (c)(17)(iii), etc.).

Eligibility under 8 CFR 274a.12 (_____) (_____) (_____)

9. Social Security Number (Include all numbers you have ever used) (if any)

17. If you entered the Eligibility Category, (c)(3)(C), in item 16 above, list your degree, your employer's name as listed in E-Verfy, and your employer's E-Verify Company Identification Number or a valid E-Verify Client Company Identification Number in the space below.

Degree: _____

10. Alien Registration Number (A-Number) or I-94 Number (if any)

Employer's Name as listed in E-Verify: _____

11. Have you ever before applied for employment authorization from USCIS?

☐ Yes (If yes, complete below)   ☐ No

Employer's E-Verify Company Identification Number or a valid E-Verify Client Company Identification Number _____

Certification

Your Certification: I certify, under penalty of perjury under the laws of the United States of America, that the foregoing is true and correct. Furthermore, I authorize the release of any information that U.S. Citizenship and Immigration Services needs to determine eligibility for the benefit I am seeking. I have read the Instructions in **Part 2** and have identified the appropriate eligibility category in **Block 16.**

Signature   Telephone Number   Date

Signature of person preparing form, if other than above: I declare that this document was prepared by me at the request of the applicant and is based on all information of which I have any knowledge.

Print Name   Address   *Signature*   Date

Remarks	Initial Receipt	Resubmitted	Relocated		Completed		
			Rec'd	Sent	Approved	Denied	Returned

Department of Homeland Security
U.S. Citizenship and Immigration Services

**I-864, Affidavit of Support
Under Section 213A of the Act**

Part 1.   Basis for filing Affidavit of Support.

1. I, _____ ,
am the sponsor submitting this affidavit of support because (Check only one box):

a. ☐ **I am the petitioner. I filed or am filing for the immigration of my relative.**

b. ☐ **I filed an alien worker petition on behalf of the intending immigrant, who is related to me as my** _____

c. ☐ **I have an ownership interest of at least 5 percent in** _____ ,
which filed an alien worker petition on behalf of the intending immigrant, who is related to me as my _____

d. ☐ **I am the only joint sponsor.**

e. ☐ **I am the** ☐ **first** ☐ **second of two joint sponsors.** *(Check appropriate box.)*

f. ☐ **The original petitioner is deceased. I am the substitute sponsor. I am the intending immigrant's** _____

For Government Use Only
This I-864 is from:
☐ the Petitioner
☐ a Joint Sponsor # _____
☐ the Substitute Sponsor
☐ 5% Owner
This I-864:
☐ does not meet the requirements of section 213A.
☐ meets the requirements of section 213A.
_____ Reviewer
_____ Location
_____ Date *(mm/dd/yyyy)*
Number of Affidavits of Support in file:
☐ 1   ☐ 2

Part 2. Information on the principal immigrant.

2. Last Name

First Name | Middle Name

3. Mailing Address Street Number and Name *(Include Apartment Number)*

City	State/Province	Zip/Postal Code	Country

4. Country of Citizenship | **5.** Date of Birth *(mm/dd/yyyy)*

6. Alien Registration Number *(if any)*
A- | **7.** U.S. Social Security Number *(if any)*

Part 3. Information on the immigrant(s) you are sponsoring.

8. ☐ I am sponsoring the principal immigrant named in Part 2 above.

☐ Yes   ☐ No (Applicable only in cases with two joint sponsors)

9. ☐ I am sponsoring the following family members immigrating at the same time or within six months of the principal immigrant named in **Part 2** above. Do not include any relative listed on a separate visa petition.

Name	Relationship to Sponsored Immigrant	Date of Birth *(mm/dd/yyyy)*	A-Number *(if any)*	U.S.Social Security Number *(if any)*
a.				
b.				
c.				
d.				
e.				

10. Enter the total number of immigrants you are sponsoring on this form from **Part 3**, Items **8** and **9**. ☐☐

Form I-864 (Rev. 10/18/07)Y

f www.facebook.com/become.citizen

Part 4. Information on the Sponsor.

			For Government Use Only
11. Name	Last Name		
	First Name	Middle Name	
12. Mailing Address	Street Number and Name *(Include Apartment Number)*		
	City	State or Province	
	Country	Zip/Postal Code	
13. Place of Residence *(if different from mailing address)*	Street Number and Name *(Include Apartment Number)*		
	City	State or Province	
	Country	Zip/Postal Code	

14. Telephone Number *(Include Area Code or Country and City Codes)*

15. Country of Domicile

16. Date of Birth *(mm/dd/yyyy)*

17. Place of Birth *(City)*	State or Province	Country

18. U.S. Social Security Number *(Required)*

19. Citizenship/Residency

☐ I am a U.S. citizen.

☐ I am a U.S. national (for joint sponsors only).

☐ I am a lawful permanent resident. My alien registration number is A-_____

If you checked box (b), (c), (d), (e) or (f) in line 1 on Page 1, you must include proof of your citizen, national, or permanent resident status.

20. Military Service (To be completed by petitioner sponsors only.)

I am currently on active duty in the U.S. armed services.   ☐ Yes   ☐ No

Part 5. Sponsor's household size.

21. Your Household Size - <u>DO NOT COUNT ANYONE TWICE</u>

Persons you are sponsoring in this affidavit:

a. Enter the number you entered on line 10.

Persons NOT sponsored in this affidavit:

b. Yourself.

c. If you are currently married, enter "1" for your spouse.

d. If you have dependent children, enter the number here.

e. If you have any other dependents, enter the number here.

f. If you have sponsored any other persons on an I-864 or I-864 EZ who are now lawful permanent residents, enter the number here.

g. OPTIONAL: If you have <u>siblings, parents, or adult children</u> with the same principal residence who are combining their income with yours by submitting Form I-864A, enter the number here.

h. Add together lines and enter the number here. **Household Size:**

For Government Use Only

Part 6. Sponsor's income and employment.

22. I am currently:

a. ☐ Employed as a/an _____

Name of Employer #1 *(if applicable)* _____

Name of Employer #2 *(if applicable)* _____

b. ☐ Self-employed as a/an _____

c. ☐ Retired from _____ since _____
   (Company Name)   *(Date)*

d. ☐ Unemployed since _____
                                    (Date)

23. My current individual annual income is: $ _____
                                    (See Step-by-Step Instructions)

f www.facebook.com/become.citizen

24. My current annual household income:

a. List your income from line 23 of this form. $ _____

b. **Income you are using from any other person who was counted in your household size,** including, in certain conditions, the intending immigrant. (See step-by-step instructions.) Please indicate name, relationship and income.

Household Size =

_____

Name	Relationship	Current Income
_____	_____	$ _____
_____	_____	$ _____
_____	_____	$ _____
_____	_____	$ _____

Poverty line for year

_____ is:

$ _____

c. **Total Household Income:** $ _____

(Total all lines from 24a and 24b. Will be Compared to Poverty Guidelines -- See Form I-864P.)

d. ☐ The persons listed above have completed Form I-864A. I am filing along with this form all necessary Forms I-864A completed by these persons.

e. ☐ The person listed above, _____ does not need to
    _____(Name)_____
complete Form I-864A because he/she is the intending immigrant and has no accompanying dependents.

25. Federal income tax return information.

☐ I have filed a Federal tax return for each of the three most recent tax years. I have attached the required photocopy or transcript of my Federal tax return for only the most recent tax year.

My total income (adjusted gross income on IRS Form 1040EZ) as reported on my Federal tax returns for the most recent three years was:

Tax Year		Total Income
_____	(most recent)	$ _____
_____	(2nd most recent)	$ _____
_____	(3rd most recent)	$ _____

☐ *(Optional)* I have attached photocopies or transcripts of my Federal tax returns for my second and third most recent tax years.

	For Government Use Only

Part 7. Use of assets to supplement income. *(Optional)*

If your income, or the total income for you and your household, from line 24c exceeds the Federal Poverty Guidelines for your household size, YOU ARE NOT REQUIRED to complete this Part. Skip to Part 8.

Household Size =

_____

Poverty line for year

_____ **is:**

$ _____

26. Your assets *(Optional)*

    a. Enter the balance of all savings and checking accounts. $ _____

    b. Enter the net cash value of real-estate holdings. (Net means current assessed value minus mortgage debt.) $ _____

    c. Enter the net cash value of all stocks, bonds, certificates of deposit, and any other assets not already included in lines 26 (a) or (b). $ _____

    d. Add together lines 26 a, b and c and enter the number here.   **TOTAL:** $ _____

27. Your household member's assets from Form I-864A. *(Optional)*

Assets from Form I-864A, line 12d for $ _____

_____
(Name of Relative)

28. Assets of the principal sponsored immigrant. *(Optional)*

The principal sponsored immigrant is the person listed in line 2.

    a. Enter the balance of the sponsored immigrant's savings and checking accounts. $ _____

    b. Enter the net cash value of all the sponsored immigrant's real estate holdings. (Net means investment value minus mortgage debt.) $ _____

    c. Enter the current cash value of the sponsored immigrant's stocks, bonds, certificates of deposit, and other assets not included on line a or b. $ _____

    d. Add together lines 28a, b, and c, and enter the number here. $ _____

29. Total value of assets.

Add together lines 26d, 27 and 28d and enter the number here.   **TOTAL:** $ _____

The total value of all assests, line 29, must equal 5 times (3 times for spouses and children of USCs, or 1 time for orphans to be formally adopted in the U.S.) the difference between the poverty guidelines and the sponsor's household income, line 24c.

Part 8. Sponsor's Contract.

Please note that, by signing this Form I-864, you agree to assume certain specific obligations under the Immigration and Nationality Act and other Federal laws. The following paragraphs describe those obligations. Please read the following information carefully before you sign the Form I-864. If you do not understand the obligations, you may wish to consult an attorney or accredited representative.

What is the Legal Effect of My Signing a Form I-864?

If you sign a Form I-864 on behalf of any person (called the "intending immigrant") who is applying for an immigrant visa or for adjustment of status to a permanent resident, and that intending immigrant submits the Form I-864 to the U.S. Government with his or her application for an immigrant visa or adjustment of status, under section 213A of the Immigration and Nationality Act these actions create a contract between you and the U. S. Government. The intending immigrant's becoming a permanent resident is the "consideration" for the contract.

Under this contract, you agree that, in deciding whether the intending immigrant can establish that he or she is not inadmissible to the United States as an alien likely to become a public charge, the U.S. Government can consider your income and assets to be available for the support of the intending immigrant.

What If I choose Not to Sign a Form I-864?

You cannot be made to sign a Form 1-864 if you do not want to do so. But if you do not sign the Form I-864, the intending immigrant may not be able to become a permanent resident in the United States.

What Does Signing the Form I-864 Require Me to do?

If an intending immigrant becomes a permanent resident in the United States based on a Form I-864 that you have signed, then, until your obligations under the Form I-864 terminate, you must:

-- Provide the intending immigrant any support necessary to maintain him or her at an income that is at least 125 percent of the Federal Poverty Guidelines for his or her household size (100 percent if you are the petitioning sponsor and are on active duty in the U.S. Armed Forces and the person is your husband, wife, unmarried child under 21 years old.)

-- Notify USCIS of any change in your address, within 30 days of the change, by filing Form I-865.

What Other Consequences Are There?

If an intending immigrant becomes a permanent resident in the United States based on a Form I-864 that you have signed, then until your obligations under the Form I-864 terminate, your income and assets may be considered ("deemed") to be available to that person, in determining whether he or she is eligible for certain Federal means-tested public benefits and also for State or local means-tested public benefits, if the State or local government's rules provide for consideration ("deeming") of your income and assets as available to the person.

This provision does **not** apply to public benefits specified in section 403(c) of the Welfare Reform Act such as, but not limited to, emergency Medicaid, short-term, non-cash emergency relief; services provided under the National School Lunch and Child Nutrition Acts; immunizations and testing and treatment for communicable diseases; and means-tested programs under the Elementary and Secondary Education Act.

Contract continued on following page.

What If I Do Not Fulfill My Obligations?

If you do not provide sufficient support to the person who becomes a permanent resident based on the Form I-864 that you signed, that person may sue you for this support.

If a Federal, State or local agency, or a private agency provides any covered means-tested public benefit to the person who becomes a permanent resident based on the Form I-864 that you signed, the agency may ask you to reimburse them for the amount of the benefits they provided. If you do not make the reimbursement, the agency may sue you for the amount that the agency believes you owe.

If you are sued, and the court enters a judgment against you, the person or agency that sued you may use any legally permitted procedures for enforcing or collecting the judgment. You may also be required to pay the costs of collection, including attorney fees.

If you do not file a properly completed Form I-865 within 30 days of any change of address, USCIS may impose a civil fine for your failing to do so.

When Will These Obligations End?

Your obligations under a Form I-864 will end if the person who becomes a permanent resident based on a Form I-864 that you signed:

- Becomes a U.S. citizen;

- Has worked, or can be credited with, 40 quarters of coverage under the Social Security Act;

- No longer has lawful permanent resident status, and has departed the United States;

- Becomes subject to removal, but applies for and obtains in removal proceedings a new grant of adjustment of status, based on a new affidavit of support, if one is required; or

- Dies.

Note that divorce **does not** terminate your obligations under this Form I-864.

Your obligations under a Form I-864 also end if you die. Therefore, if you die, your Estate will not be required to take responsibility for the person's support after your death. Your Estate may, however, be responsible for any support that you owed before you died.

30. I, _____ ,

(Print Sponsor's Name)

certify under penalty of perjury under the laws of the United States that:

a. I know the contents of this affidavit of support that I signed.

b. All the factual statements in this affidavit of support are true and correct.

c. I have read and I understand each of the obligations described in Part 8, and I agree, freely and without any mental reservation or purpose of evasion, to accept each of those obligations in order to make it possible for the immigrants indicated in Part 3 to become permanent residents of the United States;

d. I agree to submit to the personal jurisdiction of any Federal or State court that has subject matter jurisdiction of a lawsuit against me to enforce my obligations under this Form I-864;

e. Each of the Federal income tax returns submitted in support of this affidavit are true copies, or are unaltered tax transcripts, of the tax returns I filed with the U.S. Internal Revenue Service; and

Sign on following page.

f. I authorize the Social Security Administration to release information about me in its records to the Department of State and U.S. Citizenship and Immigration Services.

g. Any and all other evidence submitted is true and correct.

31. _____   _____

(Sponsor's Signature)   *(Date-- mm/dd/yyyy)*

Part 9. Information on Preparer, if prepared by someone other than the sponsor.

I certify under penalty of perjury under the laws of the United States that I prepared this affidavit of support at the sponsor's request and that this affidavit of support is based on all information of which I have knowledge.

Signature: _____   **Date:** _____

(mm/dd/yyyy)

Printed Name: _____

Firm Name: _____

Address: _____

Telephone Number: _____

E-Mail Address : _____

Business State ID # *(if any)* _____

Department of Homeland Security
U.S. Citizenship and Immigration Services

I-865, Sponsor's Notice of Change of Address

START HERE-Type or print in black ink	For USCIS Use Only

Part 1. Information About You, the Sponsor

Family Name

Given Name

Middle Name

Date of Birth *(mm/dd/yyyy)*

Place of Birth *(City, State/Province /Country)*

A-Number *(if any)*

U.S. Social Security Number

For USCIS Use Only

Returned	Receipt
Date	
Resubmitted	
Date	
Date	

Action Block

Your current status- *(Check one)*

I am a ☐ U.S. Citizen ☐ Lawful Permanent Resident

NOTE: If you became a U.S. citizen following the filing of your Form I-864, Affidavit of Support, or submission of a prior Form I-865 address change, include a copy of proof of your U.S. citizenship (example: naturalization certificate, certificate of citizenship, U.S. passport) with this notice.

Your New Home Address - Street Number and Name *(include apt. # if applicable)*

City

State or Province

Zip/Postal Code

Country

Effective Date of Change of Address

Daytime Telephone *(Area/Country Code)*

E-Mail Address *(if any)*

Remarks

Your New Mailing Address - NOTE: You do not need to complete this section if your new mailing address is the same as your new home address above.

Street Number and Name *(include apt.#, if applicable)*

C/O *(in care of)*:	City	State or Province	Zip/Postal Code

Effective Date of Change of Address	Daytime Telephone *(Area/Country Code)*	E-Mail Address *(if any)*

Part 2. Information on Sponsored Immigrant(s) *(If more than one person, continue this part on a separate sheet(s) of paper)*

Provide the requested information on the person(s) your are sponsoring:.

Family Name	Given Name	Middle Name	A-Number

Part 3. Sponsor's Signature *(Read the information on penalties in the instructions before completing this part)*

I certify, under penalty of perjury under the laws of the United States of America, that all the information provided on this notice is true and correct.

Signature

Date *(mm/dd/yyyy)*

Part 4. Signature of Person Preparing Form, If Other Than Above *(Sign below)*

I declare that I prepared this request at the request of the above person, and it is based on all information of which I have knowledge.

Preparer's Signature

Preparer's Printed Name

Date *(mm/dd/yyyy)*

Preparer's Firm Name *(if applicable)*

Preparer's Address

Daytime Phone Number *(with area code)*

Fax Number *(if any)*

E-Mail Address *(if any)*

U.S. Citizenship and Immigration Services

Old Three-Quarter Style Photo

New Passport Style Photo

Photos Must Be in Color

USCIS Is Making Photos Simpler

Washington, DC — In accordance with language specified in the Border Security Act of 2003, U.S. Citizenship and Immigration Services (USCIS) announced a change in the photo requirements for all applicants from a three-quarter face position to a standard, full-frontal face position to take effect **August 2, 2004.**

USCIS will accept both three-quarter and full-frontal color photographs until **September 1, 2004,** after which only full-frontal color will be accepted.

The application process of customers who have already submitted materials that include color photos with the three-quarter standard **will not** be affected by this change.

All photos must be of just the person. Where more than one photo is required, all photos of the person must be identical. All photos must meet the specifications for full-frontal/passport photos.

For more information on photo standards, visit the Department of State website at http://www.travel.state.gov/passport/pptphotos/index.html, or contact the USCIS National Customer Service Center at 1 800 375 5283.

List of forms that require photos is on the back

M-603 (07/04)

www.facebook.com/become.citizen

Applications and Petitions That Require Photos, and the Number Required

2 photos are required for the following forms:

I-90 – Renew or replace your Permanent Resident Card (green card)

I-131 – Re-entry permit, refugee travel document, or advance parole

I-485 – Adjust status and become a permanent resident while in the U.S.

I-765 – Employment Authorization/Employment Authorization Document (EAD)

I-777 – Replace Northern Mariana Card

I-821 – Temporary Protected Status (TPS) Program

N-300 – Declaration of Intent (to apply for U.S. citizenship)

N-400 – Naturalization (to become a U.S. citizen)

N-565 – Replace Naturalization/Citizenship Certificate

3 photos are required for the following forms:

I-698 – Temporary Resident's application under the 1987 Legalization Program for permanent resident status — file 1 photo for your application, and bring the other 2 with you to your interview

N-600K – To apply for U.S. citizenship for foreign-born child residing abroad with U.S. citizen parent

4 photos are required for the following forms:

I-817 – To apply for Family Unity Benefits

I-881 – NACARA — suspension of deportation or special rule cancellation

File the following with your photos and of others as shown below:

I-129F – Fiancé(e) Petition — file with 1 photo of you + 1 photo of fiancé(e)

I-130 – Relative petition — if filing for your husband or wife, file with 1 photo of you + 1 photo of your husband or wife

I-589 – Asylum — file with 1 photo of you + 1 photo of each family member listed in Part A. II that you are including in your application

I-730 – Relative petition filed by a person granted Asylum or Refugee status — file with 1 photo of the family member for whom you are filing the I-730

I-914 – 'T' nonimmigrant status — file with 3 photos of you + 3 photos of each immediate family member for which you file an I-914A supplement

All photos must be of just the person. Where more than one photo is required, all photos of the person must be identical. All photos must meet the specifications for full-frontal/passport photos.

For more information, visit our website at www.uscis.gov, or call our customer service at 1 800 375 5283.

Department of Homeland Security
U.S. Citizenship and Immigration Services

Instructions for N-400,
Application for Naturalization

Instructions

Read these instructions carefully to properly complete this form. If you need more space to complete an answer, use a separate sheet of paper. Write your name and Alien Registration Number (A-Number), if any, at the top of each sheet of paper and indicate the part and number of the item to which the answer refers.

What Is the Purpose of This Form?

Form N-400 is an application for U.S. citizenship (naturalization). For more information about the naturalization process and eligibility requirements, read *A Guide to Naturalization* (M-476). If you do not already have a copy of the *Guide*, you can get a copy from:

1. USCIS website (**www.uscis.gov**);

2. USCIS toll-free forms line at **1-800-870-3676**; or

3. USCIS National Customer Service Center (NCSC) at **1-800-375-5283 (TTY:1-800-767-1833)**.

When Should I Use Form N-400?

You may apply for naturalization when you meet **all** the requirements to become a U.S. citizen. The section of the *Guide* called "Who is Eligible for Naturalization" and the Eligibility Worksheet found in the back of the *Guide* are tools to help you determine whether you are eligible to apply for naturalization. You should complete the worksheet before filling out Form N-400.

If you are applying based on five years as a lawful permanent resident or based on three years as a lawful permanent resident married to a U.S. citizen, you may apply for naturalization up to 90 days before you meet the "continuous residence" requirement. You must meet all other requirements at the time that you file your application with USCIS.

Certain applicants have different English and civics testing requirements based on their age and length of lawful permanent residence **at the time of filing**. If you are over 50 years of age and have lived in the United States as a lawful permanent resident for periods totaling at least 20 years, or if you are over 55 years of age and have lived in the United States as a lawful permanent resident for periods totaling at least 15 years, you do not have to take the English test, but you do have to take the civics test in the language of your choice.

If you are over 65 years of age and have lived in the United States as a lawful permanent resident for periods totaling at least 20 years, you do not have to take the English test, but you do have to take a simpler version of the civics test in the language of your choice.

Who May File Form N-400?

To use this form you must be **ONE** of the following:

1. A lawful permanent resident for at least five years and at least 18 years old;

2. A lawful permanent resident for at least three years and at least 18 years old;

AND

You have been married to and living with the same U.S. citizen for the last three years;

AND

Your spouse has been a U.S. citizen for the last three years.

3. A member of one of several other groups eligible to apply for naturalization (for example, persons who are nationals but not citizens of the United States) and at least 18 years old. For more information about these groups, see the *Guide*.

4. A person who has served honorably in the U.S. Armed Forces;

AND

If you are at least 18 years old, a lawful permanent resident with at least one year of U.S. Armed Forces service, and you are filing your application for naturalization while still in the service or within six months after the termination of such service;

OR

You served honorably as a member of the Selected Reserve of the Ready Reserve or in active-duty status during a designated period of hostilities. You then may apply for naturalization without having been physically present in the United States for any specified period.

For more information, go to the USCIS website at **www.uscis. gov**.

NOTE: If you are married to a U.S. citizen who is employed or deployed abroad, in some circumstances you may be eligible for expedited naturalization under section 319(b) of the Immigration and Nationality Act (INA). For further assistance, see the *Guide*.

Who May Not File Form N-400?

In certain cases, a person who was born outside of the United States to U.S. citizen parents is already a citizen and does not need to apply for naturalization. To find out more information about this type of citizenship and whether you should file Form N-600, Application for Certificate of Citizenship, read the *Guide*.

Other permanent residents under 18 years of age may be eligible for U.S. citizenship if their U.S. citizen parent or parents file Form N-600 application on their behalf. For more information, see "Frequently Asked Questions" in the *Guide*.

General Instructions

Step 1. Fill Out Form N-400

1. Type or print legibly in black ink.

2. If extra space is needed to complete any item, attach a continuation sheet, indicate the item number, and date and sign each sheet.

3. Answer all questions fully and accurately. State that an item is not applicable with "N/A." If the answer is none, write "None."

4. **Write your USCIS (or former INS) A-number on the top right hand corner of each page.** Use your A-number on your Permanent Resident Card (formerly known as the Alien Registration or "Green" Card). To locate your A-number, see the sample Permanent Resident Cards in the *Guide*. The A-number on your card consists of seven to nine numbers, depending on when your record was created. If the A-number on your card has fewer than nine numbers, place enough zeros before the first number to make a *total of nine numbers* on the application. For example, write card number A1234567 as A001234567, but write card number A12345678 as A012345678.

5. Answer all questions fully and accurately.

Step-by-Step Instructions

This form is divided into 14 parts. The information below will help you fill out the form.

Part 1. Your Name *(the person applying for naturalization)*

A. **Your current legal name** - Your current legal name is the name on your birth certificate unless it has been changed after birth by a legal action such as a marriage or court order.

B. **Your name exactly as it appears on your Permanent Resident Card** *(if different from above)* - Write your name exactly as it appears on your card, even if it is misspelled.

C. **Other names you have used** - If you have used any other names, write them in this section. If you need more space, use a separate sheet of paper.

If you have **never** used a different name, write "N/A" in the space for "Family Name *(Last Name)*."

D. **Name change** *(optional)* - A court can allow a change in your name when you are being naturalized. A name change does not become final until a court naturalizes you. For more information regarding a name change, see the *Guide*.

If you want a court to change your name at a naturalization oath ceremony, check "Yes" and complete this section. If you do not want to change your name, check "No" and go to Part 2.

Part 2. Information About Your Eligibility

Check the box that shows why you are eligible to apply for naturalization. If the basis for your eligibility is not described in one of the first three boxes, check "Other" and briefly write the basis for your application on the lines provided.

Part 3. Information About You

A. **U.S. Social Security Number** - Print your U.S. Social Security Number. If you do not have one, write "N/A" in the space provided.

B. **Date of birth** - Always use eight numbers to show your date of birth. Write the date in this order: Month, Day, Year. For example, write May 1, 1958, as 05/01/1958.

C. **Date you became a permanent resident** - Write the official date when your lawful permanent residence began, as shown on your Permanent Resident Card. To help locate the date on your card, see the sample Permanent Resident Cards in the *Guide*. Write the date in this order: Month, Day, Year. For example, write August 9, 1988, as 08/09/1988.

D. **Country of birth** - Write the name of the country where you were born. Write the name of the country even if it no longer exists.

E. **Country of nationality** - Write the name of the country (or countries) where you are currently a citizen or national.

　　1. If you are stateless, write the name of the country where you were last a citizen or national.

2. If you are a citizen or national of more than one country, write the name of the foreign country that issued your last passport.

F. **Citizenship of parents** - Check "Yes" if either of your parents is a U.S. citizen. If you answer "Yes," you may already be a citizen. For more information, see "Frequently Asked Questions" in the *Guide*.

G. **Current marital status** - Check the marital status you have on the date you are filing this application. If you are currently not married, but had a prior marriage that was annulled or otherwise legally terminated, check "Other" and explain it.

H. **Request for disability waiver** - If you have a medical disability or impairment that you believe qualifies you for a waiver of the tests of English and/or U.S. Government and history, check "Yes" and attach a properly completed Form N-648, Medical Certification for Disability Exceptions. If you ask for this waiver, it does not guarantee that you will be excused from the testing requirements. For more information about this waiver, see the *Guide*.

I. **Request for disability accommodations** - We will make every reasonable effort to help applicants with disabilities complete the naturalization process. For example, if you use a wheelchair, we will make sure that you can be fingerprinted and interviewed, and can attend a naturalization ceremony at a location that is wheelchair accessible. If you are deaf or hearing impaired and need a sign language interpreter, we will make arrangements with you to have one at your interview.

If you believe you will need us to modify or change the naturalization process for you, check the box or write in the space the kind of accommodation you need. If you need more space, use a separate sheet of paper. You do not need to send us Form N-648 to request an accommodation. You only need to send Form N-648 to request a waiver of the test of English and/or civics.

We consider requests for accommodations on a case-by-case basis. Asking for an accommodation will not affect your eligibility for citizenship.

Part 4. Information About Contacting You

A. **Home address** - Give the address where you now live. Do **not** put post office (P.O.) box numbers here.

B. **Mailing address** - If your mailing address is the same as your home address, write "Same." If your mailing address is different from your home address, write it in this part.

C. **Telephone numbers** - By giving us your telephone numbers and e-mail address, we can contact you about your application more quickly. If you are hearing impaired and use a TTY telephone connection, please indicate this by writing (TTY) after the telephone number.

Part 5. Information for Criminal Records Search

The Federal Bureau of Investigation (FBI) will use the information in this section, together with your fingerprints, to search for criminal records. Although the results of this search may affect your eligibility, we do **not** make naturalization decisions based on your gender, race, or physical description.

For each item, check the box or boxes that best describes you. The categories are those used by the FBI. You can select one or more.

NOTE: As part of the USCIS biometrics service requirement, you must be fingerprinted after you file this application. If necessary, USCIS may also take your photograph and signature.

Part 6. Information About Your Residence and Employment

A. Write every address where you have lived during the last five years (including in other countries).

Begin with where you live now. Include the dates you lived in those places. For example, write May 1998 to June 1999 as 05/1998 to 06/1999.

If you need separate sheets of paper to complete section A or B or any other questions on this application, be sure to follow the instructions under **"Step 1. Fill Out Form N-400"** on **Page 2.**

B. List where you have worked (or, if you were a student, the schools you have attended) during the last five years. Include military service. If you worked for yourself, write "Self employed." Begin with your most recent job. Also, write the dates when you worked or studied in each place.

Part 7. Time Outside the United States (*including trips to Canada, Mexico, and the Caribbean*)

A. Write the total number of days you spent outside of the United States (including military service) during the last five years. Count the days of every trip that lasted 24 hours or longer.

B. Write the number of trips you have taken outside the United States during the last five years. Count every trip that lasted 24 hours or longer.

C. Provide the requested information for every trip that you have taken outside the United States since you became a lawful permanent resident. Begin with your most recent trip.

Part 8. Information About Your Marital History

A. Write the number of times you have been married. Include any annulled marriages. If you were married to the same spouse more than one time, count each time as a separate marriage.

B. If you are now married, provide information about your current spouse.

C. Check the box to indicate whether your current spouse is a U.S. citizen.

D. If your spouse is a citizen through naturalization, give the date and place of naturalization. If your spouse regained U.S. citizenship, write the date and place the citizenship was regained.

E. If your spouse is not a U.S. citizen, complete this section.

F. If you were married before, give information about your former spouse or spouses. In question F.2, check the box showing the immigration status your former spouse had during your marriage. If the spouse was not a U.S. citizen or a lawful permanent resident at that time, check "Other" and explain. For question F.5, if your marriage was annulled, check "Other" and explain. If you were married to the same spouse more than one time, write about each marriage separately.

G. For any prior marriages of your current spouse, follow the instructions in section F above.

NOTE: If you or your present spouse had more than one prior marriage, provide the same information required by section F and section G about every additional marriage on a separate sheet of paper.

Part 9. Information About Your Children

A. Write the total number of sons and daughters you have had. Count **all** of your children, regardless of whether they are:

1. Alive, missing, or dead;

2. Born in other countries or in the United States;

3. Under 18 years old or adults;

4. Married or unmarried;

5. Living with you or elsewhere;

6. Stepsons or stepdaughters or legally adopted; or

7. Born when you were not married.

B. Write information about all your sons and daughters. In the last column (Location), write:

1. "With me" - if the son or daughter is currently living with you;

2. The street address and state or country where the son or daughter lives - if the son or daughter is **not** currently living with you; or

3. "Missing" or "Dead" - if that son or daughter is missing or dead.

If you need space to list information about additional sons and daughters, attach a separate sheet of paper.

Part 10. Additional Questions

Answer each question by checking "Yes" or "No." If **any** part of a question applies to you, you must answer "Yes." For example, if you were never arrested but *were* once detained by a police officer, check "Yes" to the question "Have you ever been arrested or detained by a law enforcement officer?" and attach a written explanation.

We will use this information to determine your eligibility for citizenship. Answer every question honestly and accurately. If you do not, we may deny your application for lack of good moral character. Answering "Yes" to one of these questions does not always cause an application to be denied. For more information on eligibility, see the *Guide*.

Part 11. Your Signature

After reading the statement in Part 11, you must sign and date it. You should sign your full name without abbreviating it or using initials. The signature must be legible. Your application will be rejected if it is not signed.

If you cannot sign your name in English, sign in your native language. If you are unable to write in any language, sign your name with an "X."

NOTE: A designated representative may sign this section on behalf of an applicant who qualifies for a waiver of the Oath of Allegiance because of a developmental or physical impairment (see the *Guide* for more information). In such a case, the designated representative should write the name of the applicant and then sign his or her own name followed by the words "Designated Representative." The information attested to by the Designated Representative is subject to the same penalties discussed on **Page 7** of these instructions.

Part 12. Signature of Person Who Prepared the Form for You

If someone filled out this form for you, he or she must complete this section.

Part 13. Signature at Interview

Do not complete this part. You will be asked to complete this part at your interview.

Part 14. Oath of Allegiance

Do not complete this part. You will be asked to complete this part at your interview.

If we approve your application, you must take this Oath of Allegiance to become a citizen. In limited cases, you can take a modified oath. The oath requirement cannot be waived unless you are unable to understand its meaning because of a physical or developmental disability or mental impairment. For more information, see the *Guide*. Your signature on this form only indicates that you have no objections to taking the Oath of Allegiance. **It does not mean that you have taken the oath or that you are naturalized.** If USCIS approves your application for naturalization, you must attend an oath ceremony and take the Oath of Allegiance to the United States.

Step 2. General Requirements

Photographs. You **must** submit two identical passport-style color photographs of yourself taken within 30 days of the filing of this application. The photos must have a white to off-white background, be printed on thin paper with a glossy finish, and be unmounted and unretouched.

The photos must be 2" x 2" and must be in color with full face, frontal view on a white to off-white background. Head height should measure 1" to 1 3/8" from top of hair to bottom of chin, and eye height is between 1 1/8" to 1 3/8" from bottom of photo. Your head must be bare unless you are wearing a headdress as required by a religious order of which you are a member; however, your face must be visible. Using pencil or felt pen, lightly print your name and Alien Registration Number on the back of each photo.

NOTE: Any digital photo submitted needs to be produced from a high-resolution camera with at least 3.5 mega pixels of resolution.

Copy of Permanent Resident Card. Applicants who are lawful permanent residents of the United States must submit photocopies (front and back) of Form I-551 (Permanent Resident Card). If you have lost your Form I-551, attach a copy of any other entry document or a photocopy of a receipt showing that you have filed Form I-90, Application to Replace Permanent Resident Card.

Other Documents. Depending on the circumstances, some applicants must send certain documents with their application.

For example, if you have been arrested or convicted of a crime, you must send a certified copy of the arrest report, court disposition, sentencing, and any other relevant documents, including any countervailing evidence concerning the circumstances of your arrest or conviction that you would like USCIS to consider. Note that unless a traffic incident was alcohol or drug related, you do not need to submit documentation for traffic fines and incidents that did not involve an actual arrest if the only penalty was a fine of less than $500 or points on your driver's license.

For more information on the documents you must send with your application, see the Document Checklist in the *Guide*.

Translations. Any document containing foreign language submitted to USCIS must be accompanied by a full English language translation which the translator has certified as complete and accurate, and by the translator's certification that he or she is competent to translate from the foreign language into English.

Copies. Unless specifically required that an original document be filed with an application or petition, an ordinary legible photocopy may be submitted. Original documents submitted when not required will remain a part of the record, even if the submission was not required.

Where To File?

For naturalization applicants filing under military provisions, section 328 or 329 of the INA, and for eligible spouses of active members of the Armed Forces of the United States filing for naturalization, refer to the specific filing instructions below the general filing instructions.

If you are the applicant and you reside in Alaska, Arizona, California, Colorado, Hawaii, Idaho, Illinois, Indiana, Iowa, Kansas, Michigan, Minnesota, Missouri, Montana, Nebraska, Nevada, North Dakota, Ohio, Oregon, South Dakota, Utah, Washington, Wisconsin, Wyoming, Territory of Guam, or the Commonwealth of the Northern Mariana Islands, send your application to the USCIS Lockbox Facility at the following address:

> USCIS
> P.O. Box 21251
> Phoenix, AZ 85036

For express/courier deliveries, use the following address:

> USCIS
> Attn: N-400
> 1820 E Skyharbor Circle S, Floor 1
> Phoenix, AZ 85034

If you are the applicant and you reside in Alabama, Arkansas, Connecticut, Delaware, District of Columbia, Florida, Georgia, Kentucky, Louisiana, Maine, Maryland, Massachusetts, Mississippi, New Hampshire, New Jersey, New Mexico, New York, North Carolina, Oklahoma, Pennsylvania, Rhode Island, South Carolina, Tennessee, Texas, Vermont, Virginia, West Virginia, Commonwealth of Puerto Rico, or the U.S. Virgin Islands, send your application to the USCIS Lockbox Facility at the following address:

> USCIS
> P.O. Box 299026
> Lewisville, TX 75029

For express/courier deliveries, use the following address:

> USCIS
> Attn: N-400
> 2501 S State Hwy 121, Bldg. #4
> Lewisville, TX 75067

All naturalization applications filed under the military provisions, section 328 or 329 of the INA, should be sent to the Nebraska Service Center (NSC) regardless of geographic location or jurisdiction. In addition, spouses of members of the Armed Forces of the United States filing for naturalization should also send their application to the NSC regardless of whether they are filing from within the United States or abroad. Send your application to:

> Nebraska Service Center
> P.O. Box 87426
> Lincoln, NE 68501-7426

For express/courier deliveries, use the following address:

> Nebraska Service Center
> 850 S Street
> Lincoln, NE 68508

For further information on where to file, including if you are currently overseas, read the section in the *Guide* titled "Completing Your Application and Getting Photographed" or call the NCSC at 1-800-375-5283 (TTY: 1-800-767-1833) or visit our website at www.uscis.gov and click on "Immigration Forms."

What Is the Filing Fee?

The filing fee for Form N-400 is **$595.**

An additional biometric fee of **$80** is required when filing Form N-400. After you submit Form N-400, USCIS will notify you about when and where to go for biometric services.

NOTE: All naturalization applicants filing under the military provisions, section 328 or 329 of the INA, do not require a filing fee.

Applicants 75 years of age or older are exempt from the biometric fee. Individuals who require fingerprinting and who reside outside of the United States at the time of filing an application or petition for immigration benefits are exempt from biometric fees.

You may submit one check or money order for both the application and biometric fees, for a total of **$675.**

Use the following guidelines when you prepare your check or money order for Form N-400 and the biometric fee:

1. The check or money order must be drawn on a bank or other financial institution located in the United States and must be payable in U.S. currency; and

2. Make the check or money order payable to **U.S. Department of Homeland Security**, unless:

   A. If you live in Guam, make it payable to **Treasurer, Guam**.

   B. If you live in the U.S. Virgin Islands, make it payable to **Commissioner of Finance of the Virgin Islands**.

NOTE: Spell out U.S. Department of Homeland Security; do not use the initials "USDHS" or "DHS."

Notice to Those Making Payment by Check. If you send us a check, it will be converted into an electronic funds transfer (EFT). This means we will copy your check and use the account information on it to electronically debit your account for the amount of the check. The debit from your account will usually take 24 hours and will be shown on your regular account statement.

You will not receive your original check back. We will destroy your original check, but we will keep a copy of it. If the EFT cannot be processed for technical reasons, you authorize us to process the copy in place of your original check. If the EFT cannot be completed because of insufficient funds, we may try to make the transfer up to two times.

How to Check If the Fees Are Correct

The form and biometric fees on this form are current as of the edition date appearing in the lower right corner of this page. However, because USCIS fees change periodically, you can verify if the fees are correct by following one of the steps below:

1. Visit our website at **www.uscis.gov**, select "Immigration Forms," and check the appropriate fee;

2. Review the fee schedule included in your form package, if you called USCIS to request the form; or

3. Telephone our National Customer Service Center at **1-800-375-5283** and ask for the fee information.

NOTE: If your Form N-400 requires payment of a biometric fee for USCIS to take your fingerprints, photograph, or signature, you can use the same procedure to obtain the correct biometric fee.

Address Changes

If you change your address and you have an application or petition pending with USCIS, you may change your address online at **www.uscis.gov**, click on "Change your address with USCIS," and follow the prompts. You may also complete and mail Form AR-11, Alien's Change of Address Card, to:

U.S. Citizenship and Immigration Services
Change of Address
P.O. Box 7134
London, KY 40742-7134

For commercial overnight or fast freight services only, mail to:

U.S. Citizenship and Immigration Services
Change of Address
1084-I South Laurel Road
London, KY 40744

Processing Information

Any Form N-400 that is not signed or accompanied by the correct fee will be rejected. Any application that is not completed in accordance with these instructions, is missing pages or otherwise not executed in its entirety, or is not accompanied by the required initial evidence may also be rejected. If your Form N-400 is rejected, the form and any fees will be returned to you and you will be notified why the form is considered deficient. You may correct the deficiency and resubmit Form N-400. An application or petition is not considered properly filed until accepted by USCIS.

Requests for more information or interview. USCIS may request more information or evidence, or request that you appear at a USCIS office for an interview. USCIS may also request that you submit the originals of any copy. USCIS will return these originals when they are no longer required.

Decision. The decision on Form N-400 involves a determination of whether you have established eligibility for the requested benefit. If you do not establish a basis for eligibility, USCIS will deny your Form N-400. You will be notified of the decision in writing.

USCIS Forms and Information

To order USCIS forms, call our toll-free number at **1-800-870-3676**. You can also get USCIS forms and information on immigration laws, regulations, and procedures by telephoning our National Customer Service Center at **1-800-375-5283** or visiting our Internet website at **www.uscis. gov**.

As an alternative to waiting in line for assistance at your local USCIS office, you can now schedule an appointment through our Internet-based system, **InfoPass**. To access the system, visit our website. Use the **InfoPass** appointment scheduler and follow the screen prompts to set up your appointment. **InfoPass** generates an electronic appointment notice that appears on the screen.

Penalties

If you knowingly and willfully falsify or conceal a material fact or submit a false document with this Form N-400, we will deny your Form N-400 and may deny any other immigration benefit.

In addition, you will face severe penalties provided by law and may be subject to criminal prosecution.

Privacy Act Notice

We ask for the information on this form, and associated evidence, to determine if you have established eligibility for the immigration benefit for which you are filing. Our legal right to ask for this information can be found in the Immigration and Nationality Act, as amended. We may provide this information to other government agencies. Failure to provide this information, and any requested evidence, may delay a final decision or result in denial of your Form N-400.

Paperwork Reduction Act

An agency may not conduct or sponsor an information collection, and a person is not required to respond to a collection of information unless it displays a currently valid OMB control number. The public reporting burden for this collection of information is estimated at 6 hours and 8 minutes per response, including the time for reviewing instructions, and completing and submitting the form. Send comments regarding this burden estimate or any other aspect of this collection of information, including suggestions for reducing this burden, to: U.S. Citizenship and Immigration Services, Regulatory Management Division, 111 Massachusetts Avenue, N.W., 3rd Floor, Suite 3008, Washington, DC 20529-2210. OMB No. 1615-0052. **Do not mail your application to this address.**

Department of Homeland Security
U.S Citizenship and Immigration Services

N-400 Application
for Naturalization

Write your USCIS A-Number here:
A

Print clearly or type your answers using CAPITAL letters. Failure to print clearly may delay your application. Use black ink.

Part 1. Your Name (*Person applying for naturalization*)

A. Your current legal name.

Family Name (*Last Name*)

Given Name (*First Name*)

Full Middle Name (*If applicable*)

B. Your name **exactly** as it appears on your Permanent Resident Card.

Family Name (*Last Name*)

Given Name (*First Name*)

Full Middle Name (*If applicable*)

C. If you have ever used other names, provide them below.

Family Name (*Last Name*)	Given Name (*First Name*)	Middle Name

D. Name change (*optional*)

Read the Instructions before you decide whether to change your name.

1. Would you like to legally change your name?   ☐ Yes   ☐ No

2. If "Yes," print the new name you would like to use. Do not use initials or abbreviations when writing your new name.

Family Name (*Last Name*)

Given Name (*First Name*)

Full Middle Name

For USCIS Use Only

Bar Code	Date Stamp

Remarks

Action Block

Part 2. Information About Your Eligibility (*Check only one*)

I am at least 18 years old **AND**

A. ☐ I have been a lawful permanent resident of the United States for at least five years.

B. ☐ I have been a lawful permanent resident of the United States for at least three years, **and** I have been married to and living with the same U.S. citizen for the last three years, **and** my spouse has been a U.S. citizen for the last three years.

C. ☐ I am applying on the basis of qualifying military service.

D. ☐ Other (*Explain*) _____

Part 3. Information About You	Write your USCIS A-Number here: A

A. U.S. Social Security Number   **B.** Date of Birth *(mm/dd/yyyy)*   **C.** Date You Became a Permanent Resident *(mm/dd/yyyy)*

D. Country of Birth   **E.** Country of Nationality

F. Are either of your parents U.S. citizens? *(If yes, see instructions)*   ☐ Yes   ☐ No

G. What is your current marital status?   ☐ Single, Never Married   ☐ Married   ☐ Divorced   ☐ Widowed

☐ Marriage Annulled or Other *(Explain)*

H. Are you requesting a waiver of the English and/or U.S. History and Government requirements based on a disability or impairment and attaching Form N-648 with your application?   ☐ Yes   ☐ No

I. Are you requesting an accommodation to the naturalization process because of a disability or impairment? *(See instructions for some examples of accommodations.)*   ☐ Yes   ☐ No

If you answered "Yes," check the box below that applies:

☐ I am deaf or hearing impaired and need a sign language interpreter who uses the following language. _____

☐ I use a wheelchair.

☐ I am blind or sight impaired.

☐ I will need another type of accommodation. Explain: _____

Part 4. Addresses and Telephone Numbers

A. Home Address - Street Number and Name *(Do **not** write a P.O. Box in this space.)*   Apartment Number

City	County	State	ZIP Code	Country

B. Care of   Mailing Address - Street Number and Name *(If different from home address)*   Apartment Number

City	State	ZIP Code	Country

C. Daytime Phone Number *(If any)*   Evening Phone Number *(If any)*   E-Mail Address *(If any)*

(   )   (   )

Part 5. Information for Criminal Records Search	Write your USCIS A-Number here: A

NOTE: The categories below are those required by the FBI. See instructions for more information.

A. Gender

☐ Male   ☐ Female

B. Height

Feet	Inches

C. Weight

Pounds

D. Are you Hispanic or Latino?   ☐ Yes   ☐ No

E. Race *(Select one or more)*

☐ White   ☐ Asian   ☐ Black or African American   ☐ American Indian or Alaskan Native   ☐ Native Hawaiian or Other Pacific Islander

F. Hair color

☐ Black   ☐ Brown   ☐ Blonde   ☐ Gray   ☐ White   ☐ Red   ☐ Sandy   ☐ Bald (No Hair)

G. Eye color

☐ Brown   ☐ Blue   ☐ Green   ☐ Hazel   ☐ Gray   ☐ Black   ☐ Pink   ☐ Maroon   ☐ Other

Part 6. Information About Your Residence and Employment

A. Where have you lived during the last five years? Begin with where you live now and then list every place you lived for the last five years. If you need more space, use a separate sheet of paper.

Street Number and Name, Apartment Number, City, State, Zip Code, and Country	Dates *(mm/dd/yyyy)*	
	From	To
Current Home Address - Same as Part 4.A		Present

B. Where have you worked (or, if you were a student, what schools did you attend) during the last five years? Include military service. Begin with your current or latest employer and then list every place you have worked or studied for the last five years. If you need more space, use a separate sheet of paper.

Employer or School Name	Employer or School Address *(Street, City, and State)*	Dates *(mm/dd/yyyy)*		Your Occupation
		From	To	

Part 7. Time Outside the United States
(Including Trips to Canada, Mexico and the Caribbean Islands)

Write your USCIS A-Number here:
A

A. How many total days did you spend outside of the United States during the past five years? ☐ days

B. How many trips of 24 hours or more have you taken outside of the United States during the past five years? ☐ trips

C. List below all the trips of 24 hours or more that you have taken outside of the United States since becoming a lawful permanent resident. Begin with your most recent trip. If you need more space, use a separate sheet of paper.

Date You Left the United States *(mm/dd/yyyy)*	Date You Returned to the United States *(mm/dd/yyyy)*	Did Trip Last Six Months or More?	Countries to Which You Traveled	Total Days Out of the United States
		☐ Yes ☐ No		
		☐ Yes ☐ No		
		☐ Yes ☐ No		
		☐ Yes ☐ No		
		☐ Yes ☐ No		
		☐ Yes ☐ No		
		☐ Yes ☐ No		
		☐ Yes ☐ No		
		☐ Yes ☐ No		
		☐ Yes ☐ No		

Part 8. Information About Your Marital History

A. How many times have you been married (including annulled marriages)? ☐ If you have **never** been married, go to Part 9.

B. If you are now married, give the following information about your spouse:

1. Spouse's Family Name *(Last Name)*   Given Name *(First Name)*   Full Middle Name *(If applicable)*

2. Date of Birth *(mm/dd/yyyy)*   **3.** Date of Marriage *(mm/dd/yyyy)*   **4.** Spouse's U.S. Social Security #

5. Home Address - Street Number and Name   Apartment Number

City   State   Zip Code

Part 8. Information About Your Marital History *(Continued)*	Write your USCIS A-Number here: A

C. Is your spouse a U.S. citizen? ☐ Yes ☐ No

D. If your spouse is a U.S. citizen, give the following information:

   1. When did your spouse become a U.S. citizen? ☐ At Birth ☐ Other

      If "Other," give the following information:

   2. Date your spouse became a U.S. citizen

   3. Place your spouse became a U.S. citizen *(See instructions)*

                                          City and State

E. If your spouse is **not** a U.S. citizen, give the following information :

   1. Spouse's Country of Citizenship

   2. Spouse's USCIS A- Number *(If applicable)*
 A

   3. Spouse's Immigration Status

     ☐ Lawful Permanent Resident ☐ Other _____

F. If you were married before, provide the following information about your prior spouse. If you have more than one previous marriage, use a separate sheet of paper to provide the information requested in Questions 1-5 below.

   1. Prior Spouse's Family Name *(Last Name)* Given Name *(First Name)* Full Middle Name *(If applicable)*

   2. Prior Spouse's Immigration Status **3.** Date of Marriage *(mm/dd/yyyy)* **4.** Date Marriage Ended *(mm/dd/yyyy)*

     ☐ U.S. Citizen

     ☐ Lawful Permanent Resident **5.** How Marriage Ended

     ☐ Other _____   ☐ Divorce ☐ Spouse Died ☐ Other _____

G. How many times has your current spouse been married (including annulled marriages)? ☐

   If your spouse has **ever** been married before, give the following information about **your spouse's** prior marriage.
 If your spouse has more than one previous marriage, use a separate sheet(s) of paper to provide the information requested in Questions 1 - 5 below.

   1. Prior Spouse's Family Name *(Last Name)* Given Name *(First Name)* Full Middle Name *(If applicable)*

   2. Prior Spouse's Immigration Status **3.** Date of Marriage *(mm/dd/yyyy)* **4.** Date Marriage Ended *(mm/dd/yyyy)*

     ☐ U.S. Citizen

     ☐ Lawful Permanent Resident **5.** How Marriage Ended

     ☐ Other _____   ☐ Divorce ☐ Spouse Died ☐ Other _____

Part 9. Information About Your Children	Write your USCIS A-Number here: A

A. How many sons and daughters have you had? For more information on which sons and daughters you should include and how to complete this section, see the Instructions.

B. Provide the following information about all of your sons and daughters. If you need more space, use a separate sheet of paper.

Full Name of Son or Daughter	Date of Birth (mm/dd/yyyy)	USCIS A- number (if child has one)	Country of Birth	Current Address (Street, City, State and Country)
		A		
		A		
		A		
		A		
		A		
		A		
		A		
		A		

Add Children		Go to continuation page

Part 10. Additional Questions

Answer Questions 1 through 14. If you answer "Yes" to any of these questions, include a written explanation with this form. Your written explanation should (1) explain why your answer was "Yes" and (2) provide any additional information that helps to explain your answer.

A. General Questions.

1. Have you **ever** claimed to be a U.S. citizen *(in writing or any other way)*? ☐ Yes ☐ No

2. Have you **ever** registered to vote in any Federal, State, or local election in the United States? ☐ Yes ☐ No

3. Have you **ever** voted in any Federal, State, or local election in the United States? ☐ Yes ☐ No

4. Since becoming a lawful permanent resident, have you **ever** failed to file a required Federal, State, or local tax return? ☐ Yes ☐ No

5. Do you owe any Federal, State, or local taxes that are overdue? ☐ Yes ☐ No

6. Do you have any title of nobility in any foreign country? ☐ Yes ☐ No

7. Have you ever been declared legally incompetent or been confined to a mental institution within the last five years? ☐ Yes ☐ No

Part 10. Additional Questions *(Continued)*

Write your USCIS A-Number here:
A

B. Affiliations.

8. a Have you **ever** been a member of or associated with any organization, association, fund foundation, party, club, society, or similar group in the United States or in any other place?   ☐ Yes   ☐ No

b. If you answered "Yes," list the name of each group below. If you need more space, attach the names of the other group(s) on a separate sheet of paper.

Name of Group	Name of Group
1.	6.
2.	7.
3.	8.
4.	9.
5.	10.

9. Have you **ever** been a member of or in any way associated *(either directly or indirectly)* with:

  a. The Communist Party?   ☐ Yes   ☐ No

  b. Any other totalitarian party?   ☐ Yes   ☐ No

  c. A terrorist organization?   ☐ Yes   ☐ No

10. Have you **ever** advocated *(either directly or indirectly)* the overthrow of any government by force or violence?   ☐ Yes   ☐ No

11. Have you **ever** persecuted *(either directly or indirectly)* any person because of race, religion, national origin, membership in a particular social group, or political opinion?   ☐ Yes   ☐ No

12. Between March 23, 1933, and May 8, 1945, did you work for or associate in any way *(either directly or indirectly)* with:

  a. The Nazi government of Germany?   ☐ Yes   ☐ No

  b. Any government in any area (1) occupied by, (2) allied with, or (3) established with the help of the Nazi government of Germany?   ☐ Yes   ☐ No

  c. Any German, Nazi, or S.S. military unit, paramilitary unit, self-defense unit, vigilante unit, citizen unit, police unit, government agency or office, extermination camp, concentration camp, prisoner of war camp, prison, labor camp, or transit camp?   ☐ Yes   ☐ No

C. Continuous Residence.

Since becoming a lawful permanent resident of the United States:

13. Have you **ever** called yourself a "nonresident" on a Federal, State, or local tax return?   ☐ Yes   ☐ No

14. Have you **ever** failed to file a Federal, State, or local tax return because you considered yourself to be a "nonresident"?   ☐ Yes   ☐ No

Part 10. Additional Questions *(continued)*	Write your USCIS A-Number here: A

D. Good Moral Character.

For the purposes of this application, you must answer "Yes" to the following questions, if applicable, even if your records were sealed or otherwise cleared or if anyone, including a judge, law enforcement officer, or attorney, told you that you no longer have a record.

15. Have you **ever** committed a crime or offense for which you were **not** arrested?   ☐ Yes ☐ No

16. Have you **ever** been arrested, cited, or detained by any law enforcement officer
(including USCIS or former INS and military officers) for any reason?   ☐ Yes ☐ No

17. Have you **ever** been charged with committing any crime or offense?   ☐ Yes ☐ No

18. Have you **ever** been convicted of a crime or offense?   ☐ Yes ☐ No

19. Have you **ever** been placed in an alternative sentencing or a rehabilitative program
(for example: diversion, deferred prosecution, withheld adjudication, deferred adjudication)?   ☐ Yes ☐ No

20. Have you **ever** received a suspended sentence, been placed on probation, or been paroled?   ☐ Yes ☐ No

21. Have you **ever** been in jail or prison?   ☐ Yes ☐ No

If you answered "Yes" to any of Questions 15 through 21, complete the following table. If you need more space, use a separate sheet of paper to give the same information.

Why were you arrested, cited, detained, or charged?	Date arrested, cited, detained, or charged? *(mm/dd/yyyy)*	Where were you arrested, cited, detained, or charged? *(City, State, Country)*	Outcome or disposition of the arrest, citation, detention, or charge *(No charges filed, charges dismissed, jail, probation, etc.)*

Answer Questions 22 through 33. If you answer "Yes" to any of these questions, attach (1) your written explanation why your answer was "Yes" and (2) any additional information or documentation that helps explain your answer.

22. Have you **ever**:

    a. Been a habitual drunkard?   ☐ Yes ☐ No

    b. Been a prostitute, or procured anyone for prostitution?   ☐ Yes ☐ No

    c. Sold or smuggled controlled substances, illegal drugs, or narcotics?   ☐ Yes ☐ No

    d. Been married to more than one person at the same time?   ☐ Yes ☐ No

    e. Helped anyone enter or try to enter the United States illegally?   ☐ Yes ☐ No

    f. Gambled illegally or received income from illegal gambling?   ☐ Yes ☐ No

    g. Failed to support your dependents or to pay alimony?   ☐ Yes ☐ No

23. Have you **ever** given false or misleading information to any U.S. Government official
while applying for any immigration benefit or to prevent deportation, exclusion, or removal?   ☐ Yes ☐ No

24. Have you **ever** lied to any U.S. Government official to gain entry or admission into the
United States?   ☐ Yes ☐ No

Part 10. Additional Questions *(Continued)*	Write your USCIS A-Number here: A

E.   Removal, Exclusion, and Deportation Proceedings.

25. Are removal, exclusion, rescission, or deportation proceedings pending against you? ☐ Yes ☐ No

26. Have you **ever** been removed, excluded, or deported from the United States? ☐ Yes ☐ No

27. Have you **ever** been ordered to be removed, excluded, or deported from the United States? ☐ Yes ☐ No

28. Have you **ever** applied for any kind of relief from removal, exclusion, or deportation? ☐ Yes ☐ No

F. Military Service.

29. Have you **ever** served in the U.S. Armed Forces? ☐ Yes ☐ No

30. Have you **ever** left the United States to avoid being drafted into the U.S. Armed Forces? ☐ Yes ☐ No

31. Have you **ever** applied for any kind of exemption from military service in the U.S. Armed Forces? ☐ Yes ☐ No

32. Have you **ever** deserted from the U.S. Armed Forces? ☐ Yes ☐ No

•G. Selective Service Registration.

33. Are you a male who lived in the United States at any time between your 18th and 26th birthdays ☐ Yes ☐ No
    in any status except as a lawful nonimmigrant?

    If you answered "NO," go on to question 34.

    If you answered "YES," provide the information below.

    If you answered "YES," but you did not register with the Selective Service System and are still under 26 years of age, you must register before you apply for naturalization, so that you can complete the information below:

    Date Registered (mm/dd/yyyy) [   ]   Selective Service Number [   ]

    If you answered "YES," but you did not register with the Selective Service and you are now 26 years old or older, attach a statement explaining why you did not register.

H. Oath Requirements. *(See Part 14 for the text of the oath)*

Answer Questions 34 through 39. If you answer "No" to any of these questions, attach (1) your written explanation why the answer was "No" and (2) any additional information or documentation that helps to explain your answer.

34. Do you support the Constitution and form of government of the United States? ☐ Yes ☐ No

35. Do you understand the full Oath of Allegiance to the United States? ☐ Yes ☐ No

36. Are you willing to take the full Oath of Allegiance to the United States? ☐ Yes ☐ No

37. If the law requires it, are you willing to bear arms on behalf of the United States? ☐ Yes ☐ No

38. If the law requires it, are you willing to perform noncombatant services in the U.S. Armed Forces? ☐ Yes ☐ No

39. If the law requires it, are you willing to perform work of national importance under civilian direction? ☐ Yes ☐ No

Part 11. Your Signature

I certify, under penalty of perjury under the laws of the United States of America, that this application, and the evidence submitted with it, are all true and correct. I authorize the release of any information that the USCIS needs to determine my eligibility for naturalization.

Your Signature

Date *(mm/dd/yyyy)*

Part 12. Signature of Person Who Prepared This Application for You *(If applicable)*

I declare under penalty of perjury that I prepared this application at the request of the above person. The answers provided are based on information of which I have personal knowledge and/or were provided to me by the above named person in response to the *exact questions* contained on this form.

Preparer's Printed Name

Preparer's Signature

Date *(mm/dd/yyyy)*

Preparer's Firm or Organization Name *(If applicable)*

Preparer's Daytime Phone Number

Preparer's Address - Street Number and Name

City

State

Zip Code

NOTE: Do not complete Parts 13 and 14 until a USCIS Officer instructs you to do so.

Part 13. Signature at Interview

I swear (affirm) and certify under penalty of perjury under the laws of the United States of America that I know that the contents of this application for naturalization subscribed by me, including corrections numbered 1 through _____ and the evidence submitted by me numbered pages 1 through _____ , are true and correct to the best of my knowledge and belief.

Subscribed to and sworn to (affirmed) before me

Officer's Printed Name or Stamp

Date *(mm/dd/yyyy)*

Complete Signature of Applicant

Officer's Signature

Part 14. Oath of Allegiance

If your application is approved, you will be scheduled for a public oath ceremony at which time you will be required to take the following Oath of Allegiance immediately prior to becoming a naturalized citizen. By signing, you acknowledge your willingness and ability to take this oath:

I hereby declare, on oath, that I absolutely and entirely renounce and abjure all allegiance and fidelity to any foreign prince, potentate, state, or sovereignty, of whom or which I have heretofore been a subject or citizen;

that I will support and defend the Constitution and laws of the United States of America against all enemies, foreign and domestic;

that I will bear true faith and allegiance to the same;

that I will bear arms on behalf of the United States when required by the law;

that I will perform noncombatant service in the Armed Forces of the United States when required by the law;

that I will perform work of national importance under civilian direction when required by the law; and

that I take this obligation freely, without any mental reservation or purpose of evasion, so help me God.

Printed Name of Applicant

Complete Signature of Applicant

APPENDIX B

USCIS
Filing Fees

A significant part of the process as you complete the necessary steps toward obtaining U.S. citizenship is filing various forms. Many times, there is a fee associated with filing the required forms.

The table below will serve as a guide and will help you budget your funds as you make your way through the process. Occasionally, the fees do change. To be sure you have the most current information, double-check the USCIS Web site at www.uscis.gov under "Immigration Forms." A current fee schedule will also be included in your package if you called the USCIS to request a form. You may also call the USCIS National Customer Service Center at 800-375-5283 (toll-free) and ask for the fee information.

A number of forms require an additional $80 biometrics services fee. This fee is for USCIS to take your fingerprints and, in some cases, also your photo and signature.

Under certain circumstances the fee for some forms may be waived. If you are unable to pay the base filing fee or required biometric services fee, you may submit a fee waiver request. Whether a fee waiver is granted is at the sole discretion of the USCIS.

FORM NUMBER	TITLE	FEE	BIOMETRICS
I-90	**Application to Replace Permanent Resident Card**		
	If you are filing to register at age 14 years, your existing card will not expire before your 16th birthday, and you are filing within 30 days of your 14th birthday	**No Fee**	**No**
	If you are filing because your card was issued incorrectly due to USCIS error	**No Fee**	**No**
	If you are filing because you never received your card	**No Fee**	**No**
	All others	**$290**	**Yes**
I-102	**Application for Replacement/Initial Nonimmigrant Arrival-Departure Document**	**$320**	**No**

FORM NUMBER	TITLE	FEE	BIOMETRICS
I-129	**Petition for a Nonimmigrant Worker** NOTE: Certain employers filing H1-B or L-1 petitions must submit supplemental fees of **$750** or **$1500** or a fraud prevention fee of **$500**. To determine if you are required to pay one or more of these fees, see Form I-129 instructions.	$320	No
I-129F	**Petition for Alien Fiancé(e)**		
	General fiancé(e) petition	$455	No
	For K-3 status based on an immigrant petition (Form I-130) filed by the same U.S. citizen husband or wife	No Fee	No
I-130	**Petition for Alien Relative**	$355	No
I-131	**Application for Travel Document**		
	For Reentry Permit, Refugee Travel Document, or Advance Parole	$305	No
I-140	**Immigrant Petition for Alien Worker**	$475	No
I-191	**Application for Advance Permission to Return to Unrelinquished Domicile**	$545	No
I-192	**Application for Advance Permission to Enter as a Nonimmigrant**	$545	No
I-193	**Application for Waiver of Passport and/or Visa**	$545	No
I-212	**Application for Permission to Reapply for Admission into the United States After Deportation or Removal**	$545	No
I-290B	**Notice of Appeal or Motion**	$585	No
I-360	**Petition for Amerasian, Widow(er), or Special Immigrant**		
	If you are filing for an Amerasian special immigrant	No Fee	No
	If you are self-petitioning as a battered or abused spouse, parent, or child of a U.S. citizen or lawful permanent resident	No Fee	No
	If you are filing for a special immigrant juvenile	No Fee	No
	All others	$375	No

FORM NUMBER	TITLE	FEE	BIOMETRICS
I-485	**Application to Register Permanent Residence or Adjust Status**		
	If you are filing for adjustment as a refugee	No Fee	No
	If you are under the age of 14 years and –		
	• Filing with the I-485 application of at least one parent	$600	No
	• **NOT** Filing with the I-485 application of at least one parent	$930	No
	If you are filing for an adjustment and are over the age of 79 years	$930	No
	All others	$930	Yes
I-485A	**Supplement A to Form I-485, Adjustment of Status Under Section 245(i)**		
	If you are under the age of 17 years	No Fee	No
	If you are an unmarried son or daughter of a legalized alien and under the age of 21 years	No Fee	No
	If you are the spouse of a legalized alien under the Family Unity Program	No Fee	No
	All others	$1000	No
	NOTE: No biometric services fee is required when filing this form. However, the biometric services fee must be paid when filing the related I-485 application.		
I-526	**Immigrant Petition by Alien Entrepreneur**	$1435	No
I-539	**Application to Extend/Change Nonimmigrant Status**	$300	No
I-589	**Application for Asylum and for Withholding of Removal**	No Fee	No

FORM NUMBER	TITLE	FEE	BIOMETRICS
I-600A	**Application for Advance Processing of Orphan Petition** NOTE: Biometric services fee must be paid for the applicant, his or her spouse (if applicable), and each adult household member 18 years or older. **Previously Approved Form I-600A:** If you already have an approved Form I-600A that is about to expire and you have not yet filed a Form I-600 petition, you can request one free extension of your Form I-600A. You must submit a written request to the USCIS office that adjudicated the initial I-600A. The request must be received no earlier than 90 days prior to the expiration of the Form I-600A approval, but before the Form I-600A approval notice expires.	$670	Yes
I-600	**Petition to Classify Orphan as an Immediate Relative**		
	If based on an approved I-600A filed within the previous 18 months	No Fee	No
	If based on a pending I-600A	No Fee	No
	All others	$670	Yes
	NOTE: When petition is for siblings, only one Form I-600 with one fee ($670) is required. However, biometric services fee must also be submitted for the petitioner's spouse (if applicable) and each adult household member over the age of 18 years.		
I-601	**Application for Waiver of Grounds of Inadmissibility** NOTE: Only a single application and fee required when applying simultaneously for a waiver of health-related inadmissibility grounds under section 212(h) or 212(i) of the INA	$545	No
I-612	**Application for Waiver of Foreign Residence Requirement**	$545	No
I-687	**Application for Status as a Temporary Resident Under Section 245A of the INA**	$710	Yes

FORM NUMBER	TITLE	FEE	BIOMETRICS
I-690	**Application for Waiver of Grounds of Inadmissibility** (For legalization and special agricultural worker applicants)	$185	No
I-694	**Notice of Appeal of Decision Under Section 210 or 245A**	$545	No
I-695	**Application for Replacement of Form I-688A, Employment Authorization, or Form I-688, Temporary Residence Card (under P.L. 99-603)**	$130	No
I-698	**Application to Adjust Status from Temporary to Permanent Resident (Under Section 245A of the INA)** If filed within 31 months from the date of adjustment to temporary residence NOTE: The adjustment date is the date of filing of the application for permanent residence or the applicant's eligibility date, whichever is later.	$1370	Yes
	If filed after 31 months from date of approval of temporary resident status	$1410	Yes
I-730	**Refugee/Asylee Relative Petition**	No Fee	No
I-751	**Petition to Remove Conditions on Residence** NOTE: Each conditional resident child listed on the form who is seeking to remove the conditional status is required to submit the biometric service fee regardless of age.	$465	Yes
I-765	**Application for Employment Authorization** See form instructions for numerous fee exemptions	$340	No
I-817	**Application for Family Unity Benefits** If you are under the age of 14 years	$440	No
	All others	$440	Yes

FORM NUMBER	TITLE	FEE	BIOMETRICS
I-821	**Application for Temporary Protected Status**		
	Initial (first-time) applicants	**$50**	**Yes (see NOTE)**
	Re-registration or renewal applicants	**No Fee**	**Yes (see NOTE)**
	NOTE: Applicants between ages 14 and 65 years, inclusively, if filing for employment authorization must pay the required application fee (see I-765: Application for Employment Authorization.) Applicants under 14 years of age and not filing for an employment authorization document are exempt from paying a biometrics fee		
I-824	**Application for Action on an Approved Application or Petition**	**$340**	**No**
I-829	**Petition by Entrepreneur to Remove Conditions**	**$2850**	**Yes**
	NOTE: Each conditional resident child listed on the form who is seeking to remove the conditional status is required to submit the biometric service fee regardless of age		
I-881	**Application for Suspension of Deportation or Special Rule Cancellation of Removal (Pursuant to Section 203 of Public Law 105-100, NACARA)**		
	If filed with USCIS	**$285**	**Yes**
	Maximum payable by family when filed together (spouses and unmarried children)	**$570**	**Yes**
	If filed with the Immigration Court (Executive Office of Immigration Review) See form's instructions for detailed fee information. NOTE: A single fee will be charged by the court whenever applications are filed by 2 or more applicants in the same proceedings. The fee is not required if the USCIS refers the application to the Immigration Court. Applicants filing with the Immigration Court must submit a biometric services fee payable to the Department of Homeland Security.	**$165**	**Yes**

FORM NUMBER	TITLE	FEE	BIOMETRICS
I-905	**Application for Authorization to Issue Certification for Health Care Workers**	$230	No
I-907	**Request for Premium Processing Services** NOTE: This fee is in addition to the required filing fee for the related application or petition.	$1000	No
I-914	**Application for T Nonimmigrant Status**		
	If under the age of 14 years	No Fee	No
	All other first-time applicants	No Fee	No
N-300	**Application to File Declaration of Intention**	$235	No
N-336	**Request for Hearing on a Decision in Naturalization Proceedings (Under Section 336 of the INA)**	$605	No
N-400	**Application for Naturalization**		
	If you are filing through service in the U.S. Armed Forces (relating to Sections 328 or 329 of the INA)	No Fee	No
	All others	$595	Yes
N-410	**Motion for Amendment of Petition (Application)**	$50	No
N-470	**Application to Preserve Residence for Naturalization Purposes**	$305	No
N-565	**Application for Replacement Naturalization/ Citizenship Document**	$380	No
N-600	**Application for Certificate of Citizenship**		
	If you are filing for an adopted child	$420	No
	All others	$460	No
N-600K	**Application for Citizenship and Issuance of Certificate Under Section 322**		
	If you are filing for an adopted child	$420	No
	All others	$460	No
N-644	**Application for Posthumous Citizenship**	No Fee	No

NOTES

NOTES

NOTES

NOTES

NOTES

NOTES

NOTES

NOTES

NOTES